Dreams in the Omkoi Karen Christian Context

An anthropological research
combined with a theological study on dreams

edition afem
mission academics 42

Hans Christoph Bär

VTR

This book is part of the series "edition afem",
ed. by Prof. Dr. Thomas Schirrmacher, Dr. Bernd Brandl,
Friedemann Knödler M.A., and Thomas Mayer M.A.
http://www.missiologie.org

Bibliographic information published by the Deutsche Nationalbibliothek
The Deutsche Nationalbibliothek lists this publication in the Deutsche National-
bibliografie; detailed bibliographic data are available in the Internet
at http://dnb.d-nb.de.

ISSN 0944-1077 (edition afem – mission academics)
ISBN 978-3-95776-080-7

© 2018
VTR Publications, Gogolstr. 33, 90475 Nürnberg, Germany
http://www.vtr-online.com

Front cover:
Pepper and fire stand for the "bad dreams" Karen like to be redeemed from.
© Hans Christoph Bär

Layout: Friedemann Knödler

Drawing from his twenty five years of living among Omkoi Karen in Northern Thailand, Dr Bär has produced an invaluable study of the significance and influence of dreams in this traditional society. He demonstrates how dreams have been understood and interpreted both by those Karen who have retained their Buddhist-animist beliefs and by those who have adopted the Christian faith. His comparative study of the interpretation of dreams in biblical literature illustrates how dreams can be discerned and interpreted by Karen Christians in ways which can deliver them from fear and provide them with spiritual encouragement.

C David Harley PhD, DMin, MA
Former President of All Nations Christian College, UK,
International Director of OMF International

In this excellent anthropological and theological research study, Hans Bär draws from his extensive experience of living in Northern Thailand to show the significance of dreams among the Omkoi Karen. His study lays the groundwork for contextualized teaching for this context.

Steve Taylor DTh, Dmin
Assistant Director, Bangkok Bible Seminary

An in-depth study that combines sociological research with anthropological considerations, and biblical exegeses with theological reflections. The easy-to-read doctoral thesis takes the reader into a world of dreams normally only accessible to those fluent in the language of the Karen, familiar with their culture and trusted by these people. The study discloses a wealth of information and concludes with practical recommendations relevant for Christian communities and Christian workers, as well as theological institution engaged in ministry with people that come from an animistic background. In short: a 'dream-book' about dreams!

Sam Wunderli
Director for Southeast Asia and
Assistant General Director of OMF International

Dreams in the Omkoi Karen Christian Context is a significant contribution to the field, especially for Karen people. Bär has created an important resource not only for missionaries, but also for seminary professors and students alike. This well-researched work is a reflection of Bär's love for Karen people and provides a coverage of a number of important issues regarding dreams not commonly treated in introductory mission related books. Bär offers practical help for those who will work with people in animist culture. This is a book that is solely needed in the field. I have thoroughly enjoyed the book and highly recommend.

Karen Choi, Ph.D.
Professor of Spirituality and Christian Education
Presbyterian Theological Seminary in America

To my loving wife Beatrice
who has shared with me in the ministry among the Karen people
for over 25 years.

To our children Damaris, Lukas, Samuel and Cornelia
who have shared our lives among the Karen
for many years.

To our beloved Karen people
who have shared their lives with us and without their help
this work would not have been possible.

Table of Contents

Preface 9
Acknowledgements 10

1. Introduction 11
1.1 Statement of Topic 11
1.2 Rationale 11
1.3 The Framework 12

2. Literature Review 13
2.1 Dreams 13
2.2 The Significance of Dreams in Different Religions 14
2.2.1 Buddhism 14
2.2.2 In Greco-Roman Times 16
2.2.3 Islam 17
2.2.4 Western Psychological View of Dreams 19
2.3 The Significance of Dreams in Animism/Folk Religion 22
2.3.1 Generally 22
2.3.2 Among Aboriginals in Australia 23
2.3.3 Among People Groups in South East Asia 26
2.4 The Significance of Dreams Among the Karen 32
2.4.1 Who Are the Karen People? 32
2.4.2 The Significance of Dreams Among the Karen 44

3. Biblical Perspective of Dreams 50
3.1 Terminology for Dreams and Visions 50
3.1.1 Distinctions Between "Dreams" and "Visions" 51
3.2 Who Is Reported to Have Had Dreams? 52
3.3 Observations on Dream Passages 54
3.3.1 The Dreams of Jacob 54
3.3.2 The Dreams of Joseph (Gen 37:5-11) 62
3.3.3 Pharaoh's Dream (Gen 41:1-41) 64
3.3.4 The Dreams of Solomon 66
3.3.5 Dreams in the Book of Daniel 67
3.3.6 Dreams in the Gospel 71
3.3.7 Paul's Vision at Night (Acts 16:9-10) 72

3.4 Impact of Dreams 73

3.5 Sources of Dreams in the Bible 76
3.5.1 God Is the Giver of Dreams 76
3.5.2 Dreams from the Devil and Demons? 77
3.5.3 The Human Soul as the Source of Dreams 79

3.6 What Kind of Dreams Do We Find in the Bible? 80
3.6.1 Message Dreams versus Symbolic Dreams 80
3.6.2 Types of Dreams Taken from Cultural Dream Theory 80
3.6.3 Types of Dreams Applied to Life Situations 81

3.7 Interpretation of Dreams 82
3.7.1 Who Was Interpreting Dreams? 82
3.7.2 Reasons and Purposes of Dreams in the Bible 84

3.8 Summary 87

4. Methodology and Procedure 89

4.1 Qualitative Research 89

4.2 Cultural Issues 89

4.3 Interviewing 90

4.4 Limitations to the Validity of Research 91

4.5 Ethical Issues 91

4.6 Data Analysis 92

4.7 Biblical Critique 92

5. Results, Findings and Evaluation 94

5.1 Animist-Buddhist Compared to Christian Karen Views 94
5.1.1 Spread and Popularity of Dreams Among the Karen 94
5.1.2 Main Areas of Life Which Karen Dream About 95
5.1.3 Categorizing Different Kinds of Dreams 99
5.1.4 Understanding the Origin of Dreams 103
5.1.5 Meanings and Interpretation of Dreams 104
5.1.6 Beneficial and Detrimental Impact of Dreams 111
5.1.7 Redeeming the Experience of Dreams – Approaches by Karen 117

5.2 Biblical Critique on the Karen View of Dreams 120
5.2.1 Similarities between A Biblical and A Karen View of Dreams 120
5.2.2 Biblical Critique on the Animist-Buddhist View of Dreams 121
5.2.3 Biblical Critique on Some Karen Christians' Views of Dreams 123
5.2.4 Biblical Perspective on Redeeming the Experience of Dreams 125

6. Conclusion ... 129
6.1 Appraisal ... 129

6.2 Recommendations ... 130
6.2.1 To the Karen Christian Community ... 130
6.2.2 To Missionaries, Karen Evangelists and Pastors ... 131
6.2.3 To Theological Education Institutions and Training Centers ... 131

6.3 Further Research ... 132

Appendix A: Dreams and their meanings given by the interviewees ... 133

Appendix B: Interviews with Karen about dreams ... 141

Appendix C: Area Map ... 210

Appendix D: Glossary of Sgaw Karen Termini used ... 211

Bibliography ... 215

Lothar Käser
Preface

Dreaming is an activity that is basic to human beings all over the world. No wonder that the concept shows a spectrum of aspects, interpretations and applications in the lives of people throughout their cultures and their religions from the old stone age up to modern times. Edward Burnett Tylor, famous British anthropologist and ethnologist of religion, saw in animism the origin of religion. He developed a theory which maintained that animism originated from the experience of dreams in which human beings are unconscious and yet experience themselves as living in the real world. From this man concluded that along with his body there belonged to him a further being (at least one), in whose experience he could participate. He claimed that this conclusion led to the notion of a soul (Lat. *anima*), which complemented the body and through its presence formed an indispensable prerequisite for the life of the body.

The present volume is dealing with this subject, concentrating on the Karen people from Northern Thailand. Its author has been a missionary in the area for many years. As he learned their language he could make an emic approach to their culture, so that instead of looking for Western-European concepts of dreaming he started strictly from the vocabulary the Karen use in this field of their respective local knowledge. Moreover he compares the dreaming complex with those of other world religions including what the Bible has to say about it.

Prof. Dr. Lothar Käser

Acknowledgements

At the beginning of this project were the encouragements of OMF leaders Neel Roberts, Sam Wunderli and Arend van Dorp to pursue the DMin studies in spite of my advanced age. It has been a joy and a personal enrichment to study together with colleagues from Thailand, the Philippines and Switzerland. My thanks go to the professors at International Theological Seminary and at Bangkok Bible Seminary: Dr. Karen Choi who suggested to me to pursue the present research. Dr. David McKinley, Dr. Natee Tanchanpong and Dr. Banpot Mekstapornkul who have contributed with their advice to this work. I especially commend Dr. Steve Taylor, my dissertation mentor, for his assistance, encouragement and quick answers to my inquiries. This book is a slightly revised version of my dissertation.

I would like to acknowledge the help of Dr. Chris Joll and Dr. Buadaeng Kwanchewan from Chiang Mai University for their help on the anthropological side of this research. The teaching of Anthropology by Prof. Lothar Käser has been an inspiration to observe and ask questions during my time among the Karen. On the theological part I would like to thank Dr. David Harley for his much valued input.

Mrs. Lanette Meister has worked through the thesis improving my English writing, while David Jäggi and Christoph Meister have taken time to help me with the formatting. Thanks for your expressions of friendship.

I am grateful to the many Karen who have warmly welcomed me into their homes and have shared of their dream experiences and thoughts. Without them this thesis could not have been written. Thanks to you all, especially the senior Christian leaders, Pastor Boon Ruang and his wife as well as Mrs. Noahmo who have shared of their lives deeply. I also want to express my appreciation to Mr. Somu, Mr. Ela and Pastor Wirot who have assisted me with interviewing and then helped to transcribe the results.

I give thanks to all my faithful prayer partners who have interceded for me and encouraged me during this time.

My special "thank you" goes to my wife Beatrice, who has journeyed with me and has often run interference for me so that I could have undisturbed times of writing.

Prof. Dr. Thomas Schirrmacher and the editors of VTR publishers have made it possible to publish this research. Thanks to all of you. My gratitude extends also to Friedemann Knödler who did the layout of this book.

All honor and praise goes to God who has called me to work among the Karen and who has enabled me to do the research.

1. Introduction

1.1 Statement of Topic

This dissertation is a research work on dreams among the Sgaw Karen people and how their lives are impacted by those dreams. The main research questions are: "Can the experience of dreams among the Karen be redeemed?" and "To what extent does the experience of dreams of Karen Christians in the area south of Omkoi differ from Animist-Buddhist Karen?" A biblical perspective on dreams will provide the foundation for a biblical critique of the findings.

1.2 Rationale

In Karen culture dreams are of significance to non-Christians and many Christians alike.

- The research will show the spread and popularity of dreams among the Karen.
- It will show which areas of life (illness and death, family, relationships, agricultural circle) are most affected by dreams.
- Another aspect of the research will explore how great the impact of dreams are on the lives of the Karen people. Do dreams impact people positively or negatively?
- What is their understanding about the origin of dreams?
- Who is interpreting dreams? Do dreams of Animist and Buddhist Karen differ from Karen Christians? Or does the interpretation of dreams differ? Or both?
- How do Animist-Buddhist Karen and Karen Christians protect themselves from bad dreams?

There has not been much reflection on the theme of dreams among Karen in general. Karen Christians take dreams for granted because they occur in their animistic culture as well as in the Bible. As the Karen Christians in the hills of Omkoi district and its surroundings come from an animistic background their view on dreams might be carried over from their old traditions and beliefs and may not have been confronted or dealt with thoroughly with a Christian perspective on dreams. This study will be an attempt to give insight into the difference between an animistic world view of dreams and a biblical view of dreams in order to help Christians to differentiate between dreams which might come from God or those from other sources.

Giving a biblical perspective on dreams will lay the foundation for a biblical critique which is aimed to help to transform the world view on dreams by Karen Christians. The question concerning which similarities and differences exist between an animistic Karen view of dreams and a biblical view of dreams will be answered. Some proposals for how these issues might be addressed within the Karen Christian community are found in the final and summarizing chapter.

This study will be significant because not much attention has been given to the issue researched among the Karen people, neither by anthropologists[1] nor by Christians[2], but has an impact on their everyday life. Many Christians who have not been discipled may believe more in their dreams than in the promises of God's Word. Or do dreams support what they believe? Are dreams an expression of what their deepest beliefs are? We also will find out how some mature Christians view dreams and how they try to help young Christians who may be bothered by dreams from their old animistic beliefs. This research with its applications is an attempt to help the Karen get dreams into a biblical perspective and redeem them from their old, mainly negative, dreams which tend to draw Christians back into their old belief system.

1.3 The Framework

In many animistic cultures dreams play an important role. The study will give a selected literature review on dreams in animism with the anticipation that some facets of it will be true for the understanding of dreams in Karen culture. Within this framework the research on dreams among the Karen will be performed.

It is assumed that the animistic world view on dreams by Karen people in the district of Omkoi and its surroundings has not been deeply challenged nor thoroughly dealt with by their new Christian faith. The Christian faith may have only put a new layer over the old view, but in times of crisis, many Christians may fall back into old habits. Or do dreams help Karen to grasp their new faith in Christ? It is the aim of this research to find out more about the dreamworld of animists as well as of Christians, in particular among the Sgaw Karen people in the southern Omkoi district, Thailand. In a further step, a biblical view of dreams will be presented which will help to teach them to transform their old world view. Instead of negating the old kind of dreams only, the Christians will be encouraged to expect dreams from God and view them in the light of God's Word.

This thesis will keep the research narrowed to the meaning Karen give to dreams which will be placed into a general animistic view on dreams. It will not go into deeper psychological issues or interpretations outside the animistic world view.

---

[1] In a talk with the anthropologist and lecturer at Chiang Mai University, Dr. Kwanchewan Buadaeng, who has done her dissertation and much further research among the Karen people, she noted that there has not been any work done on dreams among the Karen people. (Talk at CMU campus on 13th Nov. 2013, 10.45-11.30 am).

[2] Dr. Hsa Mu Htaw, vice-principal at the leading Karen Baptist Theological Seminary (KBTS) in Insein, Myanmar, wrote in an e-mail to the author on 15th Sept. 2013: "I haven't seen this kind of topic among our graduated students, and there will not be any research paper here at our KBTS so far."

2. Literature Review

The theme of "dreams" is an extensive one and over the centuries a great deal of literature has been written about it. In this chapter, I will give the setting for my specific research among the Karen people. I will start with a broad overview about dreams in other religions, then narrow it down to the significance of dreams among animistic cultures with the focus on Aboriginals in Australia, followed by two people groups in South East Asia. The last section focuses on the Karen. It is mainly based on primary sources, because up until now, very little has been written about dreams among the Karen.

2.1 Dreams

The basic pattern of humans sleeping and dreaming is natural and a universal phenomenon. It is thought that all human beings who are asleep are also dreaming.[3] From ancient times people have tried to give meaning to dreams. In some cultures and religions dreaming constitutes a very significant part of life, it is viewed "as doors to higher level of insights"[4] while in other cultures and faiths it may be ignored as illusory, as for example in parts of Hinduism and Buddhism.[5]

Bulkeley, considered by many to be "the foremost scholar of dreams and dreaming today"[6] gives the following definition of dreams: "A dream is an imagined world of sights, sounds, thoughts and feelings and activities that you (either as a character in the dream or as a disembodied observer of it) experience during sleep."[7] And he adds "Dreaming has always been regarded as a religious phenomenon."[8] And *"dreaming is a primal wellspring of religious experience."*[9] Strickling goes even further in claiming that "Dreams give us a direct connection to the divine."[10]

---

[3] "When awakened at the time of intense clusters of rapid eye movements, 95 per cent of sleepers studied in labs report dreaming. From this evidence, it is generally assumed that everyone does, in fact, dream in sleep; any impression to the contrary is related to the difficulty recalling dreams." J. Allan Hobson, *Dreaming. A Very Short Introduction* (Oxford, United Kingdom: Oxford University Press, 2002), 10.

[4] Michael V. Angrosino, "Altered States of Consciousness," *Encyclopedia of Religious Rites, Rituals, and Festivals,* Ed. Frank A. Salamone, (New York, NY: Routledge, 2004), 31.

[5] Kelly Bulkeley, *Dreaming in the World's Religions. A Comparative History,* (New York, NY: New York University Press, 2008), 108. She summarizes: "In each of the three major strands of Buddhism – Theravada, Mahayana and Tantrayana – dreaming has been dismissed as a meaningless illusion and, at the same time, venerated as a harbinger of new spiritual beginnings."

[6] Amos Yong, "Book Reviews" *Pneuma 32 (2010),* 470.

[7] Bulkeley, 2.

[8] Ibid. 3. Cf. Morton T. Kelsey, J. Hall.

[9] Ibid. 6.

[10] Bonnelle Lewis Strickling, *Dreaming About the Divine* (Albany, NY: State University of New York Press, 2007), 138.

The above observations are surely applicable to this study about dreams among the Karen people who share an animistic worldview as their context. Since in animism or folk religion, religion comprises all of life, dreams are very much a part of their life and faith.

2.2 The Significance of Dreams in Different Religions

2.2.1 Buddhism

Most of the early biographies of Buddha start with a dream that his mother Queen Maya had during the time she conceived Buddha. It was during a festive time in the city of Kapilasvatthu in which Queen Maya took part. On the last of the seven days, a full moon, Queen Maya rose early, bathed in scented water, wearing splendid clothes, eating pure food giving out alms, performing the vows of the holy day. Then she went to bed and fell asleep. She experienced the following dream:

> *She was lifted up by the four guardians of the world who took her up on her couch to the Himalaya Mountains and put her under a great sala tree. Then she was bathed and dressed in heavenly garments, anointed with perfumes, and garlands of heavenly flowers were put on her. She was laid on a heavenly couch, with her head toward the East. The future Buddha, coming in the form of a superb white elephant approached her from the North. In his trunk he was holding a white lotus flower. He went around her three times and he gently struck her right side, and entered her womb.*[11]

The story of Queen Maya's dream of conceiving the Buddha has been often and reverently portrayed in paintings throughout Buddhist history. Bulkeley comments: "we should not forget that people's beliefs about dreams have a tangible impact on their actual experiences."[12] Serinity Young writes about sacred biographies of Buddhists who are thought to have come to enlightenment. These biographies are told in order to help others to attain enlightenment. "Dreams play a prominent role in these texts."[13] Further is recorded that Siddharta Gautama's wife, Gopa, had a very bad dream the night before her husband left her.[14] And some dreams of the Buddha himself are recorded as well.[15] But it has to be noted that these dreams were recorded only several hundred years later. Therefore, we do not know whether these dreams really were seen or whether they were made up, however this does show that dreams have been important in the Buddhist religion. In the foreword to Young's book, Carol Schreier Rupprecht writes: "This compelling study explores the genre of sacred biography in Indo-Tibetan Bud-

---

[11] Bulkeley, 81. Serinity Young, *Dreaming in the Lotus: Buddhist Dream Narrative, Imagery, and Practice* (Somerville, MA: Wisdom Publication, 1999), 22ff.
[12] Bulkeley, 83.
[13] Young, 8.
[14] Young, 35ff.
[15] Ibid, 25ff.

dhism to arrive at a startling conclusion: without dreams there would be no Buddha and no Buddhism."[16]

There is of course another string of tradition which would deny dreams to be important, since everything is *anicca*, illusory.

Dreams in Buddhism have been most prominent in the Tibetan tradition. There is a whole school of Dream Yoga.[17] "Tibetan Buddhists often dream of *stupas, dorjes*, and other common Buddhist symbols and deities."[18] This shows that dreams are influenced by culture and faith.

Dreams are seen as a means for reaching enlightenment: Pinoche explains this in "Dream Practice" and concludes: "If the level of the practitioner is highly advanced, the state of *chösed*[19] may manifest and dreaming will cease. ... When one ceases to dream, the dreams never arise again and clarity becomes manifest both in the waking state and in the state of dream."[20] "The present Dalai Lama (b. 1935) has shown great enthusiasm for the research of Western psychologists."[21] In 1992 he became involved with a group of researchers to discuss the topic of sleep, dreaming, and death.[22] On the other hand

> The Dalai Lama made clear his disinclination to value dreams too highly – 'if you ask why we dream, what the benefit is, there is no answer in Buddhism' – at the same time he acknowledged that some dreams (particularly vivid, recurrent ones) could be indicators of one's spiritual status.[23]

But this has not stopped the Dalai Lama to instruct initiates in dream incubation practices through special prayer and putting *kush* grass underneath the pillow for purification purposes. The initiates are told to focus on dreams which were occurring around dawn. "A good dream portended a positive ritual outcome, and a bad dream was a negative omen and must be countered by reciting a mantra and scattering water around oneself."[24] Bulkeley summarizes: "Ambivalence and paradox are the hall marks of Buddhist dream theory."[25]

---

[16] Young, xi.

[17] Francisco J. Varela, *Sleeping, Dreaming, and Dying. An Exploration of Consciousness with the Dalai Lama* (Somerville, MA: Wisdom Publication, 1997), 127. Young, 117ff.

[18] Young, 10.

[19] *Chösed* means: "4. vision of the consummation or exhausting of reality." Jakob Winkler, *Glossary of Tibetan Terms and Names for the Dzogchen Community* (Sixth version August, 2004), 3. http://www.scribd.com/doc/169835462/Glossary-of-Tibetan-Terms-and-Names-for-the-Dzogchen-Community-Winkler. Accessed on 18th February 2014.

[20] Namkhai Norbu Rinpoche, *Mi-Lam. The Dream Practice* (Arcidosso GR, Italy: Associazione Culturale Comunita Dzog-chen Merigar, 1989), 1.

[21] Bulkeley, 107.

[22] Varela, 38-39.42.124.

[23] Bulkeley, 108.

[24] Bulkeley, 108. Cf. Young, 133f.

[25] Bulkeley, 108.

2.2.2　In Greco-Roman Times

In ancient Greece you can find two different ideas about dreams. The archaic point of view is "expressed by the Homeric poets, dreams are supernatural revelations given by the gods or other supernatural figures."[26] It is often a dream figure paying a visit to a sleeping person. During this period the literature writes about seeing a dream, not experiencing a dream. These dreams were considered divine. Later on another idea was superimposed on this one. It is called the Orphic idea. "During sleep the soul left the body and communed with the gods, returning with important information, either symbolic or direct in nature."[27] The body was viewed as the prison of the soul from which it wanted to be freed. Sleep was the state which came nearest to this kind of freedom, except for death. "At the same time in this period of greatness the temples of Aescylapius[28] became important, because here a dream could be sought from the god."[29] People believed if a sick person were going to sleep in one of the temples he could be visited by a god and receive healing. Dream incubation was practiced on a wide scale. To sleep in a sacred place, maybe combined with fasting, chanting, sacrifice and purification should help to receive the much hoped for visitation of a god and the healing of the disease. "The widespread popularity of the Asclepian cult testifies to the high public regard of dreams in Greco-Roman civilization."[30] There were hundreds of dream temples in Greco-Roman society. "According to some of the extant testimonies, Asklepios himself would enter the dream and heal the dreamer with his touch, or the snake who regularly accompanied him would affect the healing."[31] On the other hand many philosophers were skeptical toward dreaming and kept it not in high esteem because it did not seem rational. Aristotle dismissed the idea that dreams could have prophetic qualities.[32] "Aristotle's main contention was that dreams are not sent by the gods, that they are natural rather than divine phenomena."[33] He believed that the gods must be rational. He dismissed so-called prophetic dreams as coincidences in which people make false connections between dreams and reality. Under him dreams were brought in as an object of analysis. Aristotle wrote two short treatises on dreams.[34] "He analyzed the basic features on sleep and dreaming, and explained them in terms of the natural laws of physics."[35] He was breaking new ground. He did not make a very great impact at first but Kelsey observes that "His ideas were gradually accepted during the Renaissance, largely through

---

[26] Morton T. Kelsey, *God, Dreams, and Revelation. A Christian Interpretation of Dreams*. Revised and Expanded Edition (Augsburg, MN: Augsburg Books, 1991), 59. In discussing dreams in the Greek world, Kelsey is relying heavily on the material of Dodds and Harrison. Ibid, 58.

[27] Ibid, 59.

[28] Others call him Asclepius or Asklepios.

[29] Ibid, 62.

[30] Bulkeley, 139.

[31] James Gollnick, "Implicit Religions in Dreams." *Implicit Religions* 8.3 (2005), 286.

[32] Cf. Charles Stewart, "Dreams" *The Routledge Encyclopedia of Social and Cultural Anthropology*, Ed. Alan Barnard and Jonathan Spencer, 2nd ed. (New York, NY: Routledge, 2010), 202.

[33] Kelsey, 70.

[34] *De Insomniis* (On Dreams) and *De Divinatione per Somnum* (On Prophesying by Dreams).

[35] Bulkeley, 152.

the church and the efforts of Aquinas, until an exaggerated Aristotelian attitude became the dominant one in Western culture."[36]

In Greco-Roman times dreams were also a means for prophesying the future. Well-known is Artemidorus' (200 A.D.) manual of dream interpretation which was originally composed of five little handbooks on the meaning of dream symbols. He "labeled those dreams that require an interpretation of symbols *allegorical dreams*, and those dreams that show or say something directly *theorematic dreams*."[37] "His text ... has been copied and translated so often that it could be the single most influential dream book in the world."[38] He left the possibility open as to whether dreams could originate from gods or not, since he held the view that all dreams have their fulfillment in their own time. His interpretations were usually concerned with the personal life of the dreamer and typically focused on similarities of dreams and waking life. Whatever was in accordance with the present culture was good and whatever deviated from it, was bad.

Kelsey concludes about dreams in the Greco-Roman time:

> *Only a few of the most skeptical cast doubts upon them as revelations of something beyond human beings, and even these skeptics believed that dreams were, at the least, important indications of the physical state of a person's life. ...The majority of the Greeks did not use their reason and logic to eliminate dreams*[39] *or other non-rational experiences from life. The Greeks used these faculties, as far as they were able, to develop all their gifts.*[40]

2.2.3 Islam

"Throughout its history, from its prophetic origins in the desert visions to its modern status as the world's second largest faith, Islam has strongly affirmed the religious power of dreaming."[41]

In the Qur'an we find several suras in which dreams play an important role. These passages have become the focus of all dream tradition in Islam. Grünebaum says, "The reality of the objective significance of the dream is guaranteed by the Holy Book."[42] The Qur'an tells that Muhammad had received dream visions from God, for example before the battle of Badr (Qu'ran 8:43)[43] or another dream is reported

---

[36] Kelsey, 72. Gollnick, 284.
[37] Gollnick, 284.
[38] Bulkeley, 162.
[39] Aristotle and Cicero were the most significant exceptions. (Note by the author).
[40] Kelsey, 78f.
[41] Bulkeley, 211.
[42] G.E. von Grünebaum, "Introduction: The Cultural Function of the Dream as Illustrated by Classical Islam." *The Dream and Human Societies*, ed. G.E. von Grünebaum and Roger Callois (Berkely, CA: University of California Press, 1966), 7.
[43] Leah Kinberg, "Dreams and Sleep." *Encyclopaedia of the Qur'an. Volume One A-D*, ed. Jane Dammen McAuliffe (Leiden, NL: Brill, 2001), 550.

through which Muhammad was confirmed that he would enter Mecca as a victor (Qu'ran 48:27).[44]

> *The Prophet Muhammad said that a good dream is one of forty-six parts of prophecy .... He also said that nothing would be left after his death except good dream visions or glad tidings .... This implies that dreams are a small but legitimate source of divine knowledge.*[45]

Seeing Muhammad in a dream, means the dream is true "for Satan cannot assume the similitude of my form."[46]

> *"Dreams played a significant role in the lives of medieval Muslim communities."*[47]

Ibn Khaldun (AD 1332-1406), an Arab Muslim historiographer and sociologist, is best known for his book "The Muquaddima". "19th-century European scholars also acknowledged the significance of the book and considered Ibn Khaldun as one of the greatest philosophers to come out of the Muslim world."[48]

According to Ibn Khaldun, "dreams are formed in one of three ways: by God, by the angels or by the Devil."[49] "First, dreams that are clear and unmistakable in their meaning and content are from God. These may be analogous to the visions of the Prophet."[50] The second may be revelations through symbols and allegories. It needs interpretation, while the last one is a confused dream without meaning and therefore needs no interpretation. It is only sent to tempt people.

Into present day, dreams among Muslims are significant. In his foreword to "Muhammad Ibn Seerins's Dictionary of Dreams" Mahmoud Ayoub argues that dreams are messengers to people from the unknown. Dreams "are often prophetic voices of the future. Hence, they have at times directed the course of the history of nations."[51] "Islamic dream beliefs also appear to have played a significant role among the Al Qaeda group in Afghanistan who planned and executed the 9/11 attacks on the U.S. in 2001."[52]

Taken the fact that the Muslim world takes dreams that seriously, it is easier to understand why Muslims who see Jesus in a dream become Christians. "We keep hearing about people who have never heard the gospel coming to Christ through

---

[44] Ibid, 551.
[45] El-Sayed El-Aswad, *Muslim Worldview and Everyday Lives* (Plymouth, UK: AltaMira Press, 2012), 201.
[46] Ibid, 202.
[47] Grünebaum, 13.
[48] Ibn Khaldun. http://en.wikipedia.org/wiki/Ibn_Khaldun. Accessed, 17th Feb. 2014.
[49] Bulkeley, 211.
[50] Gordon E. Pruett, "Through a Glass Darkly: Knowledge of the Self in Dreams in Ibn Khaldun's Muqaddima." In *The Muslim World*. (Massachusetts, MA: Northeastern University Boston), 36.
[51] Mahmoud Ayoub, "Forword." In *Muhammad Ibn Seerin's Dictionary of Dreams: According to Islamic Inner Traditions* (Philadelphia, PA: Pearl Pub. House, 1992), xii.
[52] Bulkeley, 210.

dreams (especially in Islamic contexts)."[53] But it has to be said that other Muslims dream about Mohammed and are revived or converted to Islam.[54] These religious dreams occur in many facets.

To underscore the importance of dreams in Islam, Grünebaum states that dreams play a part in virtually every aspect of Muslim life be it on personal or on community level.[55]

2.2.4 Western Psychological View of Dreams

In 1900 Sigmund Freud published his groundbreaking work "The Interpretation of Dreams." "Freud's point of departure was a defense of the traditional attitude towards dreams as significant events rather than 'mental rubbish'."[56] Freud mapped out a concept relating dreams to the unconscious side of human beings. He was the first to connect the significance of dreams to the unconscious and made an empirical study on the subject. Through his clarity in dealing with the subject his writings could not be ignored. Dreams became a subject of scientific research in the western world where it had been ignored for a long period of time. For Freud dreams became a key element in his psychoanalytic method. Freud invented a new interpretation of dreams. Up until his time there were two main methods of interpretation known. "The first of these methods envisages the dream-content as a whole, and seeks to replace it by another content, which is intelligible and in certain respects analogous."[57] Freud calls this "symbolic dream interpretation", and mentions that this "goes to pieces at the very outset in the case of those dreams which are not only unintelligible but confused."[58] The second method which was used a lot is described as the "cipher method". It uses the dream as a secret code which has to be translated into another sign which is known. If you dream about an elephant you go and look up in a dream book, what meaning the elephant may have and from there apply it to your future. As we have seen Artemidoros' dream-interpretation is a variant of this kind. But he already considered not only the dream content but also the personality of the dreamer. The same dream content may mean different things for a poor or a rich man, or for a bachelor against a husband. Freud experimented with a new kind of interpretation. He used his own dreams for it. He says: "I must insist that the dream actually does possess a meaning, and that a scientific method of dream-interpretation is possi-

---

[53] Amos Yong, "Dreaming about the Divine." *Pneuma* 32, no. 3 (January 1, 2010), 470. *ATLASerials, Religion Collection*, EBSCO*host* (accessed February 14, 2014).

[54] Robert J. Priest, Professor for anthropology writes to Christian anthropologists mailing list "fishnet@lists.bethel.edu, Anthropology of Dreams", 16 October 2013. "More specifically it would be important to do background reading on the anthropology of dreams and dream interpretation in Muslim cultures – and pay special attention to how such dreams play out in a wide variety of settings (including that of conversion to Islam)."

[55] Grünebaum, 11.

[56] Stephen Wilson, "Introduction." *The Interpretation of Dreams,* Sigmund Freud (Ware, Hertfordshire: Woodsworth Edition, 1997), viii.

[57] Sigmund Freud, *The Interpretaion of Dreams.* Translated by A.A. Brill (Ware, Hertfordshire: Wordsworth Editions, 1997), 11.

[58] Ibid, 11.

ble."[59] From his experiences he concluded: "The dream represents a certain state of affairs, such as I might wish to exist; *the content of the dream is thus the fulfilment of a wish; its motive is a wish.*"[60] Towards the end of the chapter he quotes a proverb: "'What does the goose dream of?' and answers: 'Of maize.' The whole theory that the dream is the fulfilment of a wish is contained in these two sentences."[61] Since there are many dreams which do not seem to fit into this category Freud talked of dreams with manifest content or with latent content.[62] In this way he could bend any dream to fit his theory. Freud argued that people in their wake state do not allow sexual wishes to come up, therefore they will crop up in dreams while sleeping, when the rational defense is inactive and cannot resist. Sexual wishes often come up in dreams in not so obvious or in disguised forms. "The dream disguises the repressed complex to prevent it from being recognized. ... Freud calls this mechanism, ... the *censor*."[63] The censor unconsciously helps to conceal the real meaning of the dream from the ego. The cause for the wish-fulfilling nature of the unconscious was seen by Freud in the fundamental energy in man's sexual libido which strives to gratify itself. However because it is not allowed in the wake state it disguises itself so effectively so that we do not recognize the primitive roots of personality. Freud's dream work nearly always related to (repressed) sexuality.[64] He interpreted the dream and its symbols to the sexual nature of man.[65] Freud was a rationalist, and in his thoughts dreams had to be rational. Dreams therefore were only revealing nature about the dreamer himself and could not be a message from any source from the outside. For Freud, man remained "a material being, and his energies were purely biological. This so dominated Freud's thinking that his theory of dreams was made to submit to his basic assumptions."[66]

Not all of Freud's first adherents stayed with his theory. Some appreciated his groundbreaking work but could not accept his theory of dreams or that the unconscious is reduced mainly to sexuality. Adler, for example, "believed that the will to power was the basic human drive"[67] and therefore broke away from Freud. C.G. Jung is another one who distanced himself and took his own course of dream interpretation. He wrote:

---

[59] Ibid, 14.

[60] Ibid, 31. Two pages later Freud repeats: "When the work of interpretation has been completed the dream can be recognized as a wish-fulfillment."

[61] Ibid, 43.

[62] "Let us compare and contrast the *manifest* and the *latent dream-content.*" Ibid, 46.

[63] C.G. Jung, *Dreams, from The Collected Works of C.G. Jung.* Volumes 4,8,12,16. Bollingen Series XX (Princeton, NJ: Princeton University Press, 1974), 6f.

[64] "I maintain that neurotic anxiety has its origin in the sexual life, and corresponds to a libido which has been deflected from its object and has found no employment. ... From it we may deduce the doctrine that anxiety-dreams are dreams of sexual content." Freud, 69.

[65] Ibid, 230-266.

[66] John A. Sanford, *Dreams and Healing. A Succint and Lively Interpretation of Dreams* (New York, NY: Paulist Press, 1978), 10. John A. Sanford is a Jungian analyst and an Episcopal priest.

[67] Kelsey, 172.

The interpretation of dreams as infantile wish-fulfilments or as finalistic 'arrangements' subserving an infantile striving for power is much too narrow and fails to do justice to the essential nature of dreams. A dream, like every element in the psychic structure, is a product of the total psyche. Hence we may expect to find in dreams everything that has ever been of significance in the life of humanity.[68]

Jung then speaks of this as *archetypes*.[69] "He isolated several of the important images and carefully described them. The most significant of these are the images of the shadow, the anima,[70] and the animus."[71]

He also felt that Freud had left out certain important data so that his theory could be neat and simple. For Jung, Freud had dogmatized too much. Jung wrote: "In order to do anything like justice to dreams, we need an interpretive equipment that must be laboriously fitted together from all branches of the humane sciences."[72] While Freud was a rationalist and assumed that the unconscious worked rationally, Jung on the other hand "suggested that the unconscious does not think rationally to begin with, but rather symbolically, metaphorically, in images."[73] "To be scientific about dreams, Jung urged, we must not impose upon them a theory into which they are compelled to fit, but must allow each dream to speak for itself."[74] Sanford, in accessing Jung, writes:

Jung felt that man's energies could go in many directions – into sexuality, art, creative endeavors of all kinds, or destructive directions – but that the basic drive behind man's energy was the drive to wholeness. He saw that man had a spiritual, as well as a biological nature. He felt dreams expressed man's living reality and essence; they not only portrayed the forces within man, but also were in the service of man's higher development.[75]

Kelsey, another Episcopalian priest who studied under Jung at the Jung Institute in Zurich concludes: "Jung made it his business to listen to dreams and other produc-

---

[68] Jung, 63.
[69] A definition on archetypes: "(In Jungian theory) a primitive mental image inherited from the earliest human ancestors, and supposed to be present in the collective unconscious." www.oxforddictionaries.com/definition/english/archetype. (29th May 2015). The theologian and analytical psycho therapist Hark explains: "Die archetypischen Vorstellungen und Symbole dagegen sind jene Urbilder, die in den Märchen, Mythen und Träumen der Menschheit dargestellt sind. Insbesondere enthalten die religiösen Überlieferungen der Völker und die großen Kunstwerke archetypische Motive. Diese Urbilder faszinieren, beeindrucken und beeinflussen das Erleben der Menschen." Helmut Hark, *Der Traum als vergessene Sprache. Symbolpsychologische Deutung biblischer und heutiger Träume* (opus magnum, 2004), 116.
[70] Anima – "the soul in its feminine form; figures without name and face like 'a white woman', 'a girl'." Animus – "the soul in its masculine form; figures without name and face like 'a soldier', the teacher'." Samuel Pfeifer, *Schlafen und Träumen. Schlafstörungen - Diagnose und Therapie* (Riehen, Switzerland: Psychiatrische Klinik Sonnhalde, 2009), 27. (Translation by Hans Bär).
[71] Kelsey, 178.
[72] Jung, 64.
[73] Kelsey, 172.
[74] Sanford, *Dreams and Healing*, 11.
[75] Ibid, 11.

tions of the unconscious in a way that practically no other psychologist has attempted. ... His approach is one that has something constructive to offer Christianity, something that is hard to find elsewhere."[76]

The animistic view of dreams will be explored in the next section and a Christian biblical review will be presented in chapter 3.

2.3 The Significance of Dreams in Animism/Folk Religion

2.3.1 Generally

Many animists consider dreams to be full reality. Dreams have a high significance much higher than for rationalistic westerners. Many animists consider dreams as real as their physical life. "In animistic cultures dreams are considered literal representations of reality, although they may be encased in symbols that need to be divined."[77] A dream is often seen as a window into the unseen but real spiritual world. "Dreams may therefore be used as evidence in the traditional court. For example, if a man dreams he has committed adultery with another man's wife, he is liable to pay the same fine as for an offence committed while awake."[78] Dreams are one of the most significant resources for a human being to be able to receive messages from the unseen world.[79] This is especially true in regard to sicknesses, its diagnosis, its causes and its therapy in animistic medicine.[80] But more often the illness is diagnosed through divination.[81]

Dreams are often seen as a revelation or experience from first source, they seldom need interpretation by specialists.[82] Dreams are seen as an important part of life and often they are discussed among friends and family. The meaning of dreams in a certain culture is to some degree general knowledge. Among the Karen to dream about fire or peppers means that suffering lies ahead. Going downhill means you will lose buffaloes, cows or money. Going uphill is the opposite, a very welcomed dream. The same is true if you see a lot of fish in a dream which means you are going to make a lot of money.

---

[76] Kelsey, 174.

[77] Gailyn Van Rheenen, *Communicating Christ in Animistic Contexts* (Grand Rapids, MI: Baker Book House, 1991), 186.

[78] David Burnett, *World of the Spirits. A Christian Perspective on Traditional and Folk Religions* (London, United Kingdom: Monarch Books, 2000), 49.

[79] Cf. Philip M. Steyne, *Machtvolle Götter* (Bad Liebenzell, Germany: Verlag Liebenzeller Mission, 1993), 125. A translation of: *Gods of Power*. Houston, TX: Touch Publications, 1990.

[80] Cf. Lothar Käser, *Animismus* (Bad Liebenzell, Germany: Verlag der Liebenzeller Mission, 2004), 241.

[81] Cf. Lothar Käser, *Fremde Kulturen. Eine Einführung in die Ethnologie* (Erlangen, Germany: Verlag der Evang.-Luth. Mission, 1997), 241.

[82] Träume sind Erfahrungen aus erster Quelle, die nur selten die Auslegung eines Spezialisten benötigen. Steyne, 125.

Dreams can also be warnings. In parts of Nigeria as well as in some other countries, dreaming about animals like cats, owls or goats is especially worrying.[83] To dream a bad dream brings lots of fear with it. I remember a lady in the village of Thigoglo who was a new Christian. She had been ill for more than a year. She was sitting in the house and was unable to work. Missionaries had given her vitamins and other medicine but it did not seem to help. A Thai doctor who had visited the village could not help her but commented that her sickness was caused by the spirits. Some Karen friends and I visited the village which we reached after a four to five hours walk. We then went to her house with the elders of the small church. She said that at night, she dreamed that she is falling down a big rock. The meaning was obvious: She was going to die. We then prayed for her and asked the spirits to leave in the name of the Lord Jesus Christ. After some months we heard that she was well and going out to work. At the same time people said that her husband had left her for another woman. He had cursed her so that she would die, they said. But then she got healed.[84]

If people have very bad dreams they fear that they will lose their life or somebody else will die who is near to them.

What Do Animists Think Happens When They Dream?

In many animistic cultures one may find the concept of "spirit double".[85] It is this special one who exemplifies the person in spirit. Käser calls this most important one the *"Traumego"*.[86] He writes that in many human societies dreams and their contents are viewed as experiences of the *"Traumego"* of a person.[87] At night when a person is asleep it may leave the body and travel to the spirit world. *"Kipsigis* of Kenya are typical when they say that in dreams the spirit travels while the body sleeps."[88] The dream allows the person to see what happens in the spirit world. "Ancestors and ghosts communicate with the living directly through dreams and possession and indirectly through illness."[89] The dream functions like a window, the person who dreams sees from this world into the other, the spirit world. In this kind of a dream theory the dream is thought of as being very real. Therefore, dreams can cause social friction[90] and deep personal fears.

2.3.2 Among Aboriginals in Australia

The Dreamedime is an Australian aboriginal concept. It is an epoch that started before time began and exists until today. The Dreamedime is the original while

---

[83] Cf. Steyne, 123.
[84] This happened in December 1989 while I was living in the Karen village of Sop Lahn.
[85] Lother Käser uses the term "geistartiges Doppel". Käser, *Animismus*, 107-119.
[86] The main spirit double - it could be translated as "dream ego" or maybe "alter ego". Käser, *Animismus*, 198ff.
[87] "Wir haben gesehen, dass Träume und ihre Inhalte in vielen menschlichen Gesellschaften als Erlebnisse des Traumegos des Menschen gelten." Käser, *Animismus*, 233.
[88] Van Rheenen, 185.
[89] Van Rheenen, 261.
[90] See Käser, *Animismus*, 238.

this material world is a shadow of that reality. It is the result of the original Dreamedime. "The true reality of the Dreamedime appears to us in dreams and to shamans in their journeys."[91]

Anthropologist, Lynne Hume writes:

> The central feature of Aboriginal cosmology and epistemology that is reiterated throughout Australia, despite regional variations and the vastness of the continent, is The Dreaming and its integral link between humans, land, and all that lives on the land. Variously referred to as the Dreaming, Dreamedime, Eternal Dreamedime, and the Law, The Dreaming is the sacred knowledge, wisdom, and moral truth permeating the entire beingness of Aboriginal life, derived collectively from Dreaming events.[92]

Scanner shows high respect that the Aboriginals had made "the activity of sleep, into the master-symbol to which the whole corpus of Aboriginal religious life vibrated."[93] He says:

> The Dreaming, as activity, is represented as a continuing highway between ancestral superman and living man, between the life-givers and the life, the countries, the totems and totem-places they gave to living men, between subliminal reality and immediate reality, and between the There-and-Then of the beginnings of all things and relevances and the Here-and-Now of their continuations.[94]

Even though The Dreaming is of great importance in Aboriginal life its deeper meaning has not been completely understood. The Dreaming as a philosophical concept and dreams that occur during sleep may be related or unrelated to each other. Some people visit The Dreaming in dreams. While they are asleep their soul "flies" out of their body. A medicine man may fall into trance, lying on the floor while his soul travels to The Dreamland. After such a journey he may have the power to heal. It might be a similar experience with what in the West is called astral travel. "During those incidents medicine men sometimes bring back knowledge, such as new dances and songs."[95] Dreaming is not the only way to enter The Dreaming. Hume shows that through the media of music and dancing the same can be accomplished.[96]

This all sounds very positive and one might think that this kind of dreaming must be a pleasure. But in actual fact, most dreams which are meaningful to the people are "bad dreams". Pentony recorded 80 different dreams in the Northern Kimberley region from three different tribes. "Thirty of the eighty dreams recorded were

---

[91] Christina Pratt, *An Encyclopedia of Shamanism* (New York, NY: The Rosen Publishing Group, Inc., 2007), 149.

[92] Lynne Hume, "Accessing the Eternal: Dreaming 'The Dreaming' and Ceremonial Performance" in *Zygon, vol. 39*, no. 1 (March 2004), 237.

[93] W.E.H. Stanner, "Some aspects of Aboriginal religion." *Colloquium* 9, no. 1 (October 1, 1976), 23.

[94] Ibid, 23.

[95] Hume, 248. Cf. B. Pentony, "Dreams and Dream Beliefs in North Western Australia" in *Oceania*, Vol. 32, No. 2 (Dec., 1961), 146.

[96] Hume, 250ff.

regarded by the dreamer as being 'bad' dreams. Three of the eighty were pronounced 'good'. The remainder are neutral in tone."[97] The bad dreams may be caused by magic. While the "spirit double" roams the land it may be trapped by spirits. This kind of black magic to happen would always involve a sorcerer. "The victim becomes beware of the fact that he has been the object of black magic by the content of his dreams."[98] Especially if someone dreams to be caught in a fire. This is evidence enough to know that black magic is involved. "When anything is burnt it is finished. Fire is always bad to dream about."[99]

Pentony observed that "There is a marked tendency to relate the dream closely to the material realities of the moment. Should the person be feeling ill, then the dream becomes a potent factor in the situation."[100] And he summarizes: "It seems as though the dreams which are of the most significance are those which are felt to be of dangerous nature and to be the cause of illness."[101] On the other hand conception may be due to dreaming. Fertilization happens when the father finds a "spirit child" in a dream and gives it to his spouse.[102] Whether conception is always depending on dreaming or just sometimes is not reported.

Anthropologist Tonkinson was informed by the Mardu people of the Western Desert that Aboriginals who are far from home may travel to their home in spirit. Bulkeley comments that "compelled by modernization to live far from their home territories, dream-spirit journeys have taken on special significance as means of remaining connected to the ancestral lands."[103]

In Shamanic societies as the Australian Aboriginals dreams are often the means by which future shamans are chosen. Lydia Nakashima Degarrod writes: "Whatever the means of the shamanic selection, it is primarily through dreams that shamans learn about their calling."[104] And she goes on: "The ability to dream frequently or to have prophetic dreams are some of the unusual individual characteristics that signal future shamans in many societies."[105] From this it becomes very clear that dreams in these societies play a major role.

Many more reports are written about people who dream travel and it is not restricted to specialists only.[106] "The Narrang-ga say that the human spirit can leave

---

[97] B. Pentony, "Dreams and Dream Beliefs in North Western Australia" in *Oceania*, Vol. 32, No. 2 (Dec., 1961), 149.

[98] Ibid, 145.

[99] Ibid, 147.

[100] Ibid, 148.

[101] Ibid, 149.

[102] Cf. Ibid, 146.

[103] Bulkeley, 236.

[104] Lydia Nakashima Degarrod, "Dreams and Visions" in *Shamanism. An Encyclopedia of World Beliefs, Practices, and Culture*. Ed. Mariko Namba Walter and Evan Jane Neumann Fridman (Santa Barbara, CA: ABC-CLIO, 2004), 90.

[105] Ibid, 90.

[106] Cf. Hilton Deakin, "Some Thoughts of Transcendence in Tribal Societies" in *Ways of Transcendence*, ed. Edwin Dowdy, 95-109. (Bedford Park, S.A.: Australian Association for the Study of Religion, 1992), 108. "Many other cultural groups in Oceania also shared this notion of dreaming as a

the body in sleep and communicate with the spirits of others."[107] "The human spirit is called Yambo by the Kurnai, who likewise believe that it can leave the body during sleep."[108] Lohmann writes:

> In Tahiti, many dreams represent "the wanderings of one's own soul," and are "a window opening on the supernatural world" (Levy 1973:374-77). Among the Raramuri of Mexico, souls are believed to wander outside the body during dreams, where they can gather valuable cosmological information (Merrell 1988: 60,104-105). This understanding of dreams is so common cross-culturally that Stephen refers to it as "classic" (1979:5).[109]

2.3.3 Among People Groups in South East Asia

I will pick two different people groups with animistic backgrounds from South East Asia as examples. In both people groups a lot of research on dreams has already taken place.

Dreams Among the Toraja of Sulawesi, Indonesia

The Toraja live in scattered villages in the northern highlands of south Sulawesi. Their terraced wet-rice fields are the backbone of their livelihood. This people group of over 350.000[110] is well-known for their elaborate funeral rites. Their traditional belief is called *Alukta* "which is based on the veneration of deceased ancestors and gods/spirits."[111] "Most Toraja currently consider themselves to be Christians. However, their religious and existential beliefs are still influenced by traditional ideas."[112] The ancestral figures *nene,* and spiritual beings which they call *deata* still occur in their dreams and many believe that these beings will interfere with their daily life.

Douglas Hollan holds

> Dreams cannot be understood without knowing a great deal about the cultural frames, meanings, attitudes, and beliefs within which they are constructed and interpreted. And conversely, dream thoughts and imagery may illustrate or reveal a number of important cultural themes or processes. But

---

soul journey" Bulkeley, 237.

[107] James R. Lewis and Evelyn Dorothy Oliver, *The Dream Encyclopedia* (Detroit, MI: Visible Ink Press, 2009), 25.

[108] Ibid, 25.

[109] Roger Ivar Lohmann, "The Role of Dreams in Religious Enculturation among the Asabano of Papua New Guinea" in *Ethos,* 28 (1) (2000), 81.

[110] Douglas Hollan, "The Personal Use of Dream Beliefs in the Toraja Highlands" in *Ethos,* Vol. 17, Nr. 2 (June 1989), 167. Hollan gives the figure of 350.000 people in his article which was published in 1989.

[111] Ibid, 168.

[112] Douglas Hollan, "The Cultural and Intersubjective Context of Dream Remembrance and Reporting." In *Dream Travelers. Sleep Experiences and Culture in the Western Pacific,* ed. Roger Ivar Lohmann (New York: Palgrave Macmillan, 2003), 171. In his article published in 1989 he wrote: "at least half of the Toraja highlanders now call themselves Christians." Hollan, The Personal Use, 167f.

it is equally true that dreams are not rigidly determined by cultural processes.[113]

In his paper (1989) Hollan explores how widely shared beliefs about dreams among the Toraja villagers may be used in distinct personal ways. He gives an ethnography of Toraja dream beliefs. Toraja categorize their dreams with the following three types:[114] Firstly, you will find the dream which has to do with the activities of the previous day. They are not taken as important and not much thought is given to them. A second type of dream which occurs infrequently, is similar to what we call nightmares. It is called *tauan*. It is thought that someone relives a difficult moment in life *or* that the dream may be caused by a spirit attack. The spirit may come and visit the dreamer or his soul encounters spirits during travels while the dreamer is asleep. The third type of dreams are those easy to recall and are very vivid. They are thought to be real experiences and are called *tindo*. "There are two basic subtypes: Those that are prophetic and those that are not."[115] The predictive ones "are the ones that are thought to be most meaningful and significant from a Toraja point of view."[116] They may predict fortune or misfortune.

Whether or not a given dream is prophetic is not always readily apparent. ... But generally speaking, villagers are more likely to consider a dream prophetic if (1) form and content are easily understood and made sense of using conventional, "dreambooks" interpretations (...) or (2) it has an unusual and/or intense (either positive or negative) emotional tone.[117]

Many dreams are interpreted by lay people according to widely known symbols, a kind of "dreambook" interpretation. For dreams with a strong emotional touch or those which do not fit the generally known interpretations, a dream expert may be consulted. "In either case, interpretations are never without some ambiguity since the relationship between dream symbols and the object they represent may be variable."[118] They are ambiguous also "because it is never completely certain whether the objects and events experienced in a dream should be interpreted literally or metaphorically."[119]

Hollan gives us a list of dreams by the Toraja which are thought to be "good" or "bad" dreams.[120]

---

[113] Hollan, The Cultural, 169.
[114] Hollan, The Personal Use, 168ff. The Cultural, 175.
[115] Ibid, 170.
[116] Hollan, The Cultural, 171.
[117] Hollan, The Personal Use, 170.
[118] Ibid, 170.
[119] Hollan, The Cultural, 176.
[120] Hollan, The Personal Use, 171.

"Good" Dreams	
Received gold	good rice harvest
Carry pig or buffalo meat	good rice harvest
Person's body is butchered	person will slaughter animals
Act "crazy"	receive wealth
Stand on mountain top	become a leader
Gather clouds	receive cloth
Steal objects	receive those objects/become wealthy
Swim in ocean or river	receive wealth
Jump over or cross water	become wise/clever
Followed by cats or dogs	receive buffaloes
Gored by a buffalo	buy a buffalo
Objects are thrown at dreamer	rain will fall
"Bad" Dreams	
Buffalo in the rice fields	rats will eat rice harvest
Naked	get sick
Enter a burial cave	die
Carried off by an ancestor	die
Objects are stolen/lost/carried away	lose those objects
House burns or is destroyed	lose wealth/become poor

The above table tells us that to be carried off by an ancestor is a bad dream and means death. But on the other hand, Toraja dream a lot about their ancestors. Actually the dream is the main vehicle to stay in contact with the deceased. "Such dreams are interpreted as actual communication with the soul of the deceased and are believed to foretell future prosperity."[121] In such dreams, ancestors often come and offer vegetables, cloth and medicine or convey special power to heal. In other

---

[121] Jane C. Wellenkamp, "Fallen Leaves: Death and Grieving in Toraja." In *Coping with the Final Tragedy: Cultural Variation in Dying and Grieving*, eds. D.R. Counts and D.A. Counts (Amityville, N.Y. Baywood Publishing, 1991), 131.

dreams they give advice what they should do. These dreams are taken seriously. Families may change residence because an ancestor advised them to do so or in another instance a man became a Christian because he was warned in the dream that he will die if he were not to do so.[122]

The Toraja, and most other cultures, too, distinguish between good or bad dreams. While from a psychological point of view some would hold there are neither good nor bad dreams, only good or bad interpretations of dreams.[123] Hollan shows how his interview partner Nene'na Limbong had dreamed that his dead father had come to him and wanted to take him to the afterworld. Nene'na Limbong did not want to go and in his dream he struggled against his father who dragged him along. In the end he was able to free himself from his father. Nene'na Limbong knew immediately that this was a prophetic dream and that it was foretelling his death. In fear he went to consult a dream expert "who reinterpreted *(dibori)* the dream and gave it a new meaning: the assault on Nene'na Limbong was not a sign of his impending death; rather, it was a reminder to Nene'na Limbong to feed and nurture a hungry father."[124]

Nene'na Limbong did according to the expert's advice. He killed a pig in order to feed his father. In this case, the very bad conventional interpretation of predicting his death and the awful struggle with his father was turned into a dream that showed that his father was not dangerous or harmful but only hungry and in need of food.

Hollan shows with other examples, too, that among the Toraja dreams which by conventional interpretation would have predicted misfortune of some kind may be re-interpreted. "One may enlist the services of a dream expert who can neutralize or reverse the original, ominous foreshadowing."[125] Hollan concludes: "From a Toraja point of view, all *tindo* experiences require interpretation, and the meaning of any given dream experience is always somewhat ambiguous and open to reinterpretation."[126]

From the Toraja it becomes clear that dreams in animistic culture may not only have a set of commonly known interpretations that have to be rigidly applied, but that a dream may be seen ambiguously and that gives room for personalization, reinterpretation or even manipulation of the dream.

Asabano People of Papua New Guinea

The Asabano are a small people group of semi-nomadic pig herders. In 1977 a Baptist pastor held revival meetings "in which dreams (*aluma*), visions and expe-

---

[122] Douglas Hollan, "To the Afterworld and Back: Mourning and Dreams of the Dead among the Toraja." *Ethos*, Vol. 23, No. 4 (Dec. 1995): 431.

[123] Peter Wyss, Christian counselor and former head of "White Cross" Switzerland holds this view. Personal talk on 7th September 2014 in Uster, Switzerland.

[124] Hollan, The Personal Use, 176.

[125] Ibid, 138.

[126] Hollan, The Cultural, 177.

riences of the Holy Spirit were shared, interpreted and religiously validated."[127] The movement spread quickly and in a short time most Asabano had become Christians.

Lohmann has researched in-depth about dreams in this tiny people group of Papua New Guinea. He conducted his research on dreams from 1994-95. The reason for this was that the Asabano had kept their supernatural beliefs and he was able to collect many dream stories. He found out that Asabano do not believe all dreams but that there are certain reasons why a dream is true or false. "I learned that in their minds, soul travel was only one of several sources of true dream, and that they considered false dreams possible."[128]

Dreams may also be a help in the transmission of new religious ideas. In his paper "The Role of Dreams in Religious Enculturation", Lohmann comes to the conclusion that "Dreams facilitated the reception of religious beliefs among the Asabano before, during and after their conversion to Christianity."[129] Dreams helped to receive the new belief. Dreams have not lost significance since they have become Christians but their contents have changed. Had they dreamed of wobuno[130] and other spiritual beings before, now they dream of angels, Jesus, the Holy Spirit and to them it is evidence that the message of the gospel is true. "Dreams provide Asabano with evidence for the factuality of religious statements because they provide a virtually tangible indication of truth according to their epistemology."[131]

Lindstrom makes the point here that the transmitter of cultural information, the talker, has greater credibility in Melanesian societies if what he or she has to say derives from dream experiences. I would add the observation that, if the listener then also experiences a similar dream that validates what the speaker said, the information will be accepted as proven by personal direct sensory evidence.[132]

Dreams can provide greater credibility to ideas which have been made verbally and may confirm what has been claimed before.

Before the Asabano became Christians, dreamers could obtain information about illnesses in order to know what had to be done. They were keen to know who was responsible for their plight, was it a certain spirit or was it a witch. "When cannibal witches were identified, they were killed. Informants told me of several executions that took place."[133]

Lohmann who does himself not count a Christian, has observed that the Christians dreams were different. He tells how one young mother testified that she dreamed

---

[127] Bulkeley, 240.

[128] Roger Ivar Lohmann, "How Evaluating Dreams Makes History: Asabano Examples" in *History and Anthropology*, (September 2010, pp. 227-249), 229.

[129] Roger Ivar Lohmann, "The Role of Dreams in Religious Enculturation among the Asabano of Papua New Guinea" in *Ethos,* 28 (1) (2000), 75.

[130] "benevolent anthropomorphic beings who possess fabulous powers." Ibid, 86.

[131] Ibid, 80.

[132] Ibid, 82.

[133] Ibid, 88.

of her little son who had died. In her dream he said to her: "If father comes, tell him that his suspicion that I died from cannibal witchcraft isn't true – I just died."[134] This kind of dream helped to diffuse a potentially dangerous situation to take revenge. "This is a striking contrast to the traditional practice, in which the dying named their supposed killers."[135] In Christian dreams the deceased often appear to comfort and assure their family that heaven is real and they may be united one day. While dreaming of the dead in their pre-Christian state always meant a bad omen. They feared that soon somebody will die. I am inclined to speak of the redeemed dream in these Christians who have such a strong animistic background. Lohmann concludes: "It is possible that without the influence of dreams, it would not have been possible for the Asabano to absorb and internalize exotic Christian beliefs."[136]

In another article Lohmann presents "a paradigm of the six types of cultural dream theory known from the ethnographic record, providing examples for each type."[137] "The types are: nonsense, discernment, message, generative, soul travel and visitation theories."[138] The nonsense theory is given to a dream that does not relate to reality and is therefore not useful, they are made up images. Dreams which fall under this category are automatically considered to be false. In some cultures nonsense theory may dominate but in many other cultures it co-exists with other theories. Discernment theory "holds that dreaming entails an enhanced capacity for thought and awareness."[139] If the new valuable insight cannot be explained otherwise the dream is thought to be true. A third type of dream Lohmann categorizes as the message type. Whether a message dream is to be considered true or false depends a lot on the source. If the source of the message is trustworthy and the message seems to be logical the dream will be welcomed, if the source of the message dream is known to mislead it will not be accepted. "Generative theory attributes to dreaming minds creative power to prefigure ... In order for something to exist, according to these theories, it must first have been dreamed."[140] Soul Travel Theory involves the kind of dreams that people think that their soul or life force is wandering while the body is asleep. These kinds of dreams are usually considered to be true experiences even though they may contain some wrong information. As an Asabano man named Yadibole (born about 1960) described his views in 1995, "I'm sleeping and my 'life' [soul] is going walking and seeing these things".[141] Visitation Theory is not the soul leaving the body but a messenger meeting the soul/life force. "Visitation dreams are true by definition in that they are considered not merely made up by the dreamer, but rather, genuine experiences with external agents."[142] Lohmann states that there is not just one theory

---

[134] Ibid, 93.
[135] Ibid, 93.
[136] Ibid, 97.
[137] Lohmann, Evaluating Dreams, 230.
[138] Ibid, 230.
[139] Ibid, 231.
[140] Ibid, 231.
[141] Ibid, 231.
[142] Ibid, 232.

experienced in a culture, but several. "Which theories are present will influence how people explain their dreams, and therefore how they evaluate the form and level of truth any particular remembered dream represents."[143] These six types of cultural dream theories have been a help in categorizing dreams among the Karen as well.

With the Asabano dreams about hunting, illness or death were considered to be true. If they were dreaming about killing an animal they were sure to kill one in actual life. In illness they wanted to know through dreams who was responsible for it and how to treat it. "Dreams of death command notice, pause and evaluation."[144] When someone actually died the dream was proven true.

The Asabano had undergone a profound cultural change,

> but they had not lost all connection to their ancestral wisdom. They were still dreaming. The content of their dreams may have changed, in keeping with the sociopolitically accurate observation that the Christian deity was more powerful than the Asabano spirits and ghosts. Now they dreamed more of Jesus and angels than the magical wobuno nature spirits of before. But what continued was their traditional reliance on dreaming for religious insight and guidance. Like their forbearers, the Asabano were still looking to their dreams for spiritual insight in times of difficulty, uncertainty, and collective danger.[145]

Based on Lohmann's research it will be helpful to ask questions to the Karen about what kind of dreams they dream which are important. It is thought provoking how missionaries should deal with and teach about dreams in the Christian community. Instead of denying dreams on the basis of some Bible verses it might be much more helpful to pray for dreams from God! That God may redeem their dream-life.

2.4 The Significance of Dreams Among the Karen

2.4.1 Who Are the Karen People?

Dreams are related to a people's culture.[146] They "stand squarely at the intersection of personality and culture."[147] Cultural symbols only enter the dream to the extent that they are the dreamer's personal experience. Therefore it is important to know who the Karen are, as well as their main cultural characteristics and values.

---

[143] Ibid, 232.

[144] Ibid, 235.

[145] Bulkeley, 241.

[146] "Dreams cannot be understood without knowing a great deal about the cultural frames, meanings, attitudes, and beliefs within which they are constructed and interpreted." Holland, The Cultural, 169.

[147] Donald Tuzin, "The Breath of a Ghost: Dreams and the Fear of the Dead," *Ethos* 3 (1975), 575.

Origin and History

Little is known about the early history of the Karen. The Karen reckon 2015 to be their year 2754. They look to the year of their founding to BC 739. In their legends Karen speak of coming from the land of *"Thibi Kawbi"* which some have thought may indicate Tibet and the Gobi desert. Some Karen oral traditions refer to crossing a river of "running sand" as an important event in their history. There are Chinese sources which refer to the Gobi Desert as the "river of sand".[148] It could well be that the Karen originated in an area bordering Tibet,[149] crossed the Gobi Desert and traveled through Yunnan entering northern Burma.[150] "Evidence that Karens may have lived in Upper Burma comes from references in Pagan inscriptions to Cakraw and Plaw ethnic groups."[151] Whether the Cakraw and Plaw really meant the Sgaw and Pwo Karen "remains provisional" according to Renard. But if the Cakraw mentioned are meant to be the Sgaw Karen then they played a vital role in bringing down the Pyu state in the 700's (A.D.) war. Later the

> *"growing strength of the Burmans ended the Cakraw's pre-eminence. ... The Burmans employed some Cakraws and Plaws as Buddhist temple slaves ... In a temple dedication of 1242, a list appears of thirty-one Cakraw slaves from Sagu, all with Burman names."*[152]

Cakraws also were enlisted into the Burmans army and served on outposts in Chipton, north of Kyaukse. In 1244 a Cakraw chief claimed that land as his own. Obviously, he had once occupied that land. But he lost the case.[153]

> *Actually, very little evidence is available on Karen life after these Cakraw and Plaw references until the Konbaung Wars. Contemporary Burman literature claims former Burman rulers treated the Karens well, ... Many Karens, however, have few amicable memories of Burman rule, charging them with a virulent anti-Karen bias. It could be, of course, that much of the animosity felt by Karens in the nineteenth and twentieth centuries arose in the Konbaung and the Anglo-Burmese wars when many of the Karens sided with the Mons and later the British.*[154]

After the 13th century the Karen moved further south "because no Karens were near Pagan by the 1900's."[155] They had also moved eastward over the border into

---

[148] Harry Ignatius Marshall, *The Karen People of Burma. A Study in Anthropology and Ethnology* (Bangkok, Thailand: White Lotus Press, 1997 (1922), 5.

[149] Cf. Gordon Young, *The Hill Tribes of Northern Thailand* (Bangkok, Thailand: The Siam Society, 1962), vii. "While racial and linguistic affiliations are not definitely established for these people, it is generally accepted that they are a branch of the Tibeto-Burmese stock," Ibid, 69.

[150] Gordon H. Luce, "Introduction to the Comparative Study of Karen Languages." *Journal of the Burma Research Society* 42 (1959), 11.

[151] Ronald D. Renard, *Kariang: History of Karen-T'ai Relations from the Beginning to 1923. A Dissertation for the Doctor of Philosophy in History* (Hawaii, HI: University of Hawaii, 1980), 47.

[152] Ibid, 48.

[153] Ibid, 50.

[154] Ibid, 50f.

[155] Ibid, 50.

Thailand. During the many wars between Siam and Burma the Karen were caught in between and their land was burnt and destroyed. During times of peace the Karen had to pay double the taxes of Burmese country people. The men were often taken into forced labor. Therefore Karen villages lacked strong men.[156]

Today almost all of Thailand's Karen live in the western part of the country along the shared border with Burma. The Sgaw Karen in the southern Omkoi district started to enter the country 200-300 years ago. Before them the Lawa people lived in the area, as archaeological findings have proven. Until today Karen as well as Thai are digging for wonderful decorated earthen ware in the area, which are dated from 14th-16th century, originating from the Buddhist Lawa.[157]

In 1947 the new independent state of Burma recognized the area as Karen but the Karen themselves did not think the constitution granted them sufficient autonomy or adequate territorial holdings.[158] They did not participate in talks *under* the Burmese, but they asked for an independent state. They had hopes that the English would help them in this endeavor because they had helped the British army during World War II very faithfully and effectively. But the new British labor government did not take the Karen into account.[159] Many Karen and their friends felt betrayed by the British.[160] Churchill foresaw the situation correctly when he foretold that another time of misery and ruin to come.[161] The Karen mobilized and formed the Karen National Defense Organization (*KNDO*), later called Karen National Union (*KNU*). Revolt soon broke out and a prolonged conflict was the result. The conflict remains unsolved until today. The Karen people in the hills of Burma have suffered a lot under the Burmese army. Since the change of politics in 2011, there is some hope that the conflict may be resolved. But after this prolonged civil war and extended suffering it is very hard for the Karen to trust the Burmese government.

"Estimates of the total Karen population range from three to seven millions, depending on whether the data is sourced from the Burmese government or resistance."[162] "Burma is estimated to have a population of 48.8 million (Central

---

[156] Roland Mischung, *Religion und Wirklichkeitsvorstellungen in einem Karen-Dorf Nordwest-Thailands* (Wiesbaden, Germany: Franz Steiner Verlag, 1984), 14. Mischung is professor of ethnology at Hamburg University. Even during World War II many young Karen men were forced by the Japanese to carry arms into Burma. Pathi Charloue of Long village told me his own story, and how many were killed and how he survived as a 14 year old guy.

[157] I have seen many of these sites. Until today some Lawa villages in the Hot district live side by side to Pwo Karen villages.

[158] Schrock, 802.

[159] "The British did little to ensure that Karen nationalist interests were taken into account in the brief period between the defeat of the Japanese in 1945 and the granting of independence to Burma in 1948. Charles F. Keyes, "The politics of 'Karen-ness' in Thailand." In *Living at the Edge of Thai Society*, ed. Claudio O. Delang (New York, NY: RoutledgeCurzon, 2003), 213.

[160] Benedict Rogers, *A Land Without Evil. Stopping the genocide of Burma's Karen people* (Oxford, UK: Monarch books, 2004), 73-91.

[161] In a debate on 5th Nov. 1947 Winston Churchill, leader of the opposition at that time, told parliament: "All loyalties have been discarded and rebuffed; all faithful service has been forgotten and brushed aside ... We stand on the threshold of another scene of misery and ruin." Ibid, 88.

[162] Ardeth Maung Thanwnghmung, *The "Other" Karen in Myanmar* (Langham, ML: Rowman &

Intelligence Agency, 2010), although there has been no official census since 1983."[163] As the third largest group the Karen make up about 7% of the total population in Burma.[164] In 1980 Renard estimated the Karen to number three to five million people.[165] An official census by the Hilltribe Welfare and Development Center in April 2002 shows, that there are 438'450 Karen living in just over 2000 villages in Thailand. I know of villages in Tak province which border on Chiang Mai province where not yet half of the population has been granted Thai citizenship even though they have lived in the area for many generations. Another 100'000 Karen live in refugee camps along the border. In addition, many more Karen from Burma live in Thailand illegally. By 2015, there must be over six hundred thousand Karen living in Thailand.[166]

Language

The Karen languages are hard to categorize into a linguistic family. Linguists refer to them as the Karenic group of the Tibeto-Burman family. Lebar concludes that their position within this category remains doubtful.[167] The main Karen groups are the Sgaw Karen who call themselves Praganyaw. They are the biggest group.[168] Then the Pwo Karen who call themselves Phlong. The Red Karen are also known as Kayah. The different dialects usually need translation in order to be intelligible to each other.

Livelihood and Economy

In the mountains many Karen live on subsistence farming. They plant rice in hill fields on a slash and burn basis or they may have terraced paddy fields which they can use every year. In recent years Karen in the Omkoi area have started to plant tomatoes and chilies for cash crops. In addition, Karen are raising buffalos, cows, pigs and chicken. While buffaloes and cows roam the forest, pigs and chicken are kept under or beside the house.

Traditionally, the Karen have been a self-reliant people. They have gathered their food in the forest, have caught the fish from the rivers or the men have gone hunting from time to time. They have planted cotton and worked through the whole process of weaving their own beautiful cloth. Till today, Karen like to wear their own hand-woven cloth, especially the ladies. It is a mark of their identity of being

---

Littlefield Publishers, 2012), xvii.

[163] http://www.cdc.gov/tb/publications/guidestoolkits/ethnographicguides/Burma/chapters/chapter1.pdf (22.01.2015), 1.

[164] Ibid. Operation world states a population of Myanmar at 50.495.672 for 2010 of which the Karen make up an estimated 9,24 %. Jason Mandryk, *Operation World.* Completely Revised – 7th Edition (Colorado Springs, CO: Biblica Publishing, 2010), 609.

[165] Renard, 8.

[166] The total hilltribe population is given as 914.755 people. The Karen are by far the biggest people group of what the Thai call *chao khao* (people of the mountains).

[167] Frank M. Lebar, Gerald C. Kickey, John K. Musgrave, *Ethnic Groups of Mainland Southeast Asia* (New Haven, CT: Human Relations Area Files Press, 1964), 59.

[168] Die Sgaw machen gegen die 80% aller Karen in Thailand aus. Paul und Elaine Lewis, *Völker im Goldenen Dreieck* (Stuttgart, Germany: Edition Hansjörg Mayer, 1984), 70.

Karen. They always had to buy salt from outside as well as metal tools. Until today salt is seen as very valuable.

Social Structure

The smallest unit among the Karen is the nuclear family, which occupies one household. Most households are made up of husband, wife, and any unmarried children. After marriage, the husband is usually going to live in the house of his wife. For one to three years they may live in the same house, before they will build their own. "The place of woman in the Karen culture is very much equal to that of the man. ... The house is hers, though the man provides it."[169] There are certain traits which show a clear tendency towards matrilineal structures. The Karen marry for life. Adultery or divorce is seldom and is strongly disapproved in their culture. Relatives and the village may pressurize the couple to go along with each other because otherwise the "Guardian Spirit of Water and Land" may punish the whole village.[170] If there is a divorce, the children stay with the mother.[171]

The village is the largest social unit.[172] The village is presided over by a headman who is recognized as the village's political leader by the government of Thailand. From a Karen point of view he has little power.[173] His duty is to determine the village consensus and then to follow it up. This can put him into a difficult position, as he needs to remain a "good Karen", while carrying out his duty as a headman for the government. On the village level it is the men who lead. If there is a decision to be made, all the influential people in the village will be consulted beforehand in order to find an agreement which will be confirmed on a village level meeting, where men and women are present, but is led by men.[174] Unanimity is important. Issues that are not agreed on are not acted on. On the village level, the Karen in the mountains still can exercise a certain amount of autonomy.

---

[169] Edwin J. Hudspith, "Tribal Highways and Byways: a Church Growth Study in North Thailand," M.A. Miss. Thesis, Fuller Theological Seminary Pasadena, 1969, 258.

[170] Hans Bär, *Heilsgeschichtlicher Bibelunterricht. McIlwains Programm 'Building on Firm Foundations' im Einsatz unter den Karen im Bezirk Omkoi (Nordthailand)* (Bonn, Germany: Verlag für Kultur und Wissenschaft, 1998), 108.

[171] In order to appease the "Guardian Spirit of Water and Land" certain rites have to be performed. Yamamoto writes: "Though the rite is performed by either a wife or a husband, importance is predominantly attached to the wife. The sacrificial animals, the ritual place (house) and the participants (children) are all identified as the wife's belongings." Kumiko Yamamoto, "Religion and Religious Change in a Hill Karen Community of Northwestern Chiang Mai Province," *JSS* Volume 79, (1991), 136.

[172] "in Thailand until half a century ago, for a majority of the Karen, the village was the largest political unit, and the village ritual leader was a leader among equals." Yoko Hayami, *Between Hills and Plains. Power and Practice in Socio-Religious Dynamics among Karen*. Kyoto Area Studies on Asia, Volume 7 (Kyoto, Japan: Kyoto University Press, 2004), 27.

[173] This is changing because the influence of the Thai administration is growing and Karen recognize that they need able representatives in the local and regional Thai administration.

[174] I have attended such meetings and once asked a question about a decision to be taken. This created an awkward situation since the Karen had agreed beforehand and the meeting was only to confirm and inform the village of the decision.

Cultural Values

Harmony can be seen as the highest value in Karen culture. It expresses itself in their desire to live in harmony with nature through the excellent fallow system they have developed in their agricultural circle. They try to live in harmony with the unseen powers through the annual celebrations in which they feast the guardian spirits of the village. "They attempt to maintain harmony in relationships within the village by submission to the acknowledged leaders, and harmony with their neighbours by avoiding conflict whenever possible."[175]

If there is conflict between families in the same village, it is often resolved in that one of the conflicting clan will establish a satellite village. I have seen such a satellite village being reintegrated into the mother village after some years, after the conflict was resolved. I agree with Steyne who writes:

> *The idea of reconciliation, the need to restore harmony or bring balance or equilibrium back to man's experience of his world, are very much a part of man's religious beingness. ... The concern for reconciliation does not arise out of a sense of guilt or even shame, but rather that of fear and the knowledge that disharmony plugs the conduit of blessing.*[176]

Values are transmitted by their oral tradition. Karen have lots of stories about *orphans*. Karen identify with the deprived and underprivileged orphan who by his whit will overcome the obstacles and be victorious. Hovemyr emphasizes the Karen self-identification as underprivileged orphans, but with a sense of moral superiority.[177] "Orphans have to cope without protection from parents and ritual support; so they must be clever, highly moral and develop supernatural powers."[178] "The orphan theme provides a means of communication that reaches the heart of the Karen."[179] I have also been impressed by their *social sensitivity*. It is often Karen who lead orphanages and are working in this kind of institution.

Traditional Karen culture stands for *high moral values* which in many ways are similar to biblical standards. Unmarried young people are not supposed to have any intimate relationship. Karen husbands and wives stay together for life. Adultery is a major taboo. Harmony and family go hand in hand, Karen strife for both.

The Karen think very highly of *education*. The legend of the "Golden Book" mentioned before has shown them the value of education. While missionaries built schools for Karen in Burma already 150 years ago, in Thailand the Karen had no such opportunity. "Thailand was quite unlike British Burma in that almost no

---

[175] Paul and Elaine Lewis, *Peoples of the Golden Triangle* (London, UK: Thames and Hudson Ltd, 1984), 10. Cf. Lewis, *Goldenes Dreieck*, 71.

[176] Philip M. Steyne, *Gods of Power* (Houston, TX: Touch Publications, 1990), 147f.

[177] Anders Hovemyr, *In Search of the Karen King* (Uppsala, Sweden: Studia Missionaria Uppsaliensia, 1989).

[178] Mikael Gravers, "Waiting for a righteous ruler: The Karen royal imaginary in Thailand and Burma," *Journal of Southeast Asian Studies*, 42, 2 (June 2012), 348.

[179] Hudspith, 263f.

missionaries preached to the Sgaws or Pwos. Few became Christian, fewer joined the civil service and almost none received a higher education."[180]

Today for many Karen their number one goal is to obtain a good education. They feel left behind if they do not have educational opportunities equal to the rest of Thailand and the world.

This short outline on who the Karen are, also shows the major challenges these people face in today's world. Strong traditional values are confronted with educational, economic and social changes. Under these circumstances it is not surprising that many Karen are looking for a new faith with which they can rise to these challenges.

Religion

Traditionally Karen people are animists who practice ancestor worship. Over the last decades ancestor worship among Thai Karen has diminished tremendously. The so called '*au qai*'[181] ritual which has been performed for the ancestors has nearly died out. Even in very remote villages, only a few families still carry out this ritual which is led by the oldest woman of the family. Many Karen are just fed up with the demands of the ancestors to sacrifice their chicken, pigs and buffaloes to them so that an ill person will get better. This kind of economic reasoning is the main explanation in addition however, it is very impractical to call all the family members together when they are working far away in Chiang Mai or Bangkok. Many have become Christians and have stopped this ritual as well as many other animistic rituals. But it is not only the Christians who have stopped the '*au qai*' tradition. Many non-Christian Karen have told me that they have stopped the ancestor worship by having performed what they call a '*hsai k'si*' ritual.[182] This is a ritual offered by specialists to help the Karen cut themselves off completely from their ancestors. In this ritual, a person is injected with a liquid which is so horrendous for the ancestors ('*mü qa*') that the ancestors will not dare to come near to them anymore. Keyes and Mischung speak of tattooing the persons to signify that they have undertaken this rite.[183] Mischung observes that the ritual does not always succeed but that the '*mü qa*' still may come and demand food, for example if someone has become ill and the patient has seen his parents or grandparents in a dream asking for food.[184]

---

[180] Ronald D. Renard, "Studying peoples often called Karen." In *Living at the Edge of Thai Society*, ed. Claudio O. Delang, (New York, NY: RoutledgeCurzon, 2003) 11. The earliest known Sgaw graduate, Mr Thom Nithithom from Mae Sariang, received his degree from Chulalongkorn University in about 1960 to become a lawyer.

[181] The Karen in Burma call it '*ta aw Bgha*' (to eat the Bgha). Marshall, 248.

[182] This is not a new cult as Keyes was thinking it might be but rather a means to get rid of the duty of ancestor worship. They may still decide to become Buddhist or Christians later. Cf. Mischung, *Religion*, 179ff.

[183] Charles F. Keyes, *Ethnic Adaptation and Identity. The Karen on the Thai Frontier with Burma* (Philadelphia: Institute for the Study of Human Issues, Inc., 1979), 132. Mischung speaks of ritual tattooing ("rituellen Tatauierung"), 181.

[184] Mischung, *Religion*, 184. Buadaeng notices: "despite the near disappearance of the cult, the ancestor spirits still heavily influence their descendants. ... Consequently, propitiation of ancestor spirits

Even though the '*au qai*' ritual has been widely abandoned the animistic Karen still perform a lot of different ceremonies, rituals and offerings in order to appease the many different spirits and powers. This is especially the case if someone falls ill. Karen want to know the cause of the illness or accident for they believe that such things must always have some spiritual reason. This is investigated using different methods of divination. In order to be successful in healing the illness, the cause needs to be known beforehand.

Often a '*ki cü*'[185] ritual will be performed. '*Ki cü*' rituals can have many different meanings, one of the most important is the '*ki cü kau k'la*' in order to call back the '*kl'a*'. Or before they plant rice or do an important work they may offer small sacrifices ('*lü ta*') on the way entering the village.[186]

In addition to these many different spirits and ancestor spirits, Karen believe in God, who created all things. They call him '*Ywa*'.[187] He has been known through their mythology and oral tradition. '*Ywa*' once created everything but then he went to a place where nobody can go. But he will return to his orphaned children. In their oral tradition the Karen are the "oldest brother". The white man is the youngest. At the beginning God gave each one a book. As long as they lived according to this book everything went well. But the oldest did not care much about the book but went to the fields to work. He forgot the book on the porch from where it fell down and was eaten by the pigs and chicken. Since then the Karen live in ignorance and hardship. But they kept the hope that one day the younger white brother will bring back the book.[188] Some Karen saw the coming of the first missionaries to Burma as the fulfillment of this myth.[189]

Karen have told me stories about creation, Adam and Eve and the temptation as well as the flood which are amazingly similar to the biblical stories.[190] The Karen also have some prayers to '*Ywa*'[191] but prayers to different spirits predominate.

---

is worked into contemporary religious practice, even when Karen have become Christian or Buddhist." Kwanchewan Buadaeng, *Negotiating Religious Practices in a Changing Sgaw Karen Community in North Thailand*. A thesis submitted in fulfillment of the requirements for the degree of Doctor of Philosophy (University of Sydney, 2001), 52.

[185] A wrist tying ritual.

[186] For more details on propitiation rituals and different spirits: Buadaeng, 70-102. Mischung, *Religion*, 189-221.

[187] '*Ywa*' is the word used for God in the Bible.

[188] I have heard the story myself. It has many different versions but the essence is the same. It explains why the Karen are not as prosperous as other groups. Cf. Renard, 2. Hudspith, 264f. Mischung, *Religion*, 25. Buadaeng, 37.

[189] Lewis, 71. When the English arrived in Burma many Karen greeted them enthusiastically as the young brother who brings back the "Golden Book", which they identified as the Bible. Many Karen became Christians. Cf. Mischung, *Religion*, 25.

[190] Francis Mason, *The Karen Apostle*. Revised by H. J. Ripley (Boston, MA: Gould, Kendall, and Lincoln, 1847), 97-99. Copyright: BiblioLife, LLC

[191] "The days of the Mon kings, of the Burman kings, and of the Siamese kings are past, runs one prayer to Ywa, and the day of the Karen king is yet to come, when the Karen will dwell within the great town, the high city, the golden palace." Theodore Stern, "Ariya and the Golden Book: A Millenarian Buddhist Sect Among the Karen." *The Journal of Asian Studies* 27, 2 (1968): 304.

The '*Ywa*' tradition[192] have helped the Karen to become Christians, because missionaries told them stories which sounded familiar to them.[193] But besides there a many legends about '*Ywa*' which are very different from any story in the Bible. Some Christian Karen say the Buddhist will tell you those.[194]

Beside the '*Ywa*' tradition which has become prominent among Christians, animistic Karen are much more occupied with the works of '*mü gaw li*' (devil). Among new Christians, I have observed that they often refer to '*mü gaw li*' and how to counter his temptations and evil intentions much more than to '*Ywa*'.

Mischung summarizes his investigation into traditional Karen religion, saying that in comparison to other tribal people the Karen religion is poor in motives.[195] Their religious perception is determined mainly in *negative* themes.[196] Their ritual praxis serves the coping with the negative structural reality. A positive perspective is missing.[197]

The Concept of '*k'la*'

Since '*k'la*' play a significant role in dreams it will be necessary to explain the term. What Larchrojna terms 'soul' is what the Karen name '*k'la*', which might be translated "life principle (shade)"[198] while the Karen word '*tha*' or '*sa*' describes the emotions and the will of a person and may be translated "soul" or "heart". The moral values are also given to the '*tha*' not to the '*k'la*'. Under the heading "our good or evil actions not chargeable to the '*k'la*'," Wade writes: "When we sin it is not our '*k'la*' that sins, it is our '*tha*' that sins. And good people's glory does not belong to the '*k'la*' but to the good heart."[199] "The '*k'la*' of human beings is sometimes spoken of in the same way as we speak of ghosts, or apparitions; the departed spirit; it appears to answer to the term 'angel' as used in Ac. 12:15 'it is his angel.'"[200] The '*k'la*' equates about the term which Lothar Käser uses for "spirit

---

[192] "The third conception in the religious traditions of the people is embodied in the 'Y'wa' legend, which tells of the placing of the first parents in the garden by 'Y'wa,' the Creator, their temptation to eat of the forbidden fruit by a serpent or dragon, etc. This story so closely resembles that of the ancient Hebrews, as also certain western Asiatic traditions, that one finds it difficult not to believe that all these traditions somehow had a common origin. Were the 'Y'wa' legend marked by distinctive features, we might regard it as one exhibiting only a general resemblance to other traditions extant in other parts of the world, but its parallelism with the account in Genesis precludes this view of the case," Marshall, 210f.

[193] The father of my former language informant told me in a talk in Omkoi, 12th Aug. 1996.

[194] Buadaeng reports some of these stories. Buadaeng, 40f.

[195] "Im Vergleich zu Religionen mancher anderer 'Naturvölker' ist die der Karen von einer auffälligen Motiv-Armut." Mischung, *Religion*, 226.

[196] „ist die religiöse Vorstellungswelt der Karen überwiegend von *negativen* Themen ... bestimmt." Mischung, *Religion*, 227.

[197] "dass der überwiegende Teil ihrer rituellen Praxis der Bewältigung einer negativ strukturierten Wirklichkeit gewidmet ist, ohne dass dem ein entsprechend elaborierter positiver Sinnkomplex gegenüberstünde." Mischung, *Religion*, 228.

[198] Marshall, 218.

[199] Wade, *Thesaurus*, 449. Translation from Karen by the author.

[200] Wade, *Thesaurus*, 445.

double" who does not live in a person but very near to it, and who may wander about while dreaming.[201] The Thesaurus, which contains a wealth of cultural insights which were compiled by missionaries and Karen, comments:

> *The Karens speak of the 'k'la' of the living man, as distinct from, but intimately connected with the body; a spirit which existed prior to the body, and will survive its dissolution. The body with the animal life, and mind, are subject to its power and influence so far as health and disease, life and death are concerned. It may, therefore, be termed man's Genius, or Guardian spirit. It is supposed capable of leaving the body and wandering about at pleasure, particularly when the bodily senses are locked up in sleep; but if, as often happens, it is by any means detained beyond the usual time, disease ensues; and if permanently detained, death is the consequence; hence, in illness, offerings are made to the 'k'la' to induce it to return.*[202]

From this text we can conclude that dreams do not only predict illness but are the cause of it, because the *'k'la'* may be caught by spirits and cannot return to his body.

"The *'k'la'* is supposed to be capable of being frightened away from the body by those things which frighten the man."[203] At a funeral, I have observed that Karen Animist and Buddhist do not allow children and women to go to the funeral site in fear that their *'k'la'* will be frightened away. The *'k'la'* of women and children are seen as weaker than the *'k'la'* of men and therefore are more easily attacked by spirits.[204] Some Christian women take part and go to the funeral site because they believe that they are protected by God and also that the spirit of the deceased will be with God. Therefore they do not fear anymore.

For Karen it is a great offense if somebody does frighten another person. Karen believe that the *'k'la'* will leave that person and that the person may become ill. If this happens the person who has made the offence may have to pay a fine and if the victim is an Animist or Buddhist, he has to pay the cost of a ritual to call back the *'k'la'*.

Mischung mentions the following five main reasons why the *'k'la'* go missing:[205]

a. The *'k'la'* distanced themselves too far from the body and therefore stray in the surroundings.

b. They have been caught by spirits in the forest.

c. The *'kau k'ca'* keep the *'k'la'* caught, sometimes without reason, sometimes because the owner was disrespectful towards them.

---

[201] Käser, *Animismus*, 109-119.

[202] Jonathan Wade, *Thesaurus of Karen Knowledge, Vol.1*, (Rangoon, Burma: U Maung U, 1963). First Published in Karen: Jonathan Wade and Sau Kau-Too (compilers). *Thesaurus of Karen Knowledge*. (Tavoy, Burma: Karen Mission Press, Vol. I, 1847), 448.

[203] Wade, *Thesaurus*, 450.

[204] Cf. Buadaeng, 48.

[205] Mischung, *Religion*, 130.

d. The dead have allured the '*k'la hko hti*' into the '*plü kau*'.
e. The ancestors feel neglected by their descendants and therefore do not let the '*k'la*' go.

Each time a calling back ceremony has to be performed.

The Thesaurus notes the following about the '*k'la*' in relation to dreams: "The time of sleep seems to be the most common occasion on which the '*k'la*' thus wanders from the body. When in these wanderings it holds intercourse with evil beings, the sleeper in the mean time has evil dreams."[206] People think the '*k'la*' go out when they dream and they may be caught by spirits, and not come back. So they have to sacrifice to the spirits so they let them go and then they have to make a "calling back '*k'la*' ceremony" by tying the hand wrist.

Generally speaking animistic Karen in the Chiang Mai province believe that they possess thirty-three '*k'la*'.[207] Three of them are important, one is the 'head *k'la*' (*k'la hkö hti*) which resides on the head where the fontanel[208] is located. The other two are sitting behind the left and right ear.[209] According to Mischung the three embody the positive side of the human vitality which stands against the hostile nature while the thirty minor '*k'la*' embody the destructive, uncontrollable aspect of the human vitality, its animalistic component.[210] The '*k'la hko hti*' is the most crucial one. Some even call it a good or a pure one.[211] If it leaves, a person dies. It then goes to the '*plü kau*' from where it may come back to be reincarnated in

---

[206] Wade, *Thesaurus*, 452f.

[207] Appendix B, 14P: "Our forefathers said there are 33. There is one behind each ear and one on the fontanelle. During the night they wander, they say. They go out to other houses to the fields and they go and eat what is left there. But the three main '*k'la*' do not wander away." Appendix 64Ch. Mischung, *Religion*, 122. Hinton also speaks of 33 "souls". Peter Hinton, "The Pwo Karen of Northern Thailand: a Preliminary Report." Unpublished paper (Chiang Mai, 1969) 33. "The Karen in the present study believed there were 33 or more *kala* which reside in each human's body." Kinuko Omori, Lawrence P. Greksa, "Morbidity and Mortality Patterns, Health Beliefs, and Health Risk Factors of Karen Highlanders of Northwest Thailand," in *Southeast Asian Journal*, Vol. 30, No. 4 (Dec 1999), 796. In some villages in Tak province some informants spoke of seven 'k'la' which corresponds with the number given in the *Thesaurus*. See Appendix 38Luwa, 45S and 63Jae. In the *Thesaurus* we find some sources which interpreted the 'k'la' very negatively, they said: "The 'k'la' is sometimes spoken of as *seven* beings; it is, however always used in the singular number; ... According to *some*, the seven are constantly devising means to destroy the body, which is protected by another genius, called 'tso'. The 'tso' has its residence on, or about the head, from which eminence it watches approaching evil, and prevents it." Wade, *Thesaurus*, 450. "If the 'tso' is going away from above us, we will die." Wade, *Thesaurus*, 452 (Translation from Karen by the author). See also Cross, 311. The description of the '*tso*' is about the same as my informants made of the main '*k'la*' ('*k'la hko hti*' or '*k'la wi: wa:*'). Buadaeng gives the number of 37 '*k'la*' of which 32 are away residing in some wild animals like tigers or gibbons. Buadaeng, 47. I have never heard of that number, but some of the '*k'la*' are given the names of wild animals but they should still be around the person. If staying away they are called back.

[208] Fontanel = '*hko hti*'.

[209] Appendix B, 14P. Similar in Mischung, *Religion*, 123.

[210] Mischung, *Religion*, 123.

[211] Appendix B, 64Ch: "The one who cannot walk is a good one. Because he stays with you on the fontanel. When this one goes away you will die.".

another person.[212] Somu's mother[213] was sure that this happened with some of her thirteen children of which only six have survived. She told me that one of her small children with a remarkable birthmark died after she had had a bad dream about fire. Later she dreamed that she would conceive and she did. When she gave birth to this child it had the same birthmark at the same place. She was sure that it was the same *'k'la'*, and that the deceased child had come back.

The thirty other minor *'k'la'* are not as important, they are not very useful and they like to wander because they like eating. But they are still important for the well-being of the person.[214] My informants said that the main *'k'la'* is not leaving, if it leaves the person dies.[215] Mischung writes that the main *'k'la'* may go off sometime in order to meet the deceased (*'plü'*) in the afterworld (*'plü kau'*). But this happens at high risk because the *'plü'* may want to keep him there which would mean that the person dies.

The Land of the Dead (*'plü kau'*)

The *'plü kau'* is another part of animistic Karen cosmology which correlates a lot with dreams of the Karen. It is thought that if a Karen dies a normal death, the appointed time of the *'k'la hko hti'* is expired. Therefore, the *'k'la hko hti'* of the deceased goes back into the realm of the dead as *'plü'* (dead). The other 32 *'k'la'* disappear after some time. They do not have further significance. If someone dies a violent death, people fear that his *'k'la'* will not be able to enter the *'plü kau'* immediately because his appointed time has not come yet to return. He therefore becomes a forest spirit which is much feared.

The *'k'la hko hti'* which goes back to the *'plü kau'* may be reborn into the world. In this respect the Buddhist concept of reincarnation sounds familiar to the Karen. Even some Christians still think that their relatives who they have lost, will be reincarnated into this world.[216] One of my informants explained,

> *Your father has died and you dream that the father comes to you and asks you to come to him as well. That is when your father has already died. And then your wife gets pregnant. That meant that your father had come back (in the womb of your wife). ... If the child then is born and has the same mark as your father, then it is confirmed that this is the case.*[217]

The land of the dead (*'plü kau'*) is thought to be upside down or like a mirror image. The sun rises in the west and goes down in the east. When it is day here, it is night in the realm of the dead. The mouth of the river is the spring over there.

---

[212] "There is a belief that *k'la* of the deceased can enter a person at birth. This belief is also found among the Karen in Burma (Marshall 1997[1922]: 218) and the Burmese themselves (Spiro 1978). It is similar to the Buddhist notion of the reincarnation." Buadaeng, 49.

[213] Talk in her house in Mor Kler Khi, 2nd June, 2014.

[214] I remember a Karen man calling all his *'k'la'* back outside a village we had just visited. He wanted to make sure that they all come with him so that he will stay well.

[215] Appendix B, 64Ch.

[216] Appendix B, 14P; 38M; 38MM.

[217] Appendix B, 14P.

When it is rainy season in this world it is dry season in the land of the dead. Everything is the opposite way to what it is here. The '*plü kau*' is the negative pole of Karen cosmology.

The '*plü kau*' can be divided into two realms. One is the '*doo s'wau*' where most dead Karen are thought to be; the other is the '*doo lau ra*' where those who have sinned ('*ma ta dä ba*') a lot during their lifetime will be kept. Literally, the first means "forest villages" against "forest of rolling down."[218] The '*doo lau ra*' is comparable with what Christians call hell. The separation of those who arrive at the '*plü kau*' into the '*doo s'wau*' and the '*doo lau ra*' is done by a guard called '*hkoo sei hkau klai*'. He weighs the relative sin of each '*plü*' who arrives there.[219] The '*doo s'wau*' can be thought of a pleasant place. Using the term "heaven" for it, would be misleading or would have to be explained. In Karen thinking people who are in the '*doo s'wau*' still have to work as they worked in this world. One of my main informants explained,

> *Regarding those who have died, some still dream of them that they do fields, some build nice houses, others not so nice. So they think if you die you will still have to work. They believe in this: You still have to do fields and build houses and they think it is that way. They believe, after death they still have to do things. They do not believe that they are with God in His kingdom. They still have to do things. Therefore, when a person dies, they give him knives, rice seeds and potatoes and other things to plant.*[220]

Karen dream a lot about the '*plü*'. In dreams their '*k'la*' may visit the '*plü kau*'. "Sometimes I dream like doing things here. There are young people there, too. I go to villages and I eat with people."[221] Their own '*k'la*' will meet with those in the realm of the dead. This can be dangerous because the '*k'la*' may be allured to stay there[222] or it may be caught by other spirits on the way back. This will lead to perilous sickness.

2.4.2 The Significance of Dreams Among the Karen

Quite a lot of research has been undertaken on Karen customs, practice of ancestor worship ('*au qai*')[223] and the spirit world of the traditional Karen as well as about their mythology[224] and their poems ('*hta*').[225] A study in anthropology and ethnol-

---

[218] 'doo' means forest. 's'wau' means village. 'lau ra' means roll down or to drop.

[219] Cf. Mischung, *Religion*, 141.

[220] Appendix B, 67BR.

[221] Appendix B, 54Ch. Cf. 57A.

[222] Cf. Appendix B, 28Ch.

[223] Buadaeng, Hayami, Marshall, Mischung, Wade, Yamamoto.

[224] Saw Hay Moo, *Doing Theology in the Karen Church: The Gospel as Incarnation (John 1:1-14) within the Karen YWA (God) Tradition*. A Dissertation for the Doctor of Missiology (Pasadena, CA: Fuller Theological Seminary, 2002). Francis Mason, *The Karen Apostle*. Revised by H. J. Ripley. (Boston, MA: Gould, Kendall, and Lincoln, 1847). Copyright: BiblioLife, LLC.

[225] Roland Mischung, „When it is better to sing than to speak: the use of traditional verses (*hta*) in tense social situations." In *Living at the Edge of Thai Society*, (130-150), ed. Claudio O. Delang (New York, NY: RoutledgeCurzon, 2003). Mischung, Religion, 243-252.

ogy about the Karen in Burma was written by Harry Ignatius Marshall in 1922,[226] or the findings which Jonathan Wade collected in the Thesaurus give great insights.[227] However not much attention has yet been given to the theme of dreams, which plays a significant role in everyday life of the Karen people, neither in these early works nor in other research.

Marshall as well as Cross[228] mention that the spirits of notoriously evil persons in this earthly life or those who were put to death because of major criminal offences are called '*ta mü qa*' or '*ta mü ta qa*'. They appear in dreams as wild animals or as 'pongyis', Burmese Buddhist monks. They "are usually seen by sick persons whose spirits ('*k'la*') they are seeking and on which they subsist."[229] Wade writes: "The '*ta mü qa*' (this word transliterated from Burmese Karen script by the author) appear to persons in dreams in the shape of dogs, elephants, Burmans, Burman priests, vultures".[230]

While a person sleeps his '*k'la*' may leave his body and roam. "When in these wanderings it holds intercourse with evil beings, the sleeper in the meantime has evil dreams it is owing to the protection of the '*so*' that these imaginary evils do not become real ones."[231] In a short reference to dreams Mason wrote: "The sensation in sleep, called 'night mare,' is produced, the Karens say, by a 'Na' being seated on the region of the stomach."[232]

Somphob Larchrojna, in his master thesis about Karen medicine refers to dreams on several occasions, since dreams are often connected with illnesses. "Dreams were believed to show the wanderings of one's soul."[233] "Should one dream about someone dead, for instance, one's wrists would quickly be bound to recall one's soul from the afterworld, lest one should fall ill and even die."[234] He writes of an instance where both the father of a sick child and the diviner dreamed "that the spirit of a grandparent begged them to remove the wrist and neck bindings, so he could take the child with him."[235] After the bindings were removed the child died. Larchrojna also mentions two instances of exorcism because people who were

---

[226] Harry Ignatius Marshall, *The Karen People of Burma. A Study in Anthropology and Ethnology*, (Bangkok, Thailand: White Lotus Press, 1997 (1922).

[227] Jonathan Wade, *Thesaurus of Karen Knowledge, Vol.1*, (Rangoon: U Maung U, 1963). First Published in Karen: Jonathan Wade and Sau Kau-Too (compilers). *Thesaurus of Karen Knowledge*. (Tavoy, Burma: Karen Mission Press, Vol. I, 1847).

[228] E.B. Cross, "On the Karens." In *Journal of the American Oriental Society* 4 (1854): 312f.

[229] Marshall, 229.

[230] Wade, *Thesaurus*, 458.

[231] Ibid, 453. Tongkham Song Saeng, *Demonology among the Karens* (Bachelor of Theology Thesis. Chiang Mai, Thailand: The Thailand Theological Seminary, 1964), 15. Song Saeng cites Wade word by word without giving any hint to the source. Much of his thesis is based on Thesaurus, Vol. 1, 442-486.

[232] Francis Mason, "Religion, Mythology, and Astronomy among the Karens" in *Journal of the Asiatic Society of Bengal*, Vol. XXXIV, No. III, Part II (October 1865), 211.

[233] Somphob Larchrojna, *Karen Medicine*, (A thesis submitted in fulfillment of the requirements for the Master of Arts degree. Sidney, Australia: Sidney University, 1975), 39.

[234] Ibid, 39.

[235] Ibid, 94.

frightened by nightmares.[236] Finally, he mentions that "if a woman had a strange or beautiful dream after sexual intercourse, she would conclude the next morning that she had conceived."[237]

From these references we get a glimpse of how different dreams are experienced and how much they interfere with everyday life.

The Japanese anthropologist, Hayami, writes: "Many times when I visited a Karen person, I was told 'I dreamed last night that you were coming'."[238] I have had a similar experience, when visiting the home village with a student. The father received his son with the words: "I dreamed last night that you were coming with salt."[239] Hayami has interpreted this kind of reception as "a tendency to regard a social event, such as a meeting of two persons, as the fulfillment of a predestined fate. ... In fact, I had been told this so many times, that I began to be dubious, considering it a Karen form of social nicety."[240]

But when I asked Somu's father what he dreamed to know that we were coming, he said: If in a dream I see my son sitting, I know he is not coming, but if he gets up, I know he is coming.

In his dissertation Roland Mischung[241] refers to dreams in several instances. He explains which role *'k'la'*[242] play in dreams. The thirty bad or minor *'k'la'* like to wander and the person in question will dream about things which are going to happen to him. If he has a happy dream he may receive money or have success but more often he dreams about things that mean he will get into troubles.[243] Or if somebody dreams of a dead person or feels strongly for that person the non-Christian Karen will perform a wrist-binding (*'ki cü'*) ceremony. It will help him to dispatch from the dead person.[244] The dead persons who have gone into the afterworld (*'plü kau'*) can appear in dreams. People fear such dreams because when dead people (*'plü'*) appear they do not only come to frighten the living but they allure the *'k'la'* to the *'plü kau'*.[245] I remember the widow of the headman in Sop Lahn telling me that she had dreams in which her deceased husband came and asked her to go with him.

---

[236] Ibid, 107, 112.

[237] Ibid, 117.

[238] Hayami, *Between Hills*, 29.

[239] Visit to Mor Kler Khi with Somu on 2nd June 2014. Unlike Hayami, I have not heard this very often.

[240] Ibid, 29.

[241] Roland Mischung, *Religion und Wirklichkeitsvorstellungen in einem Karen-Dorf Nordwest-Thailands*. (Wiesbaden, Germany: Franz Steiner Verlag, 1984). Mischung is professor of ethnology at Hamburg University.

[242] The concept of *'k'la'* is explained in his book on pages 122-136.

[243] Ibid, cf. 124.

[244] Ibid, cf. 126,131.

[245] Ibid, 139.184.

Mischung comments that a few of his informants claimed that they could see the great spirit(s) of the land (*'kau k'ca'*) in dreams who appeared as old men – a few as women – in traditional Karen dressing.[246]

Mischung's mentioning of dreams in various contexts are very interesting, but they are not in the focus of his work. However, it becomes clear that the *'k'la'* and the dead (*'plü'*) and the land of the dead (*'plü kau'*) play an important role when it comes to dreaming.

Yoshimatsu writes: "The original soul (main *'k'la'*) in the realm of the dead sometimes contacts human beings in this world through dreams (because face to face contact with any soul (*'k'la'*) causes immediate death of mortals)."[247] That would mean that dreams are essential for animistic Karen to get into contact or be contacted by the afterworld.

The Karen Animist believes that the thirty minor *'k'la'* may travel through dreams.[248] "They not only can travel around the world, but also to other worlds. Through dreams, minor souls may transform their shape to a water buffalo, bird or butterfly."[249] I have hardly found any evidence for these last statements.

From Mischung and Yoshimatsu's research it is clear that the *'k'la'* and the *'plü kau'* play an important role in dreams.

Just how significant dreams are among the Karen was shown to me in the following experiences when I walked with my wife to several remote mainly animistic/buddhistic villages from 1st - 9th August 2012. In practically all the villages we heard people talk about their dreams, without us asking questions. Let me give you some examples.

While we were guests at Atipa's house in Toplakhi, he gave testimony as to how he had become a Christian. His wife was ill and nobody could help. The Baptist pastor Sumee from Topladae had come to visit him. Atipa and his wife were ready to become Christians, but Atipa's mother did not want him to become a Christian. The next night, while the evangelist slept in his house, Atipa had such a wonderful and positive dream. He told his mother about it and said to her that he was going to believe in Jesus.[250] The dream had helped him to overcome the resistance of his mother.

In the village of Thibokhi we were guests with the evangelist couple Supopa and Supomo. Supomo had not been well for the last six months. She had had severe pain in her abdomen. She had been consulting many different doctors. We once

---

[246] Ibid, 191.

[247] Kumiko Yoshimatsu, "The Karen World: The Cosmological and Ritual Belief System of the Sgaw Karen in North Western Chiang Mai Province." *Final Research Report Presented to the National Research Council of Thailand, Bangkok.* 13.

[248] Cf. Chumpol Maniratanavongsiri, Religion and Social Change: Ethnic Continuity and Change among the Karen in Thailand with Reference to the Canadian Indian Experience. A Thesis for the Degree of Master of Art. (Peterborough, Ontario, Canada: Trent University, 1993). 29. Also Mischung, 124.

[249] Maniratanavongsiri, 29.

[250] My talk with Atipa and his wife in his house in the evening of 1st Aug. 2012.

took her out to McCormick hospital in Chiang Mai for a thorough checkup. On this evening the Christians who had come for two days of training, were all going to pray for Supomo. Before they prayed, she said that she had had a dream at the beginning of her illness. She had dreamed several times that somebody asked her to carry children on her back but she was not able to do it. She also dreamed that somebody had come and asked her to cook a meal even though that person could cook well. She felt she could not do it. It was too much for her. After Supomo became ill, she said that she did not dream these dreams anymore.[251] We could see that Supomo believed that at the beginning she had had a dream and now she had gotten into trouble as the dream had forewarned. At that time, we were tempted to give a psychological interpretation of the dream, since we knew that she had worked so hard that year. She always stayed in Thibokhi because she had to look after the hostel with 10 children and her husband was often away in other villages.[252]

The next day we walked to Chroetha. We had come to Repomo's and her husband's Repopa's house. They said that they would like to become Christians. Repomo comes from a Christian family but when she married an unbeliever she went back to the old way. Now, after six years, her husband was willing to become a Christian and they wanted to make a new start with Christ. While we were sitting in their bamboo hut, the first thing Repomo told us was that she had had a bad dream the night before. She dreamed about spirits and that she was naked. This bothered her and made her afraid.

We explained that the spirits might not be happy about her decision to become a Christian, and that we would specifically pray for her regarding this dream so that it would have no ill effect on her. She was relieved.[253]

When we came back to Chiang Mai, on the same day Supomo's son, Mr. Gula phoned from Bangkok where he was studying at a Bible Seminary. He asked how his mother was and whether she was better. I had to tell him that we had prayed for her again and that she still was having some pain before our visit with her. Mr. Gula then mentioned that he had had a dream the previous night. I could tell that he was bothered by it, but he did not tell me what his dream was about.[254] Within just ten days, we had had many experiences with dreams, each of which caused the person involved to take some immediate action.

Following are three additional, more recent examples of how dreams are perceived and how they influence the respective person's life.

A very loving Karen friend of mine who has had a history of fears had gone to another village to teach the Bible. At night he dreamed that he had lost his flip flop shoes. People interpreted the dream to mean that he had lost his wife's love. He was so concerned about his dream that he left the village immediately to run

---

[251] Supomo giving testimony on her illness on 5th Aug. 2012 in Thibokhi, Tak Province.

[252] We all prayed and taught her not to put her faith in such a dream but to renounce it and trust God to heal and restore her. Later we gave her some medicine and when we met her on Oct. 1st 2012 she was happy and told us that she has been healed.

[253] Talk in the house of Repomo in Chroetha, on August 7th 2012.

[254] Phone call of Mr. Gula on 9th Aug. 2012.

back home to his house. He was afraid that his wife may have been unfaithful to him. This kind of reaction was not out of the blue, but the dream seemed to confirm the suspicions and fears which he had already carried with him since his twins were born two years earlier. The twins were a girl and a boy and in olden days some Karen believed that if they were not identical twins, they were not from the same father. Sometimes one of the twins was even killed. Some people made comments about it when his twins were born. Even though the hospital staff explained the matter to him differently, somehow this lie nagged at him and the dream caused new friction and sadness in their marriage. While talking to him he did not say that he believed the dream but that people gave that interpretation. But taken from his actions there is no doubt that he believed the dream more than anything else.

It was New Year 2009, at six o'clock in the morning a phone call jolted us out of bed. It was Noh Chila, the wife of the caretaker family in our Omkoi hostel. She had been married for several years without ever having been pregnant. She sounded excited when she told us that she had dreamed that she would give birth to a boy. Therefore, she had decided to return to her village home in expectancy of a pregnancy. My wife tried to calm Noh Chila down and asked her and her husband to stay on as caretakers for the time being. My wife told Noh Chila that it was great that she felt that God had promised her a boy, but that perhaps she would still have to wait a while as in the case of Sara. However, the same day she and her husband left. We prayed for them that they really would have a baby. A bit more than a year later, she was able to hold her baby boy in her arms and we praised God together!

In the village of Mae Lahn, at the regional Christmas celebration 2011 which was attended by several hundred Karen Christians, the main speaker was the very gifted preacher and evangelist, Loue Poh. He is the accepted leader among Karen Christians in the area and is invited to speak at Karen and Thai Christian meetings. He started his Christmas message with the statement that God had shown him in a dream that the Karen Christians in the area had been adulterous in their relationship to God. Adultery is one of the severest sins in Karen culture. Whenever it happened in the old days, the couple might have had to leave their village. Loue Poh then preached a powerful message about Hosea and some passages from Ezekiel. That he had dreamed about it gave the message a very current and serious tone.

The evangelist Supopa even told me[255] that he knows of one case where a man was killed because somebody had dreamed that he had sinned against him that means to have put a death spell (*'lo ta'*) on him. Supopa, however, thought that the victim had done nothing wrong.

From all these examples it has become very clear that many Karen pay great attention to dreams. Dreams are discussed among family and relatives. It is clear that even after they have become Christians, dreams still play a significant role.

---

[255] Interview with Supopa in the village of Thibokhi, 3rd Aug. 2012, on MP3.

3. Biblical Perspective of Dreams

When I was a young missionary living in the Karen village of Sop Lahn, a young Christian lad came up to our house and told me the dream he had seen. He was very concerned about it. I could not understand everything about the dream due to lack of language. But I answered him, quoting Jeremiah 23:28 where it says: "Let the prophet who has a dream tell his dream, but let the one who has my word speak it faithfully. For what has straw to do with grain? declares the Lord."

Was this an appropriate answer? How should Christians respond to the high significance of dreams in some cultures? What is the biblical attitude or teaching with regard to dreams? In order to answer this question we will now turn to the Scripture to investigate the significance that dreams have played in the biblical narrative and the way in which they are understood and interpreted. Even though dreams and visions are sometimes mentioned in the same sentence and on some occasions are used interchangeably, in this study I will concentrate on stories and passages which explicitly refer to dreams and in some instances to "visions at night" which might be another expression for dreams.

3.1 Terminology for Dreams and Visions

The Hebrew word for dream is *chalom* or *chelem*, the verb is *chalam*.[256] For "to see" the Hebrew words are *chazah* and *raah*. From these roots the words *chazon/chezev* and *marah/mareh*[257] with some variations of it are used. The words for "seer" are *chozeh*[258] and *roeh*.[259]

> *The most common way of saying 'to dream' is to use the internal object hlwm hlmty, 'I dreamed a dream'. This expression is, however, used only of symbolic dreams. Message-dreams are simply introduced by the formula bhlwm, 'in a dream', preceded by the verb describing the way in which God intervenes.*[260]

In the New Testament we find the following words for dreams ἐνύπνιον (*enupnion*) in Acts 2:17, and ἐνυπνιάζομαι (*enupniazomai*) in Acts 2:17 and Jude 8. The clas-

---

[256] *Chalam*, to dream has got the same roots as "to be in good liking." Robert Young, *Analytical Concordance to the Holy Bible,* Eighth Edition (London, UK: Lutterworth Press, 1977), 271-272. Or according to Gesenius „gesund sein" (to be healthy). Wilhelm Gesenius, *Hebräisches und Aramäisches Handwörterbuch über das Alte Testament* (Berlin, Germany: Springer Verlag 1962), 234. An interesting note to the meaning of "to be healthy": Scientific results show that dreaming is important for our health. People who have been regularly disturbed in their sleep during their dreaming phase have become psychologically disturbed.

[257] According to R. Young *chazon/chezev* is used for vision and the main use of *marah/mareh* is for appearance, vision, sight and countenance.

[258] Coming from the same roots as *chazon/chezev*.

[259] Derived from the very common word *raah* which is also used for seeing visions or dreams. Cf. Gesenius, 734-736. Samuel was called a *roeh*/seer (1Sam 9:11) or the prophet Gad, was David's *chozeh*/seer (2Sam 24:11). It is a former term for "prophet" (*nabi*) (1Sam 9:9).

[260] Jean-Marie Husser, *Dreams and Dream Narratives in the Biblical World* (Sheffield, UK: Sheffield Academic Press, 1999), 89.

sic word for dreams ὄναρ (*onar*) is used in Mt 1:20; 2:12.13.19.22 and 27:19.[261] Luke, who reports many dream-visions in Acts, does not use ὄναρ. He uses ὅραμα (*horama*) and also ὀπτασία (*optasia*) which are translated as vision. Once, in Acts 2:17, he uses ὅρασις (*horasis*).[262] Hanson, in his widely recognized study, observes that it is not unusual that an author prefers one term over the other and that Luke strongly prefers ὅραμα.[263] Hanson then uses the ambiguous term "dream-vision". Does Luke's expression "a vision appeared to Paul in the night"[264] mean a vision that can be distinguished from a dream? Or could it be that Luke did not want to use ὄναρ, he expresses the meaning of "dream" with the expression "vision in the night".

3.1.1 Distinctions Between "Dreams" and "Visions"

In scholarly circles there is some debate about distinctions between dreams and visions. "Dreams" and "visions" are often used in close connection or in parallel (Nu 12:6; Job 33:15; Is 29:7; Dan 2:28; 4:2; 7:1; Zech 10:2; Joel 2:28). This would seem to indicate that the terms are being used interchangeably. "They are of one piece in the Hebrew."[265] Others have argued for a clear distinction between the two.[266] James Miller argues that those passages are "poor proof of the identity between dreams and prophetic visions," because "it is common for poets to link terms which would normally remain distinct in prose."[267]

Husser concludes from his research in the Old Testament: "It seems likely that, in classical prophecy, dreams and visions are two distinct phenomena, although visions can *also* take place at night."[268] Hubbard follows this string of thought saying, "The basic difference between *dream* (Heb. *chalom* ...) and *vision* (Heb. *chizzayon* ...) is that the dreamer is usually asleep, while the visionary is awake during the reception of the revelation."[269]

In Greek language it also seems quite hard to distinguish between dreams and visions. Hanson in his study about visions and dreams in the Greco-Roman literature comes to the conclusion that it is impractical if not impossible to distinguish between dreams and visions. John B.F. Miller follows this conclusion when he writes

> *In English, one may distinguish these experiences in modern usage. This distinction is based usually on whether the one having the experience is asleep*

---

[261] Walter Bauer, *Wörterbuch zum Neuen Testament* (Berlin, Germany: Walter de Gruyter, 1971).

[262] "act of seeing, sight, vision" Young, 1027.

[263] John S. Hanson, "Dreams and Vision in the Graeco-Roman World and Early Christianity." *ANRW*. Edited by H. Temporini and W. Haase (New York, NY: De Gruyter, 1980), 1408.

[264] Acts 16:9. Similar Acts 18:19.

[265] Kelsey, 33. Tending towards this view, John B.F. Miller.

[266] Husser, 151. Jepsen, "chazah" *TDOT* 4: 283, 290, arguing that *chazah* (visions) are clearly distinguished from dreams.

[267] James Miller, "Dreams and Prophetic Visions." *Biblica* 71 (1990), 401.

[268] Husser, 151.

[269] David Allan Hubbard, *Joel and Amos. An Introduction and Commentary* (Leicester, UK: Inter-Varsity Press, 1989), 70.

("dream") or awake ("vision"). Such a distinction, however, is not so common in the literature of late antiquity that is preserved in Greek.[270]

On the other hand "Dream interpreters like Artemidorus, for instance, distinguish between varying types of dream experience."[271]

Ira Milligan comments on the distinction: "There is a difference between a dream and a night vision. A night vision requires little or no interpretation. In addition to the actual vision seen, a night vision usually has a voice speaking that gives the primary meaning and message of the vision. For example: Acts 16:9-10."[272]

Taking into account the different arguments it becomes clear that dreams and visions in some texts are written as parallelisms and are used interchangeably. It could well be that when Luke speaks about visions at night, he was thinking of dreams without using the word explicitly. But in the majority of visions recorded in the Bible, it is clear that they are reported as visions as distinct from dreams. It is also clear that God speaks through dreams or through visions. Some prophets are critical of dreams (Jer 23:25-31) and also of delusive visions (Ez 13:6-7.23). For the present study I will investigate those passages in Scriptures which speak of dreams explicitly.

3.2 Who Is Reported to Have Had Dreams?

The first dream that is mentioned in the Bible is given to King Abimelech as a warning about him having taken Sarah as his wife. The dream caused him to correct his behavior and to fear God (Gen 20:3ff).[273] It is interesting to note that about half of the receivers of dreams mentioned by name were people outside the covenant of God while the other half belonged to God's people. Those outside the covenant people who are mentioned by name include Abimelech (Gen 20:3), and Laban, the father-in-law of Jacob. He pursued Jacob after he had fled from Laban. God came to Laban in a dream and warned him not to enter into a dispute with Jacob (Gen 31:24). – Both – Pharaoh's chief cupbearer and chief baker, who were thrown into prison where Joseph had been incarcerated for some time, – had dreams which Joseph, by the grace of God, was able to interpret (Gen 40:3-23). Through dreams God revealed to Pharaoh that there would be seven years of abundance after which seven years of famine would follow. God wants Pharaoh to take

---

[270] John B.F. Miller, *Convinced that God had Called Us: Dreams, Visions and the Perception of God's Will in Luke-Acts* (Leiden, NL: Brill, 2007), 9. Miller follows Hanson. The title of his book (dissertation) expresses this stance. He speaks about dreams in Luke-Acts even though the classical term "dream" is never used by Luke.

[271] John B.F. Miller, 9 (Footnote).

[272] My translation of "Es gibt einen Unterschied zwischen einem Traum und einem Nachtgesicht. Eine nächtliche Vision erfordert wenig oder gar keine Auslegung. Zusätzlich zu der eigentlichen Vision, die gesehen wird, kommt es bei einem Nachtgesicht häufig vor, dass durch eine hörbare Stimme die wesentliche Bedeutung und Nachricht der Vision vermittelt wird. Hier ein Beispiel: Apostelgeschichte 16:9-10." Ira Milligan, *Träume deuten, Träume verstehen. Ein biblisches Handbuch, um Gottes Stimme zu hören. Mit Bedeutungswörterbuch* (Berlin, Germany: Aufbruch-Verlag, 2007), 14.

[273] In the parallel story in Genesis 12, we are not told how God warned Pharaoh about taking Sarai as his wife, but it is possible that this was also through a dream.

the appropriate measures to rescue the people. (Gen 41:25.28). Again it was Joseph who was enabled by God to interpret the two dreams (Gen 41:1-36). A Midianite soldier told his dream to his friend while Gideon was listening (Judges 7:13-15).[274] Nebuchadnezzar had two dreams (Dan 2 + 4). In the first one, God was revealing to the king what was going to happen in the future. God had given the content of the dream in a vision to Daniel who then could interpret it. In the second dream, Nebuchadnezzar dreamed of a huge tree which was cut down. Through the interpretation given by Daniel, God showed the king as in a mirror what was going to happen to him. In Job 33:15-18[275] we read that God speaks to men through dreams in order "to preserve his soul from the pit."[276] During the time in which God allowed Satan to attack Job, he reports that he is terrified by dreams[277].

In the New Testament we find two instances where God gave dreams to people outside his covenant: The Magi were warned in a dream "not to go back to Herod, so they returned to their country by another route" (Mt 2:12). At the end of Matthew's gospel, Pilate's wife warned her husband, who was about to judge Jesus, to have nothing to do with him (Mt 27:19).[278]

The following are those within the covenant people of God who are mentioned to have received dreams from God. It is recorded that Jacob dreamed three times.[279] The first dream was about the well-known stairway (Gen 28:12-15). The next concerned the mating of his sheep (Gen 31:10-12). Later an angel of God appeared to him in a dream and asked him to return to his native land at once (Gen 31:11.13). Joseph dreamed twice about himself and his family (Gen 37:5-11). Some prophets had dreams. God told Miriam and Aaron, "When a prophet of the Lord is among you, I reveal myself to him in visions, I speak to him in dreams" (Nu 12:6). An exception to this is that God spoke to Moses face to face[280] which gives much clearer revelation than a vision or a dream. It tells us that the Torah is not based on dreams or pictures but on direct words from God. King Saul had received revelations from God through dreams but in later years, after having disobeyed the Lord, God did not reveal himself to Saul through dreams anymore (1Sam 28:6.15). While King Solomon was offering sacrifices at Gibeon "the Lord appeared to Solomon during the night in a dream, and God said, 'Ask for whatever

---

[274] "A round loaf of barley bread came tumbling into the Midianite camp. It struck the tent with such force that the tent overturned and collapsed." His friend then gave the correct interpretation that this must be "the sword of Gideon son of Joash, the Israelite. God has given the Midianites and the whole camp into his hands".

[275] "In a dream, in a vision of the night, when deep sleep falls on men as they slumber in their beds, he may speak in their ears and terrify them with warnings, to turn man from wrongdoing and keep him from pride, to preserve his soul from the pit, his life from perishing by the sword."

[276] Actually, the present experience of many Muslims. Cf. Tom Doyle, Greg Webster, *Träume und Visionen. Wie Muslime heute Jesus erfahren.* 23 Geschichten (Giessen, Germany: Brunnen Verlag, 2013).

[277] Job 7:13-15: "When I think my bed will comfort me and my couch will ease my complaint, even then you frighten me with dreams and terrify me with visions, so that I prefer strangling and death, rather than this body of mine."

[278] "Don't have anything to do with that innocent man, for I have suffered a great deal today in a dream because of him."

[279] Richard L. Ruble, "The Doctrine of Dreams." *Bibliotheca Sacra,* (1968), 361.

[280] Nu 12:8: "With him I speak face to face, clearly and not in riddles".

you want me to give you.'" (1Kings 3:5-15). After Solomon had finished building the temple, "the Lord appeared to him a second time, as he had appeared to him at Gibeon" (1Kings 9:1-9). Daniel was not only given visions and the gift of interpreting dreams but he had an apocalyptic dream vision[281] himself about "four great beasts, each different from the others, came up out of the sea."[282] In addition he was given the interpretation of it in a dream-vision (Dan 7:1-28). In the New Testament Joseph received four dreams, all in connection with the birth and childhood of Jesus (Mt 1:20; 2:13.19.22). Three times it says, "an angel of the Lord appeared to him in a dream,"[283] while once he was warned in a dream[284] not to go back to Judea. "Interestingly, Jesus never mentioned dreams."[285] Obviously, as the promised prophet like Moses[286] he had the same direct contact to God as Moses and even more intimate like a son with his father. The prophet Joel prophesied towards an age to come that when the Spirit will be poured out on all people "Your sons and daughters will prophesy, your old men will dream dreams, your young men will see visions" (2:28). This prophecy is cited affirmatively in Acts 2:17 in the speech of Peter on the day of Pentecost. Reading all these biblical accounts of men and women who have dreamed as well as the promises that God will give dreams and visions to his people, we may expect people to have revelations from God through dreams even in the present day.

3.3 Observations on Dream Passages

Firstly, I will take a broad look of what the different passages mean and how Bible teachers have interpreted the texts over time. Special attention is given to the dreams of Jacob.

In the later part of this chapter (3.4-3.8) we will get the different observations focused to the main statements.

3.3.1 The Dreams of Jacob[287]

Jacob's First Dream (Gen 28:10-19)

Jacob's dream of a stairway "is a supreme display of divine grace, unsought and unstinted."[288] At this time Jacob was fleeing from his brother Esau. He was not

---

[281] Dan. 7:1: "In the first year of Belshazzar king of Babylon, Daniel had a dream, and visions passed through his mind as he was lying on his bed. He wrote down the substance of his dream." (NIV).

[282] Dan 7:3.

[283] Mt 1:20; 2:13; 2:19.

[284] Mt 2:20.

[285] Ruble, 362.

[286] Dt 18:15: "The LORD your God will raise up for you a prophet like me from among your own brothers. You must listen to him." Dt 18:18: "I will raise up for them a prophet like you from among their brothers; I will put my words in his mouth, and he will tell them everything I command him.".

[287] Gen 28:10-19; 31:10-12; 31:11.13.

[288] Derek Kidner, *Genesis. An Introduction and Commentary* (Illnois, IL: Inter-Varsity Press, 1967), 158.

looking for God. God surprised him with this dream and God did not rebuke him for anything but promised him endless blessing. Blessings reaching from the past – from his grandfather Abraham and his father Jacob – to the unknown future, from this spot in the desert to the four corners of the earth and from his person to all generations to come. God's plan of salvation is revealed to him through this dream. However, this dream has not always been interpreted as "a supreme display of divine grace". As Steinmetz points out: "The story of Jacob's dream has had a particularly rich history of interpretation in Western Christendom."[289] In his article, Steinmetz shows how three medieval Bible expositors[290] interpreted this passage and how Luther saw it. He first cites Anders Nygren's classical study,[291] which came to the conclusion that Luther rejected the three interpretations, namely that "medieval theologians identified Jacob's ladder with the ladder of grace and merit, the analogical ladder of speculation, and the anagogical ladder of mysticism."[292] Steinmetz shows that the medieval representative's exposition and Luther's are much more intertwined. While Lyra and Denis are mainly interested in the literal sense[293] of the text, Hugh of Saint Cher offers two other kinds of interpretation, namely the allegorical or mystical[294] and the moral which shows the significance of the text for the Christian ethics. They are all concerned to show Jacob as a hero without any doubts in the promises of God. He does receive this revelation from God because his heart is prepared for it through the suffering he has gone through and because of his ascetic practices, which they think, is shown in his choosing of a stone for a pillow. "Denis and Lyra identify the ladder in Jacob's dream as Christ."[295] Hugh prefers a mystical interpretation in which

> *He identifies the ladder not only with Christ, but also with the Bible, the cross, the sacrament of penance, and the cloistered life. The angels are not only the spirits who ascend to contemplate Christ and descend to serve him, but also preachers, the four evangelists, the doctors, imitators of Christ, the penitent, and the monks. Denis adds good priests, virtuous prelates, and contemplatives to the list of 'angels'.*[296]

Denis also gives an explanation of what occurs in the dream. He thinks that angels insinuated the images into Jacob's mind. "Such a vision is not a hallucination, because the prophet is also given an intellectual understanding of the sensible

---

[289] David C. Steinmetz, "Luther and the ascent of Jacob's ladder." *Church History* 55, no. 2 (June 1, 1986), 180.

[290] "Hugh of Saint Cher, a thirteenth-century Dominican who taught at the University of Paris; Nicholas of Lyra, a fourteenth-century Franciscan, often thought to be a convert to Christianity from Judaism because of his knowledge of rabbinic literature; and Denis the Carthusian, a fifteenth-century monastic reformer and ally of Nicholas of Cusa." Steinmetz, 182.

[291] Anders Nygren, *Agape and Eros, Part I and Part II* (Philadelphia, PA: The Westminster Press, 1953), 621-637.

[292] Steinmetz, 180.

[293] Not as literal interpretation in today's theological understanding with its historical criticism, but in the literal sense how the story presents itself in Genesis 28.

[294] Looking for a "deeper" meaning in the passage which is not obvious in the text.

[295] They refer to John 1:51. Steinmetz, 185.

[296] Steinmetz, 185.

images."[297] But Denis looks at the dream as the lowest form of prophetic vision, and when it says that Jacob saw God in his dream, he really saw only a sensible image of God.

Luther was acquainted with medieval commentators. He does for example "not agree with the medieval tradition that holds that Jacob was prepared for his vision by his virtues (...), he does agree that Jacob was prepared for his vision by his troubles."[298] Luther does not give a theory about dreams. He accepts the fact that God can reveal himself in dreams but only as far as these agree with the Word of God. "As Luther sees it, Jacob already had been made a patriarch and an heir of the covenant of Abraham through Isaac's blessing."[299] The dream is a confirmation of the blessing Isaac had conferred on him.[300] In contrast to the medieval commentators Luther takes delight in uncovering Jacob's weaknesses, because the weaknesses of the saints comfort him more than their virtues. "The triumph of God is a triumph in the midst of human frailty."[301]

Luther does not reject the ladder of grace and merit as Nygren suggests. Rather, he redefines it as a ladder of grace and good works. The ascent to God is by grace alone. The Word justifies sinners absolutely by imputing to them the righteousness of Christ. Justified sinners, however, descend to their neighbors in good works which are performed in response to grace and out of gratitude for God's mercy. Works are not rejected, but they play no role in the ascent to God.[302]

Steinmetz sees Luther's exegetical contribution more in what he adds than in what he rejects. What he adds is his own theological insights about the doctrine of justification. But in this he is not satisfied with a theoretical and analytical exegesis "until he has put us with Jacob in the middle of that lonely field, made Jacob's terror and homesickness our own, and laid our heads on Jacob's comfortless pillow."[303]

Compared to the medieval commentators and even to Luther, Calvin in his commentary[304] is very sober. Referring to Numbers 12:6, Calvin accepts this dream as

---

[297] Steinmetz, 184.

[298] Steinmetz, 188.

[299] Ibid. Taken from *D. Martin Luthers Werke. Kritische Gesamtausgabe*, 61 vols. (Weimar, Germany: 1883-), 43.595.36.

[300] I question this interpretation. Isaac had blessed Jacob twice (Gen 27:27-29; 28:1-4). The second time he blesses him with the words, "May he give you and your descendants the blessing given to Abraham, so that you may take possession of the land … the land God gave to Abraham" (Gen 28:4). Isaac prays that the promises given to Abraham will come on Jacob and he mentions explicitly only the promise of the land. In the dream God reveals himself in very similar words as he did it to Abraham. It is at Bethel that God promises the whole blessing of Abraham to Jacob. It includes the blessing, "All people on the earth will be blessed through you and your offspring" (Gen 28:14). This is much more than a confirmation of the blessings given by Isaac. It is though the fulfillment of Isaac's prayer for Jacob.

[301] Steinmetz, 190.

[302] Steinmetz, 189.

[303] Steinmetz, 192.

[304] John Calvin, *Commentary on Genesis - Volume 2* (Grand Rapids, MI: Christian Classics Ethereal

a revelation of God[305] but later comments, "Moses again affirms that this was no common dream; for when any one awakes he immediately perceives that he had been under a delusion in dreaming."[306] Commenting on the audition in the dream he noticed: "Mute visions are cold: therefore the word of the Lord is as the soul which quickens them. The figure, therefore, of the ladder was the inferior appendage of this promise."[307] Calvin's very much down to earth exposition can be seen in the following comment: "Other commentators argue, with more subtlety, that the stone was a symbol of Christ, on whom all the graces of the Spirit were poured out, that all might draw out of his fullness; but I do not know that any such thing entered the mind of Moses or of Jacob."[308]

Further, Calvin dismisses the interpretation of some Hebrews who see the ladder as a figure of the Divine Providence, "for the Lord has given another sign more suitable."[309] In referring to John 1:51 he suggests that the ladder is a symbol of Christ.[310]

Jakob Kroeker, a German pietist, accepts that God has spoken through dreams but his comments suggest that he did not give much significance to dreams in the Bible. He says: "Wenn es sein musste, dann wurde das ewige Wort Fleisch auch in einem Traum."[311] Or: "Gottes Offenbarung – wenn zunächst auch nur durch einen Traum – hatte nicht vergeblich geredet."[312] Hellmuth Frey, sees the dream as a quiet message to Jacob who is on his flight into a foreign land: "Die Türen der Heimat hinter dir schließen sich, aber die Türen des Himmels über dir öffnen sich."[313] He then compares the "door of heaven" to the door of the lost Paradise which is closed until the one will come who will reopen it for humanity.[314]

Library). The reformer Calvin lived 1509-1564.

[305] Ibid, 91.

[306] Ibid, 95.

[307] Ibid, 93. Calvin does not comment on dreaming in Gen 20:3.6 where God came to Abimelech in a dream and spoke to this heathen in a dream. Cf. John Calvin, *Commentary on Genesis – Volume 1* (Grand Rapids, MI: Christian Classics Ethereal Library), 401-404.

[308] Ibid, 96.

[309] Ibid, 92.

[310] Calvin and Luther, like many others "followed the interpretation of Augustine, equating the ladder with the 'Son of Man' (John 1:51)." Kenneth A. Mathews, *The New American Commentary. An Exegetical and Theological Exposition of Holy Scripture. Genesis 11:27-50:26* (Nashville, TE: Broadman and Holman Publishers, 2005), 444.

[311] "If it had to be then the eternal Word became flesh in a dream, too." (Translation: Hans Bär). Jakob Kroeker, *Patriarchen. Die Grundlagen des Glaubens* (Giessen, Germany: Brunnen Verlag, 1959), 209.

[312] "God's revelation – even if **only** through a dream – was not spoken in vain." (Translation: Hans Bär). Ibid, 210. Similar Henry M. Morris: „This theophany was in the form of a dream. Though not the only way – or even the usual way – in which God had appeared to men in these ancient times, such a means was certainly used on many occasions. This does not mean, of course, that any supernatural significance is normally to be ascribed to dreams. It is only that, when Scripture so indicates, God has used this means." Henry M. Morris, *The Genesis Record. A scientific and devotional commentary on the book of beginnings* (Grand Rapids, MI: Baker Book House, 1976), 447.

[313] "The doors of your home country are closing behind you, but the doors of heaven above you are opening." (Translation Hans Bär). Hellmuth Frey, *Das Buch des Kampfes. Kapitel 25-35 Des Er-*

Liberal theologians like Claus Westermann and other followers of Source criticism determine the dream beginning and ending in v.12.[315] Others see dreams as fiction.[316] The vision in the dream is attributed to "source E" and God's verbal message to "source J".[317] In his article, Peleg shows that it makes more sense to treat v. 12-15 as one entity. Jacob's dream includes both a "dream theophany"[318] and a "symbolic dream". In his symbolic understanding of the dream Peleg interprets the going up (*alah*) and the going down (*yarad*) of the angels of God. Usually, angels are messengers of God but in this dream they do not speak. The verbs *alah* and *yarad* indicate movement in opposite direction. He shows that the "going up" (*alah*) has positive connotation and "going down" (*yarad*), negative.[319] He interprets the going down with leaving the Promised Land, and the going up with returning to it.[320] *Alah* is used to come near to God and *yarad* to go away from God.[321] The words are used this way in Jonah 1:2: "Its wickedness has come up (*alah*) before me." 1:3: "sailed to Tarshish to flee from (*yarad*) the Lord." Jonah

---

sten Buches Mose (Stuttgart, Germany: Calwer Vereinsbuchhandlung, 1938), 80.

[314] Ibid, 81.

[315] Claus Westermann, *Biblischer Kommentar Altes Testament. Genesis* (Neukirchen-Vluyn, Germany: Neukirchener Verlag, 1981), 551. "Die elohistische Fassung des Traumgesichtes schloss mit V. 12. Es war also ein ganz stilles und wortloses Traumbild von grosser Feierlichkeit, das sich vor dem Schläfer aufgetan hatte." Gerhard von Rad, *Das Alte Testament Deutsch. Das erste Buch Mose. Genesis* (Berlin, Germany: Evangelische Verlagsanstalt, 1972), 229.

[316] "Husser makes several general observations. (1) The dream reports we have are literary creations either from monumental inscriptions or from epic sources, all of which have been redacted. (2) Even though these reports are fictions, they contain elements of authentic dream experiences of people in that age." Robert Karl Gnuse, "Book Review on Husser, Jean-Marie." *Dreams and Dream Narratives in the Biblical World.* Sheffield, UK: Sheffield Academic Press, 1999." *The Catholic Biblical Quarterly,* 61 (2000), 522.

[317] Yitzhak Peleg, "Going up and going down: a key to interpreting Jacob's dream (Gen 28,10-22)." *Zeitschrift für die Alttestamentliche Wissenschaft* 116, no. 1 (January 1, 2004), 9.

[318] "in "dream theophany", the God appears in the dream and delivers his message orally, while in a "symbolic dream", the message is delivered in a visual-symbolic manner, which therefore requires interpretation." Ibid, 1.

[319] Ibid, 8. This is a very interesting observation, since one of the most common known interpretation of the meaning of dreams among the Karen is, going up is a good dream – going down is a bad dream. See more details under point 4.1.5.

[320] When Jacob was about to leave the Promised Land in order to go to Egypt he went to visit Beer-sheba and "God spoke to Israel in a vision at night" (Gen 46:2). "He said: Do not be afraid to go down (*yarad*) to Egypt for I will make you in a great nation there" (Gen 46:3). Some interpreters think it was a dream again. Theodor H. Gaster speaks regarding dream incubation: "The only clear instance in the Bible is the story of Jacob at Beer-Sheba." Theodor H. Gaster, "Dreams. In the Bible," *Encyclopaedia Judaica,* Vol. 6 (Jerusalem, Israel: Keter Publishing House, 1971), 209. "Other interpreters took 'ascending and descending' to be cryptic symbolism in a dream-revelation that refers to the rise and fall of world empires, an interpretation that joins Jacob's dream to the dreams and visions about the rise and fall of world empires in the book of Daniel (this exegetical motif is found in *Gen. Rab.*)." Ronald S. Hendel, "The ladder of Jacob: ancient interpretations of the biblical story of Jacob and his children." *Interpretation* 62 no 2 (April 2008), 183.

[321] If God is in heaven, ascending means exultation and proximity to God, descending means remoteness and moral decline.

left the land in order to escape from God. "Thus we strengthen the supposition of the basic development of the negative metaphorical meaning of this term."[322]

"*According to the 'dream theophany' model – the story describes and means to explain how Beth-El became a sacred place. ... according to the model of the 'symbolic dream' – the story tells about Jacob who leaves Israel in order to return in the future.*"[323]

"The recorded stories of Jacob show us impressively that a dream is not a separate event but it stands in connection to the word, prayer and blessing."[324] We can see this in the vow Jacob took after he had anointed the stone.[325]

Summary of How Dreams Have Been Interpreted Over Time

In medieval times Bible expositors loved to allegorize Bible passages, including the dream narratives. The reformers, like Luther and Calvin accepted that dreams can come as a revelation from God. But those are special dreams and cannot be compared with common people's dreaming. Liberal commentators with their rational expositions see dreams as not very relevant or even as fiction. Karl Barth in his ten volume dogmatic ignored the theme of dream. He does not make any reference to it,[326] even though he was shaken by a dream and said that he normally takes dreams seriously.[327] German Pietists and Evangelicals[328] usually go along with the reformers and are often very skeptical. They reason, now we have the Holy Spirit and the Word of God who guide us. We do not need dreams anymore, and some may even warn to observe dreams.[329] But Joel 2:28/Acts 2:17 suggests

---

[322] Ibid, 9.

[323] Ibid, 12.

[324] "In den Jakobsgeschichten stellt die Überlieferung eindrucksvoll dar, dass der Traum nicht ein separates Ereignis ist, sondern zum Wort, zum Gebet und zum Segen in Beziehung steht." (Translation by the author). Hark, 34.

[325] Genesis 28:20-22.

[326] Karl Barth, *Die kirchliche Dogmatik: Registerband* (Zürich, Switzerland: EVZ-Verlag, 1970).

[327] Eberhard Busch records: "One morning I met Karl Barth despondent. 'What has happened to you', I asked him. He said: 'This night I had a bad dream. I dreamed that a voice spoke to me: Would you like to see hell once?' And I answered in good spirits: 'For sure, I would like to see it, for I have been interested in it for a long time.' Then, a window opened before me and I saw an endless desert which sight cut me to the quick, and in the middle of it sat one desolate person. Then the window closed and the voice said: 'This is threatening you!'. Offhandedly, I said to him: 'A dream ...' He resisted this fiercely: 'Oh no, normally dreams have to be taken seriously.'" Eberhard Busch, *Glaubensheiterkeit: Karl Barth, Erfahrungen u. Begegnungen* (Neukirchen-Vluyn, Germany: Neukirchener Verlag, 1986), 85. (Original in German).

[328] It is hard to find any expositors who deal with the theme of dreams on a theological level. Hansjörg Bräumer is one of the few who has written an excursus on it. See Hansjörg Bräumer, "Exkurs III: Träume und ihre Deutung im Alten und Neuen Testament." In *Das erste Buch Mose*, 3. Teil (Wuppertal, Germany: R. Brockhaus Verlag, 1990), 112-130.

[329] "Seit Pfingsten geschieht jedoch die normale Leitung der Gläubigen durch den Heiligen Geist, und wir sollten ungewöhnlichen Vorgängen oder Träumen gegenüber äusserst vorsichtig bleiben." Gerhard Maier, *Matthäus-Evangelium*, (Stuttgart: Hänssler-Verlag, 1979), 24-25. "We emphasize again, as Christians we should not go after dreams." He then quotes J. A. Bengel, a well-known German pietist and Bible expositor who said: "He who can use common means, does not look for uncommon ones." Ibid, 37. (Translation Hans Bär). Why should Maier count dreams to the un-

that when the Holy Spirit comes on all believers, people without regard to their gender and status will have dreams. Expositors and writers from the evangelical Pentecostal and charismatic movement give greater attention to dreams, especially to the Joel/Acts passage. Milligan even writes of dreams as "God's primary means of communication."[330]

Jacob's Second and Third Dream (Gen 31:10-12; 31:11.13)

Coming back to the biblical records, it is most interesting that God revealed himself again to Jacob through a dream, when the time had come for Jacob's return to the Promised Land.[331] The fact that the Lord introduced himself in the dream as *the God of Bethel, where you anointed a pillar and where you made a vow to me,* was a powerful reminder for Jacob[332] to return. It must have reminded him that God has always been with him through all the years even when Laban had cheated him, and that he will be with him as he had promised him at Bethel. This dream theophany was a great encouragement not to stay with Laban's clan but to return to the Promised Land. When Jacob had departed from Laban "the angels of God met him" (Gen 32:1). When Jacob saw these angels he must have been reminded of the angels he had seen in his dream. The term "angels of God" (*malaki Elohim*) is only used here and in the dream of Jacob (Gen 28:12) and is clearly distinguished to the *malak Jahwe* which stands always in the singular.[333] Jacob met these angels before he left the Promised Land and again when he entered it. How he met them at his return we do not know, was it in a vision or a dream? In any case, it was a confirmation to Jacob that he was on the right track despite his worries concerning how he would meet his brother Esau.

Besides the two dreams – before leaving and then before returning to his homeland – Jacob had had another peculiar symbolic dream which he told his wives Rachel and Leah. He saw "that all the male goats mating with the flock are streaked, speckled or spotted" (Gen 31:12). Even though his father-in-law had cheated him several times, God was still in control and gave him great blessings. Whether Jacob saw this dream before he put fresh cut branches which he had partly peeled into the watering troughs so that the sheep would bear streaked, speckled or spotted young[334] we do not know. If he had done this before he had dreamed, it would have meant a correction to Jacob's thinking. It was not his trickery that had helped him, but God had done this for him. If Jacob had done his trickery after having had the dream, the dream would have meant a promise which Jacob believed. Perhaps he wanted to help in his own way towards the fulfillment

---

common means? We dream every night!

[330] Ira L. Milligan, *Understanding the Dreams You Dream. Biblical Keys for Hearing God's Voice in the Night* (Shippensburg, PA: Destiny Image Publishers, 1997), 1. Is it *primary* means? *Primary* in which sense?

[331] Genesis 31:10-13.

[332] Cf. Shimon Bakon, "Genesis 31: Jacob's peculiar dream." *Jewish Bible Quarterly* 40, no. 4 (October 1, 2012), 259.

[333] "Es sind himmlische Wesen, streng unterschieden von dem singularischen *malak Jahwe.*" Westermann, 554, 615.

[334] Genesis 30:37-43.

of the promise of God. Either the dream was a confirmation and the giving of the right interpretation of what had happened or it was a promise from God to Jacob.

The reason Jacob told those two dreams to his wives at an important junction of his life, was not by chance. He wanted to win their support to leave their family and follow him to his native land. They recognized God's speaking through dreams to Jacob and they replied: "So do whatever God has told you" (Gen 31:16).

How Important Are the Dreams of Jacob?

Firstly, it becomes very clear that God uses dreams to lead people.

Secondly, God dignifies the dream to implement a decision in the history of salvation, namely to install Jacob as the agent of God's promises which he had given to Abraham and Isaac before. This covenant has an impact on the whole earth. Could God not have taken other means to relate this far reaching decision to Jacob? Of course he could have but our God chose the dream to be his vehicle.

All three dreams were given in crisis situations. When Jacob was fleeing from home, alone, on his way to a foreign land.[335] When Laban had cheated him ten times and done everything he could in order to stop Jacob from getting any more sheep. When Laban's sons turned against him and "Laban's attitude toward him was not what it had been,"[336] and the time had come to return to his native land to meet his brother Esau.

All three dreams contained encouragements and teachings from God. The one at Bethel was the most important one. The dream showed Jacob that God had chosen him and given him the blessing which he had so greatly desired, and which his father had spoken over him. Through him and his offspring all peoples on the earth would be blessed. In addition, God promised to be with him wherever he went and he would bring him back to his land.

The dream taught Jacob to fear the Lord which is expressed in his waking thoughts, "Surely the LORD is in this place, and I was not aware of it." He was afraid and said, "How awesome is this place!"[337]

When his father-in-law cheated him, God still blessed him and watched over him. The dream confirmed to Jacob that God had his hand in it when all the flocks gave birth to speckled or streaked young. Most likely God taught him through this dream that he does not need his trickery, and that his focus on the mating of his flock should change to the more important task of his life.[338]

---

[335] When Jacob later returned to Bethel he said: "I will build an altar to God, who answered me in the day of my distress" (Gen 35:3).

[336] Genesis 31:1-2.

[337] Genesis 28:16-17.

[338] Simon Novak makes a point that Jacob in his second dream saw a mirror of himself looking for wealth only. "... see all the goats leap upon – *alah* – the flock are streaked, speckled and grizzled." (Gen 31:10). The *alah* of the goats is in contrast to the angels in the first dream who ascended (*alah*) to God. Novak writes: "Twenty years with Laban has changed him: he now dreams of speck-

The third dream confirmed to Jacob that he should go back to the land of his fathers.[339] It was also a strong reminder to the first dream he had dreamed.[340] It taught Jacob that after more than twenty years God had not forgotten His promises to him, nor the vow he had made to God. God is faithful and absolutely reliable.

3.3.2 The Dreams of Joseph (Gen 37:5-11)

The two dreams of Joseph are symbolic dreams. Since there is no explanation given by God, the dreams need interpretation. In the first dream, Joseph is harvesting the field with his brothers. While they were binding sheaves of grain, suddenly Joseph's "sheaf rose and stood upright, while your sheaves gathered around mine and bowed down to it."[341] After Joseph had told them this dream his brothers were the interpreters of it. They understood the dream and asked: "Do you intend to reign over us? Will you actually rule us?"[342] The brothers "recognize that the vision prophesies his power, splendor and supremacy over them."[343] His brothers accuse Joseph that he intends to become their king as they question him about the interpretation of his dream. However, they go too far in their interpretation, Joseph never became a king nor did he interpret the dream in that way.

Joseph had another dream and he told it to his brothers. "I had another dream, and this time the sun and moon and eleven stars were bowing down to me."[344] Usually you cannot see sun, moon and stars at the same time. But these bowed down not in front of his star but before himself. When he had told the dream to his father, his father gave an interpretation in the form of a reproachful question: "What is this dream you had? Will your mother and I and your brothers actually come and bow down to the ground before you?"[345] Yet, Jacob kept the matter in mind. If Joseph really dreamed it, and he did not doubt that, he could not easily dismiss it. He was familiar with dreams and maybe he was reminded of his own dreams. He "keeps the matter in mind" as later the same is reported of Mary, when she had heard of the epiphany of the angels (Lk 2:19). "It is a dream that can have significance for the future."[346] It shows that a dream is not always significant for the immediate

---

led, grizzled and streaked flock, mirroring the fact that all his energy is now focused on acquiring possessions; the acquisition of wealth has become his highest aspiration. The vision of the ladder had been replaced by the vision of the mating flock! This is what Laban has done to him. Jacob is shocked. He is stung by the irony of the same Hebrew term *alah* used in the two dreams, in the first for the angels ascending, and in the second one, for the mating of the goats." Simon Novak, "Jacob's two dreams," in *Jewish Bible Quarterly*, 24, no 3 (1996), 189-190.

[339] Compare Genesis 31:3 with 31:13.

[340] "I am the God of Bethel, where you anointed a pillar and where you made a vow to me" (Gen 31:13).

[341] Genesis 35:6.

[342] Genesis 35:8.

[343] Original in German: Die Brüder "erkennen, dass das Gesicht ihm Kraft und Grösse und künftige Überlegenheit über sie voraussage." E. L. Ehrlich, "Der Traum im Alten Testament" in *BZWA*, 73, Berlin, Germany, 1953, 60.

[344] Genesis 35:9.

[345] Genesis 35:10.

[346] "Trotzdem ‚behält er die Sache' (wie Lk 2:19); es ist ein Traum, der etwas für die Zukunft bedeuten kann." Claus Westermann, *Genesis*, 3. Teilband (Neukirchen-Vluyn, Germany: Neukirchener Ver-

presence but for long term. On the other hand the dream had an immediate negative impact on Joseph's brothers. They were jealous of him and hated him even more. Still the essence of the dream came true after many years.[347] Russell Hendel sheds light on the dream from another angle. He contends that "the Bible interprets dreams of prophets and kings[348] as well as dreams with divine symbols as indicating long-term communal and spiritual events.[349] In contrast, dreams without divine symbols that occur to ordinary people,[350] deal with immediate personal matters."[351] The dream of Joseph differs from it. There is no divine indication but it has long-term effects because, according to Russell, Joseph believed in its prophetic nature. His brothers interpreted "Joseph's dream as personal wishes and fantasies, not as coming from God."[352] They "explicitly interpret *bowing* personally, indicating Joseph's desire to *rule over us* (Gen 37:8)."[353] They think it is a quest for power on Joseph's side. According to Russell, Joseph did not interpret his dream on a personal but on a community level. If he thought that he would have a special role in saving his family, what could the *bowing* of his brothers and even of his father and mother mean?[354] "Joseph interpreted the bowing in his dreams as symbolically indicating thanks; he would help his family who would bow in thanks. In contrast, his brothers interpreted the bowing in terms of power."[355] This could explain why Joseph told his dreams so happily to his family, thinking that he would help them all to succeed. "Joseph took a seemingly ordinary dream with ordinary physical content and treated this dream as if it were prophetic, giving it a meaning of spiritual content."[356] In conclusion, Hendel asks, why does the Bible allot such an amount of time and attention to the treatment of a personal dream of an immature teenager?

---

lag, 1982), 30.

[347] "Joseph would later become the 'prince among his brothers' (Dt 33:16) and receive 'the rights of the firstborn' (1Ch 5:2), at least the double portion of the inheritance, since his father adopted his two sons (48:5)." *NIV Study Bible*, Fully Revised (Grand Rapids, MI: Zondervan, 2002), 63.

[348] "For example, Genesis Rabah 89:4, commenting on the biblical passage, And Pharaoh was dreaming (Gen 41:1), states: 'Is Pharaoh the only person who dreamed? But because he was a king his dreams had special significance for the world.' This midrash alerts us to the biblical point of view that the dreams of kings, like the dreams of prophets, have special significance." Russell Jay Hendel, "Joseph: a biblical approach to dream interpretation." In *Jewish Bible Quarterly* 39, no. 4 (October 1, 2011), 238.

[349] Dreams of Pharaoh (Gen 41:25) and Nebuchadnezzar (Dan 2:28).

[350] Pharaoh's cup bearer and chief baker (Gen 40). In the NT Pilate's wife (Mt 27:19).

[351] Hendel, 231. This statement may be generally true but not in all instances. For example, Jacob's dream about the speckled and striped sheep or Laban's dream when he ran after Jacob were dreams with divine symbols but dealt with immediate personal matters.

[352] Ibid, 232.

[353] Ibid, 232.

[354] "The Bible interprets the act of bowing in four distinct ways. Bowing can indicate (a) thanks (e.g. Gen 24:26,48,52), (b) acknowledgement of power (e.g. Gen 33:3; Gen 49:8), (c) worship (Ex 20:5), and (d) greeting (Ex 18:7; Gen 18,2; Gen 19,1)." Ibid, 234.

[355] Ibid, 234.

[356] Hendel, 236. "The midrash interprets the sheaf dream prophetically, an indication of future events that would happen in many years." Ibid, 235f.

> To teach us that those personal dreams dealing with social or even physical needs can be treated with prophetic methods. Joseph's dream, ordinary developmental dreams for teenagers, when properly treated with prophetic methods, led to the reestablishment of the Jewish national destiny. This dream interpretation method is based on a) a communal service, b) a long-term approach, c) non-sexual interpretation, and d) the non-transparency of dream content.[357]

Taking the dream with the interpretation above, Ryle may be correct in assuming that Josef gained such stamina from the dream that it carried him through all the years no matter what he had to endure.[358] He kept the vision which God had given him in dreams and in the end, he could encourage his brothers: "You intended to harm me, but God intended it for good to accomplish what is now being done, the saving of many lives."[359] Dreams – when dealt with rightly – can turn out to be a great blessing.

There are no other dreams reported from Joseph. But he received the gift from God to interpret dreams. His first challenge to interpret dreams happened when he was imprisoned and both his fellow inmates, the King's cup bearer and chief baker, had dreamed (Gen 40:1-23). They both were sad because nobody was there to interpret the dreams. "Then Joseph said to them, 'Do not interpretations belong to God? Tell me your dreams.'"[360] He then gave to each one a personal interpretation which came true.

3.3.3 Pharaoh's Dream (Gen 41:1-41)

Only after two years, when the Pharaoh had a dream which nobody could interpret, did the cupbearer remember Joseph and tell the Pharaoh about him. Because the King had dreamed, the dream had prophetic and long-term meaning.[361] We observe that Joseph was very direct and careful to explain to Pharaoh that he cannot make the interpretation himself,[362] but that God would reveal to the King what he is about to do.[363] By this testimony the Pharaoh became convinced that "the spirit of God"[364] was in Joseph. In time God confirmed the dream and made it come true.[365]

---

[357] Ibid, 237.

[358] Cf. James Ryle, *Ein Traum wird wahr. Spricht Gott auch heute durch Träume und Visionen?* (Fürth, Germany: Verlag R. Hassmann, 1999), 103.

[359] Genesis 50:20.

[360] Genesis 40:8.

[361] "Bes. der König als Mittler zw. Göttern und Menschen wurde als Adressat von Traumbotschaften angesehen (z.B. Gudea von Lagasch; Sphinxstele Thutmosis' IV, 14. Jh. v.Chr.. Nabonid von Babylon, 6. Jh. v.Chr.)" "Especially the King as an intermediary between gods and people was seen as the receiver of dream messages (E.g. Gudea of Lagasch; Sphinxstele Thutmosis' IV, 14th century B.C.; Nabonid of Babylon, 6th B.C.) (Translation Hans Bär). Matthias Albani, "Traum/Traumdeutung. Alter Orient und Altes Testament," in *RGG4*, Vierte, völlig neu überarbeitete Auflage, Band 8 (Tübingen, Germany: Mohr Siebeck, 2005), 566.

[362] "While Pharaoh naturally thought of expertise in the 'science' of dreams, Joseph almost explosively disavowed this whole approach (the exclamation, *It is not in me,* is a single word)." Kidner, 195.

[363] Genesis 41:16.25.28.32.

[364] Genesis 41:38: "Can we find anyone like this man, one in whom is the spirit of God?".

[365] Cf. Psalm 105:19. Joseph's dream interpretation is spoken of as "the word of the LORD" which

Newman points to the ancient Egyptian belief that the goddess Hathor was the daughter of Ra, the sun god. "She was visualized as a gigantic cow stretched over the heavens, taking care of the Milky Way, which the Egyptians called the Nile in the Sky."[366] She was responsible for the Nile to overflow so that the land would be fruitful. In some instances she would appear as seven Hathors which strikes a strong resemblance to Pharaoh's dream of seven cows. Newman concludes, "Joseph's interpretation thus drew upon Egyptian symbols well-known to Pharaoh and used them effectively to explain the whole dream. That is why it rang true in the ears of Pharaoh."[367] Knowing the Egyptian culture well may have helped Josef to interpret the dreams. As we have seen before, dreams are often culturally bound.

Summary of the Dreams of Joseph and Pharaoh

We find that all these dreams were symbolic dreams and needed interpretation. Joseph's dream about the sheaves was interpreted by his brothers. His dream about sun, moon and stars was interpreted by Jacob. Joseph interpreted the dreams of the cupbearer and the baker which were related to their professions as well as the two dreams of Pharaoh. All these symbolic dreams were without spoken words. The pictures needed interpretation. The text makes it very clear that the interpretation of dreams is a gift of God.[368] All the magicians and wise men of Egypt could not interpret them to Pharaoh.

The function of dreams in the stories of Joseph are

- To help Joseph to look up to God in times of great distress, knowing his life still had a higher purpose, giving him strength to trust God.

- The dreams given to Joseph were not in order to claim power over his family but to serve them as their savior.

- To open the door for witnessing to the Highest God in front of the cupbearer, baker and Pharaoh. Joseph's clear testimony to the Pharaoh gives honor to God.

- To preserve God's covenant people through times of disaster.

God's revelation in dreams to Pharaoh shows God's concern for all the people in this world. God's representative at the court of Pharaoh played the key role by interpreting the dreams. Using the gift God had given him.

---

proved him true.

[366] Stephen Newman, "Pharaoh's Dreams: An Extended Interpretation." In *Jewish Bible Quarterly* 40, no 4 (Oct.-Dec. 2012), 254.

[367] Ibid, 254.

[368] See also Daniel 2:27.

3.3.4 The Dreams of Solomon[369]

The first dream occurred at Gibeon where the bronze altar stood. Solomon loved the Lord and he offered a thousand burnt offerings on the altar. Did Solomon go to "high place" of Gibeon in order to receive dreams from God, as Ehrlich suggests? Ehrlich writes, "This dream is the only example where an incubation[370] is clearly described in the OT."[371]

The two dreams reported of Solomon are message dreams. In the first dream God initiates a conversation with Solomon saying to him, "Ask for whatever you want me to give you."[372] Solomon asks for "a discerning heart to govern your people and to distinguish between right and wrong."[373] Or as the writer of the Chronicles put it: "Give me wisdom and knowledge, that I may lead this people."[374] God is very pleased with Solomon's decision for he did not ask for wealth, riches or honor. God answers his prayer and in addition God will give him the riches and honor for which he had not asked. Then he concludes the conversation with the following promise, "And if you walk in my ways and obey my statutes and commands as David your father did, I will give you a long life."[375] Concerning the revelation, Matthew Henry comments, "It was in a dream, when he was asleep, his senses locked up, that God's access to his mind might be the more free and immediate."[376]

In the second dream which occurred after Solomon had built the temple and the palace, God gave him a straightforward message in a dream, telling Solomon that if he were to follow the statutes of the Lord, God would establish his royal throne over Israel forever. But if he or his sons were going to worship other gods, God would cut off Israel from the land and He would not dwell among them. In this dream God explained the blessing and the curse to him. It was obviously a stern warning after all the success Solomon had had. God could see the danger Solomon was in and He was fighting for the heart of Solomon.

In summary, these two dreams were from God. This can be seen that the conditions which God set in both dreams were in agreement with God's known Word at that time. These dreams were very significant for Solomon's life. The Bible re-

---

[369] 1Ki 3:4ff; cf. 2Ch 1:2ff; 1Ki 9:1ff; cf. 2Ch 7:11ff.

[370] "Dream incubation is a practiced technique of learning to 'plant a seed' in the mind, in order for a specific dream topic to occur, either for recreation or to attempt to solve a problem." "Dream Incubation," *Wikipedia, the free encyclopedia.* https://en.wikipedia.org/wiki/Dream_incubation. (Accessed 21st July 2015.)

[371] E. L. Ehrlich, "Traum." In *RGG*, 6. Band, 3. Auflage (Tübingen, Germany: J.C.B.Mohr, 1962), 1004. Translation by the author. Whether this was really an incubation is up to discussion because the text gives us no hint that Solomon did it in order to receive a message from the Lord. It is only written, that he loved the Lord which seems to be the motivation behind his sacrifices.

[372] 1Kings 3:5.

[373] 1Kings 3:9.

[374] 2Chronicles 1:10.

[375] 1Kings 3:14.

[376] Matthew Henry, *Matthew Henry's Commentary on the Whole Bible. New Modern Edition. Volume 2, Joshua to Esther* (Peabody, MA: Hendrickson Publishers, 1991), 463.

ports that the Lord appeared to him three times,[377] twice in a dream, the third time God told Solomon that because he had abandoned God, he would lose the kingdom.[378] *The first dream was like an initiation of Solomon's kingship.*[379] The promise of God and its fulfillment in Solomon's wisdom led Israel to the peak of its history. The promises of the Old Testament that the nations will come to Zion was fulfilled during this time. Solomon did well to take these dreams seriously. They made an immediate impact on his life. After the first dream he went back to Jerusalem offering sacrifices "before the ark of the Lord's covenant"[380] which was surely a wise move in obedience to God.

3.3.5 Dreams in the Book of Daniel

"Daniel could understand visions and dreams of all kinds" because God had given him knowledge and understanding.[381] Daniel chapter 2[382] reports that Nebuchadnezzar had a dream that troubled him. He wanted his magicians, enchanters, sorcerers and astrologers to tell him what he had dreamed and then give the meaning for it. It may well be that he had forgotten the dream. In eastern superstition there was a saying: "If a man cannot remember the dream he saw (it means): his (personal) god is angry with him."[383] Until it was recalled and interpreted it hung over him as an evil dream bothering him. This may explain why the king was so insisting and angry when his wise men could not tell him his dream. He therefore threatened to kill them all, including Daniel and his friends. When Daniel heard what was about to happen he asked the king to wait so that he might be able to tell him the dream. Daniel was very much aware that he could not do it by himself, but only by the power of the living God whom he trusted. Therefore, he went to his friends and "urged them to plead for mercy from the God of heaven concerning this mystery, so that he and his friends might not be executed with the rest of the wise men of Babylon."[384] During the night, God revealed the mystery to Daniel in a vision and Daniel praised the God of heaven. To the King's question regarding whether he would be able to tell him the dream and interpret it for him "Daniel replied: No wise man, enchanter, magician or diviner can explain to the king the mystery he has asked about, but there is a God in heaven who reveals mysteries."[385] And he continues, "As for me, this mystery has been revealed to me, not

---

[377] Besides, in connection with the building of the temple and its dedication, God revealed himself to Solomon in other forms, when it says, "The word of the LORD came to Solomon" (1Kings 6:11) and "the glory of the LORD filled his temple" (1Kings 8:11).

[378] 1Kings 11:9-11.

[379] While it is mentioned that King Saul and King David received the Holy Spirit there is no mentioning of it with King Solomon. But after this dream it becomes obvious that God's Spirit is in him and has given him wisdom.

[380] 1Kings 3:15. Instead of sacrificing on the "high places."

[381] Daniel 1:17.

[382] Daniel 2:4 – 7:28 is in Aramaic. It contains all the dream accounts of this book.

[383] Joyce G. Baldwin, *Daniel. An Introduction and Commentary* (Leicester, UK: Inter-Varsity Press, 1978), 88.

[384] Daniel 2:18.

[385] Daniel 2:27f.

because I have greater wisdom than other living men, but so that you, O king, may know the interpretation and that you may understand what went through your mind."[386]

Another translation of the last words reads "that you may know the thoughts of your mind." This sentence is amazingly similar to what modern psychology thinks about dreams. "It reveals to us the thoughts of our unconscious mind. The word 'mind' can literally stand for the word 'heart'."[387] It means our innermost being. By having understood a dream we may become aware of our innermost thoughts.

Daniel then tells and interprets the dream for Nebuchadnezzar. It shows the future kingdoms and the coming of God's kingdom. Daniel closes his interpretation with the words, "The great God has shown the king what will take place in the future. The dream is true and the interpretation is trustworthy."[388]

In Daniel chapter 4 Nebuchadnezzar had another dream about a tree.[389] He tells the story himself, except the passage when he was insane which is told in the third person (vv. 28-33). He starts with praising the Most High God whose "kingdom is an eternal kingdom; his dominion endures from generation to generation."[390] The king comes to this conclusion after the experiences of the dream in chapter 4. The enormous tree had grown large and strong "and its top touched the sky."[391] "In one of Nebuchadnezzar's building inscriptions, Babylon is compared to a spreading tree (cf. v. 22)."[392] But then he saw a holy messenger coming down from heaven who called in a loud voice: Cut down the tree and trim off its branches; strip off its leaves and scatter its fruit. But the stump and roots should remain in the ground.[393] When Daniel heard the dream he was terrified, but after some encouraging words from the king he said: "You, O king, are that tree!"[394] He then communicated the judgment of the Most High God to the king that the kingdom will be taken away from him "until you acknowledge that the Most High is sovereign over the kingdoms of men."[395] Daniel advises him, "Renounce your sins by doing what is right, and your wickedness by being kind to the oppressed."[396] "Here is no passive determinism. On the contrary, the writer urges an incentive to a change of life-

---

[386] Daniel 2:30.
[387] Sanford, *God's forgotten*, 90.
[388] Daniel 2:45.
[389] "Scholars of ancient literature have recognized the tree mentioned in Nebuchadnezzar's dream as an important symbol in Babylonian writing. This symbol was 'congruous' with Nebuchadnezzar himself and his kingdom, since Babylon had long thought of itself as the center of the world." Jason A. Garison, "Nebuchadnezzar's Dream: An Inversion of Gilgamesh Imagery." *Bibliotheca Sacra* 169 (April – June 2012), 182.
[390] Daniel 4:3.
[391] Daniel 4:11.
[392] NIV, 1325.
[393] Cf. Daniel 4:13-15
[394] Daniel 4:22.
[395] Daniel 4:25.
[396] Daniel 4:27.

style."[397] One year later, when Nebuchadnezzar was boasting about his kingdom the dream was fulfilled. Nebuchadnezzar was removed from power as the dream had suggested. Only when Nebuchadnezzar raised his eyes toward heaven his sanity was restored and he praised the Most High.[398]

Daniel made it clear to Nebuchadnezzar that a dream asks for right action. He encouraged him to take the necessary steps to avoid God's judgment on him. But a year later, the king obviously had forgotten Daniel's admonition and the dream was fulfilled with all the consequences foretold for the ruler.

Here we have an example of how God used a dream to bring this world ruler to change his heart. God brought about his conversion. "Never again will he live like a man who thinks he is the center of the universe. Never again will he fall into the trap of thinking that the world is turning around himself."[399] "The point of the passage is that God confronts pride."[400] This is Nebuchadnezzar's own conclusion: I "praise and exalt and glorify the King of heaven, because everything he does is right and all his ways are just. And those who walk in pride he is able to humble."[401]

Daniel 7 constitutes the climax "and it is the high point in relation to the whole book."[402] It tells us that Daniel himself had a dream of four great beasts coming out of the sea.[403] The four beasts stand for four kingdoms. The four kingdoms correspond to the kingdoms in the dream of Nebuchadnezzar in chapter 2. But Daniel's dream shows the fourth beast as extraordinary. It had ten horns and another horn was growing between them and it replaced three of the others. Daniel also sees how "the Ancient of Days" took his seat. "The court was seated, and the books were opened."[404] The fourth beast with the horn was speaking boastful words, until "it was slain and its body destroyed and thrown into the blazing fire."[405] Then Daniel looked,

and there before me was one like a son of man, coming with the clouds of heaven. He approached the Ancient of Days and was led into his presence. He was given authority, glory and sovereign power; all peoples, nations and men of every language worshiped him. His dominion is an everlasting dominion that will not pass away, and his kingdom is one that will never be destroyed.[406]

---

[397] Baldwin, 114.
[398] Daniel 4:34.
[399] Stuart Olyott, *"Unbestechlich!" Daniel – Treue um jeden Preis* (Friedberg, DE: 3L Verlag, 2001), 78. (Translation by the author).
[400] Garison, 179.
[401] Daniel 4:37.
[402] Baldwin, 137.
[403] "To the Hebrews the sea was both dangerous and mysterious, a restless element (Is 57:20) but not beyond the Lord's power to tame (Ps 107:23-29). The nations were like the sea (Is 17:12,13). Baldwin, 138.
[404] Daniel 7:10.
[405] Daniel 7:11.
[406] Daniel 7:13-14.

In Daniel's dream it is not a stone which grows to an everlasting kingdom, instead he sees the King of kings receiving all power from the Ancient of Days.

Daniel was troubled in spirit and he "approached one of those standing there and asked him the true meaning of all this."[407] It is in the dream-vision that Daniel asks the meaning of his dream.[408] One of the angels was willing to give him the interpretation. Daniel understood the meaning of the first three beasts, but concerning the fourth beast, its horns and the special horn, he desired to be better informed. The horn which grew up afterwards is another king but different from the other. "He will speak against the Most High and oppress his saints."[409] But then the court in heaven will sit and take his power away and completely destroy him forever. Afterwards the kingdom of heaven is handed over to the saints, the people of the Most High. The dream deeply troubled Daniel,[410] but he kept the matter to himself.[411]

In the first place, we see that Daniel wrote down the substance of his dream. It was an apocalyptic dream. He not only saw many pictures but also heard voices and he engaged in a conversation with a heavenly being in order to find out the meaning to the dream. The interpretation of this tremendous dream-vision[412] was not Daniel's but came from heaven. It is the only dream in the Bible which was interpreted not by man but by an angel. This shows that apocalyptic dreams may be difficult to interpret. It also shows the tremendous importance of this dream and that the meaning is absolutely trustworthy. The book of Daniel "is a clear demonstration of the regard in which dreams were held."[413]

From the dreams reported in Daniel we gain new significant insights.

- Firstly, God reveals himself in a dream so that the dreamer may know the thoughts of his mind.

- Secondly, God uses a dream to bring a person to repentance. Here it is the most powerful king of that time.

- Thirdly, God uses a dream to predict the ultimate triumph of the kingdom of God.

---

[407] Daniel 7:16.

[408] "The visionary situation continues for Daniel is able to approach *one of those who stood there*" Baldwin, 144. "The dream continues even while the question about the fourth beast is being asked" Baldwin, 145.

[409] Daniel 7:25.

[410] "The personal cost of receiving divine revelation is never underestimated in the Old Testament (cf. Je. 4:19; Ezk. 3:15; Zc. 9:1; 12:1, AV, RV), and the book of Daniel insists here ... on the anxiety and psychological turmoil involved receiving, even at God's hand, understanding of the future course of history." Baldwin, 143.

[411] Daniel 7:28.

[412] "Daniel had a dream and visions passed through his mind as he was lying on the bed." Daniel 7:1.

[413] Sanford, *God's forgotten*, 89.

3.3.6 Dreams in the Gospel[414]

Five dreams are recorded around the birth and childhood of Jesus. Four of those dreams were given to Joseph and one to the Magi. "The conveying of God's instructions *in a dream* is a striking feature of the infancy narratives."[415] Three times it is said about the dreams to Joseph, "an angel of the Lord appeared to him in a dream and said."[416] Does that mean that each time a sort of stereotypical messenger came to Joseph and delivered his message, or is it more likely as Sanders supposes, that all we have is the interpretation of the dream? The dream itself is not told only the message which the dream contained. "What the actual dream might have been we have no way of knowing."[417] Twice it simply says, "Having been warned in a dream".[418] The warning once came to the Magi and once to Joseph. Again, we do not know what the actual dream was like, but we know both the Magi and Joseph understood the message of the dream. "This guidance of Joseph's movements by direct revelation emphasizes God's direction of Jesus' birth and childhood to conform to the scriptural pattern."[419] Schweizer observes that the angel speaks in the "I" form of God as in the Old Testament. Effectively, he is the incarnational action of God.[420]

That God revealed himself to the Magi through a dream shows God's love and care in meeting individuals where they are, because "Revelation by dreams was a regular feature in the culture to which these Magi belonged."[421] God communicated with them in a language they were familiar with.

Joseph and the Magi obeyed to what they were told in the dream and in this way God's plan was accomplished. If Joseph had taken the dream lightly, his whole family and especially Jesus would have been in danger of being killed. The story shows clearly that dreams can be very important.

Another dream of warning is reported in Matthew. When Pilate was about to judge Jesus, his wife had a dreadful dream that night the meaning of which she conveyed to her husband, "Don't have anything to do with that innocent man, for I have suffered a great deal today in a dream because of him."[422] This dream was another witness to the innocence of Jesus.[423] Unfortunately, her husband did not listen to her but made a judgment which he knew was not right. So he became the

---

[414] Mt 1:20-25; 2:12; 2:13-15; 2:19-21; 2:22-23; 27:19:

[415] R.T. France, *Matthew. Tyndale New Testament Commentaries* (Leicester, UK: Inter-Varsity Press, 1985), 78.

[416] Matthew 1:20; 2:13; 2:19.

[417] Sanders, *God's forgotten*, 187.

[418] Matthew 1:12; 2:22.

[419] France, 78. The dreams around the birth of Jesus are of a very different genre than those reported around the birth of the Buddha, see 2.2.1 Buddhism.

[420] "Er ist gewissermassen das gestaltgewordene Wirken Gottes." Eduard Schweizer, *Das Evangelium nach Matthäus* (Göttingen, Germany: Vandenhoeck & Ruprecht, 1981), 21.

[421] France 84.

[422] Matthew 27:19.

[423] Cf. Matthew 26:60; 27:4.24.54.

tragic figure in the story of salvation. Also, while this Gentile woman was open to the voice of God, the Jewish leaders of the time were deaf to it.

In conclusion what have we learned about dreams in the gospel?

- ○ God uses dreams in order to prepare the unique incarnation of his son. Through dreams he assigns different roles individuals are to play within salvation history.
- ○ God uses a dream to reveal to the judge's wife that Jesus is innocent indeed.
- ○ God gives clear warnings through dreams.
- ○ God speaks to some people in dreams more than to others.
- ○ God communicates through dreams to his own people as well as to people who do not know him.
- ○ To take heed of dreams from God, turns into blessing for the respective person.

3.3.7 Paul's Vision at Night (Acts 16:9-10)

In Acts it is reported twice that Paul had a vision at night,[424] once that the Lord stood near Paul in the night[425] and another time an angel of God stood by him in a stormy night and gave him a message of encouragement.[426] Many commentators think these were dreams.[427] Heininger thinks that, within Acts, only the passage 16:8-10 qualifies with a certain right to be called a symbolic dream.[428] Wikenhauser makes a clear distinction between visions at night or visions during the day and he examines only the former as dreams.[429] But as I have mentioned before, Luke speaks of a vision (horama) and never uses the classical word, "onar", for dream. Nevertheless, it shows us how Paul's team were interpreting the dream-vision to what they should do. The interpretation was unanimous and they decided

---

[424] Acts 16:9: "During the night Paul had a vision of a man of Macedonia standing and begging him, 'Come over to Macedonia and help us.'" Acts 18:9f: "One night the Lord spoke to Paul in a vision: 'Do not be afraid; keep on speaking, do not be silent. For I am with you, and no one is going to attack and harm you, because I have many people in this city."

[425] The Lord told him, "Take courage! As you have testified about me in Jerusalem, so you must also testify in Rome" (Acts 23:11).

[426] Acts 27:23-25.

[427] Bräumer, 116. Kelsey, 93f. John B.F. Miller, Michael James Day, "The Function of Post-Pentecost Dream/Vision Reports in Acts." Sanford, CA: *God's forgotten*, 79.

[428] "Innerhalb der Apg kann allein 16:8-10 mit gewissem Recht als (symbolischer) Traum qualifiziert werden." Bernhard Heininger, "Traum/Traumdeutung. Neues Testament," in *RGG4* Vierte, völlig neu überarbeitete Auflage, Band 8 (563-574) Tübingen, Germany: Mohr Siebeck, 2005.

[429] "Das NT spricht öfters von Gesichten und zwar von solchen, die von Menschen in wachem, und solchen, die im Schlafzustande empfangen werden. Die zweite Art, die man in der Traumgesichte bezeichnen kann, findet sich nur bei Mt und in der Apg." Alfred Wikenhauser, „Die Traumgeschichte des Neuen Testaments in religionsgeschichtlicher Sicht." In *Pisciculi: Studien zur Religion und Kultur des Altertums: Franz Joseph Dölger zum sechzigsten Geburtstag dargeboten von Freunden, Verehrern und Schülern*. Edited by T. Klauser und A. Rücker. Antike und Christentum Ergänzungsband I (Münster, Germany: Aschendorf, 1939), 320.

to follow the call of the man in the vision and entered Europe. All four appearances at night speak into crisis situations and were strong encouragements to Paul and to some people around him, when he needed them most. Miller, who has written his dissertation on dream-visions in Luke-Acts, comments on the above passage:

> *I have suggested that Paul's vision at Troas (Acts 16:9-10) is worthy of special attention because it differs from Luke's other dream-visions in a number of interesting ways. ... the vision offers a divine directive, despite the absence of a divine figure in the vision itself. The majority of Luke's dream-visions feature an angelic intermediary. Paul's dream vision at Troas, on the other hand, features a "Macedonian male." God is not mentioned until the characters interpret Paul's experience: "we immediately sought to go to Macedonia, convinced that God had called us to proclaim the good news to them" (Acts 16:10).*[430]

We conclude from these passages of Paul's visions at night that Paul experiences the dream-visions as divine encouragement in times of crises. Secondly, in these difficult situations, Paul receives divine directives. He follows these directives but not without consulting his fellow workers about its meaning.[431]

After having examined most of the recorded dreams in the Bible, we now take a closer look at the impact these dreams have had on the dreamers and their immediate environment.

3.4 Impact of Dreams

Whenever the dreamer obeyed to the dream which God had given it had great impact. Abimelech, for example, gave Sarah back to Abraham and in addition a lot of sheep, cattle and slaves. He also said to Sarah with his tongue-in-cheek, that he would give to her "brother" 1000 shekels so that she will be completely vindicated. "Then Abraham prayed to God, and God healed Abimelech, his wife and his slave girls so they could have children again."[432] The impact of a dream was often fear of God, worshiping God and acknowledgment of God.

Jacob was shaken to the ground by his dream in Bethel. He stood in awe of God.[433] "He did not dismiss the message from heaven carelessly with the words: 'It is only a dream.' Jacob took the message very seriously and he tested it."[434] He was afraid. He sensed the presence of the LORD and the holiness of God. He felt he was at the gate of heaven. These impressions caused Jacob to take action. He took the stone which he had placed under his head, anointed it and set it up as a

---

[430] John B.F. Miller, 138.
[431] Acts 16:10.
[432] Genesis 20:17.
[433] Genesis 28:17.
[434] "Er wirft diese Botschaft des Himmels nicht achtlos beiseite, etwa mit den Worten: 'Das ist ja nur ein Traum!' Jakob nimmt die Botschaft ganz ernst und testet sie." (Translation: Hans Bär). Rheinhold Ruthe, Lydia Ruthe-Preiss, *Traumbotschaften. Deutungshilfe für die Seelsorge* (Wuppertal, Germany: R. Brockhaus Verlag, 1994), 114.

pillar,[435] a place to remember God. He gave the place a new name, Bethel, which means "house of God". He then made a vow to God that "the LORD will be my God and this stone that I have set up as a pillar will be God's house, and of all that you give me I will give you a tenth."[436] Jacob made these promises under the following conditions: "If God will be with me and will watch over me on this journey I am taking and will give me food to eat and clothes to wear so that I return safely to my father's house."[437] Some expositors think that Jacob set these conditions because he lacked faith or as a type of horse-trading. Ruthe speaks of "reality testing." Jacob tests his dream to accuracy. He is not tempting God. We like to say: "Dreams are like foam."[438] But Jacob actually shows us one way that we can test the truth of a dream. If you God, confirm the dream message, then I will take it as your message to me.[439]

The second dream of Jacob was a confirmation that the first dream had come true. Jacob does not hesitate to take action on the third dream and leave Aram in order to return to his native country.

When he was back in the country he kept his promises as the following passage shows:

> So Jacob said to his household and to all who were with him, 'Get rid of the foreign gods you have with you, and purify yourselves and change your clothes. Then come, let us go up to Bethel, where I will build an altar to God, who answered me in the day of my distress and who has been with me wherever I have gone. So they gave Jacob all the foreign gods they had and the rings in their ears and Jacob buried them under the oak at Shechem.[440]

After Jacob had told his wives Leah and Rachel that God had spoken to him in a dream to return to his country of God's promise, they followed him gladly with the words, "So do whatever God has told you."[441]

Gideon worshiped God.[442] Nebuchadnezzar acknowledged God and praised him.[443] "The human ruler is finally to be an agent of divine will, a vehicle through which the greatness and sovereignty of God are universally made known."[444]

Sometimes dreamers suffered in a dream[445] or were afraid and troubled after they had dreamed. This was the case with Nebuchadnezzar and Daniel.[446] Sometimes

---

[435] "A thing set up, a standing pillar, *matsebah*." Young, 752. The same word in v. 22.
[436] Genesis 28:21-22.
[437] Genesis 28:20-21.
[438] A German proverb: "Träume sind Schäume."
[439] Cf. Ruthe, 120. (Original in German).
[440] Genesis 35:2-4. This important action was part of the dream's impact on Jacob.
[441] Genesis 31:16.
[442] Judges 7:15.
[443] Daniel 2:47; 4:37.
[444] Seow, 73.
[445] Job 7:13ff; Matthew 27:19.
[446] Daniel 4:5.19; 7:15.

dreams caused a negative reaction by the dreamer or with the people who felt affected by it. Job, after having nightmares, says that he prefers strangling and death.[447] Joseph's brothers hated him for the dreams and his father rebuked him.[448] King Herod was furious after the Magi had obeyed the dream and did not return to him "and he gave the orders to kill all the boys in Bethlehem and its vicinity who were two years old and under."[449]

The dream of Pilate's wife had no obvious impact because her husband did not heed it.

Many dreams though have had a positive impact on the dreamers. Laban was restricted in his wrath against Jacob through the dream God gave him. But this had a positive effect on his relationship with Jacob. They made peace and Laban even blessed his daughters and their children.[450] Joseph was put in charge of the whole land of Egypt, while Nebuchadnezzar placed Daniel in a high position and even his friends were promoted.[451] Joseph was released from his nagging negative thoughts and he took Mary home as his wife.[452]

The theologian Werner Jentsch writes in regard to Joel 2:28,

> *Wann und wo es Jahwe gefällt, macht er Träume gleichsam zu Gefäßen seiner Gnade, zu Wegen für sein Wirken. An solche Träumer, die Geistträger sind, denkt der Prophet Joel, wenn er für das Ende der Tage die Ausgießung des Geistes auf charismatische Personen ankündigt: Das prophetische Charisma ist dann kein Monopol der Propheten mehr, sondern erstreckt sich auf das ganze Gottesvolk.*[453]

What a tremendous impact this has had. As we can see, dreams are much more than empty, meaningless occurrences. God has often spoken through dreams which have made an amazing difference to the respective person and sometimes to all of mankind.

---

[447] Job 7:15.
[448] Genesis 37:8.10.
[449] Matthew 2:16.
[450] Genesis 31:55.
[451] Genesis 41:41; Daniel 2:48-49.
[452] Matthew 1:24.
[453] "Wherever it may be, Jahwe uses dreams as vessels of His grace and as ways of His works. When the prophet Joel announces the pouring out of the spirit on charismatic people at the end of days, he thinks of such *dreamers* who are *spirit filled:* The prophetic charismatic gift will be no longer the monopoly of prophets but will extend to all people of God." (Translation by the author). Werner Jentsch, *Der Seelsorger: Beraten, Bezeugen, Befreien. Grundzüge biblischer Seelsorge* (Moers, Germany: Brendow, 1984), 267f.

3.5 Sources of Dreams in the Bible

3.5.1 God Is the Giver of Dreams

It is made very clear that all three dreams which are reported of Jacob came from God. Angels appeared and God Himself spoke to Jacob in the first dream, while in the second, the angel of God spoke to him about the sheep. In the third dream, it was "the God of Bethel" that appeared and spoke to him. Before Jacob left for Egypt, God appeared to him "in a vision at night" and encouraged him with the promises that God would make him into a great nation there, that God would be with him and bring him back, and that Joseph's own hand would close his eyes.[454]

This same truth that God is the giver of dreams is most clearly expressed in Numbers 12:6. After Aaron and Miriam had rebelled against God, God instructed them: "Listen to my words: 'When a prophet of the LORD is among you, I reveal myself to him in visions, I speak to him in dreams.'" In contrast, God spoke to Moses face to face. However, prophets were not the only receivers of God's dreams but kings, as well. At one stage God revealed himself to Saul in dreams, but not in later years when he had continually disobeyed God.[455] All the dreams that are told in the Bible and at which we have already looked had their origin in God. Job 33:15-18 makes it clear that God may communicate to any man when he is asleep. We notice the positive assessment of dreams as a form of divine revelation.

In Jeremiah 31:26 God spoke to Jeremiah about the restoration of Israel while he was asleep. He concludes, "At this I awoke and looked around. My sleep had been pleasant to me." "Jeremiah had evidently received the previous divine revelation (beginning 30:3) in a dream."[456] This being the case it shows us that God spoke to Jeremiah in dream-visions even though he was very skeptical of revelations through dreams because of its misuse.

God speaks through the prophet Joel about the Day of the Lord and he says, "And afterward, I will pour out my Spirit on all people. Your sons and daughters will prophesy, your old men will dream dreams, your young men will see visions."[457]

> *This prophecy – a prophecy of programmatic importance for the text of Acts – depicts the widespread dissemination of God's spirit resulting in widespread prophetic activity. The vehicles of this far-reaching divine communication are dreams and visions.*[458]

In that age prophecies, dreams and visions will occur not only to a few but to the people who have received God's Spirit. The source of dreams is the Holy Spirit. Peter sees this prophecy of Joel being fulfilled on the day of Pentecost.[459] That means that, in our last days, the gift to have dreams through God's Spirit will be

---

[454] Genesis 46:3-4.
[455] 1Samuel 28:6: "The Lord did not answer him by dreams or Urim or prophets.".
[456] NIV, 1193.
[457] Joel 2:28.
[458] John, B.F. Miller, 44.
[459] Acts 2:16-17.

present. "Distinctions of age, sex, and social class would be swept away in this common spiritual endowment."[460] Hans Walter Wolff comments,

> *If Joel sees prophetic existence as being established through dreams and visions, the Jeremianic polemic against dreamers (Jer 23:25) is apparently completely foreign to him; he is rather influenced in this respect by the Torah.*[461]

And Calvin writes, "When God manifested himself to the Prophets, it was usually done ... by dreams and visions, as it is said in Numbers 12: this was as we may say, the ordinary method."[462] Calvin does not comment on the fact that this text is not only relevant for the prophets but for all believers today.

3.5.2 Dreams from the Devil and Demons?

Deuteronomy 13:1-5[463] provides help in distinguishing dreams from God or from other sources. God provides quality control for dreams and visions. "The coming to pass of a predicted sign and wonder (v. 3) would normally be one indication of the validity of the prophet."[464] But only dreams which are in accordance with the revealed will of God are dreams sent from God. Dreamers who lead God's people astray have to be punished by death. Not only the evil itself, but also the evildoer, had to be eliminated.

From this text we can conclude that there are dreams which are given by other sources, otherwise the stern warning would not be necessary. God allowed this to happen in order to test the faith and obedience of His people.[465] The sign or wonder coming true is not enough. The dream must be checked against the revealed will of God in His Word. It must lead to God, not away from Him.

---

[460] Leslie C. Allen, *The Books of Joel, Obadiah, Jonah and Micah* (Grand Rapids, MI: Williams B. Eerdmans Publishing, 1976), 99.

[461] Hans Walter Wolff, *Joel and Amos: A Commentary on the Books of the Prophets Joel and Amos* (Philadelphia, MA: Fortress Press, 1977), 66.

[462] John Calvin, *Commentaries on Joel, Amos, Obadiah (Extended Annotated Edition).* (Altenmünster, DE: Jazzybee Verlag Jürgen Beck, 2012), 25.

[463] "If a prophet, or one who foretells by dreams, appears among you and announces to you a miraculous sign or wonder, and if the sign or wonder of which he has spoken takes place, and he says; 'Let us follow other gods' (gods you have not known) 'and let us worship them,' you must not listen to the words of that prophet or dreamer. The LORD your God is testing you to find out whether you love him with all your heart and with all your soul. It is the LORD your God you must follow, and him you must revere. Keep his commands and obey him; serve him and hold fast to him. That prophet or dreamer must be put to death, because he preached rebellion against the Lord your God, who brought you out of Egypt and redeemed you from the slavery; ..."

[464] Peter C. Craigie, *The Book of Deuteronomy* (Grand Rapids, MI: Williams B. Eerdmans Publishing, 1976), 223.

[465] "The performance of a sign or wonder did not mean that the gods advocated by a false prophet or dreamer had any real power, but only that the true God would permit certain things to happen in order to test und thereby strengthen his people." Peter C. Craigie, *The Book of Deuteronomy* (Grand Rapids, MI: Williams B. Eerdmans Publishing, 1976), 223. The question is whether Craigie takes the power of 'the gods' seriously enough – they may well have power in the limits God is giving it to them.

Job had nightmares[466] during the time when God had given him into the devil's hand.[467] Job saw God as the source of his nightmares for he had no idea what was going on in the unseen world. It is obvious that the devil was using his power to cause Job suffering even in dreams at night. Andersen comments on the passage: "Even sleep gives him no relief from terrors. For then God – it can only be He – comes in horrible nightmares."[468] I do not agree on the emphatic "it can only be He", because the background tells us that Job was in the devil's hand. The dream came from God only in as far as God gave Job into the hand of the devil though limiting the devil to spare Job's life.

Even though God revealed himself to Jeremiah at night, as we have seen, Jeremiah is very skeptical of dreams because of their misuse by false prophets.[469] They say that they have dreamed but actually they lie (23:25). They "prophesy the delusions of their own minds" (23:26). Their dreams make people forget God's name (23:27). He then commands, "Let the prophet who has a dream tell his dream, but let the one who has my word speak it faithfully. For what has straw to do with grain?" (23:28). "Indeed, I am against those who prophesy false dreams" (23:32). He warns the people not to listen to those interpreters of dreams.[470] Zechariah looks at dreams very similar to Jeremiah. He says, "diviners see visions that lie; they tell dreams that are false, they give comfort in vain."[471] The consequences of these practices are far reaching for God's people: "Therefore the people wander like sheep oppressed for lack of a shepherd."[472]

In summary, we can say that false dreams can come through lying spirits[473] or they can be made up by false prophets. Behind those lies is the father of lies.[474] In this case the ungodly source of the dream is crystallized by the sinful life of the dreamer.[475]

When Jesus was tempted by Satan, Satan "showed him all the kingdoms of the world and their splendor."[476] We are not told how this happened, but it must have been by some supernatural means. The story shows us that the devil is able to cast vision or dreams in order to tempt and lead people astray.

---

[466] Job 7:13-15: "When I think my bed will comfort me and my couch will ease my complaint, even then you frighten me with dreams and terrify me with visions, so that I prefer strangling and death, rather than this body of mine."

[467] Job 2:6.

[468] Francis I. Andersen, *Job. An Introduction and Commentary* (Leicester, UK: Inter-Varsity Press, 1976), 137.

[469] Jeremiah 23:25-32

[470] Cf. Jeremiah 27:9; 29:8.

[471] Zechariah 10:2.

[472] Zechariah 10:2.

[473] 1Kings 22:22: "I will go out and be a lying spirit in the mouths of all his prophets, he said.".

[474] Cf. John 8:44.

[475] Robert Rüegg und Ewald Rieser, *Träume und Bilder und ihre Deutung in biblischer Sicht* (Zürich, Switzerland: Vereinigte Bibelgruppen, 1973), Abs. 22.

[476] Matthew 4:8.

Another hint that some dreams have their source in Satan is given in Jude 8.[477] Martin Holland comments, those dreamers despise the revealed order of God. They put their uncontrollable dreams in its place. They commit sexual sins.[478]

We can summarize that dreams may well come from Satan and his demons even though these will not be outside the ultimate control of God.

3.5.3 The Human Soul as the Source of Dreams

There are a number of passages "that reveal an attitude towards dreams similar to that found in Aristotle: Isa 29:8 and Eccl 5:2 relate dreams to a physical and psychological circumstance of the dreamer."[479] In Ecclesiastes, dreams are seen as the product of "many cares" and "Much dreaming and many words are meaningless. Therefore stand in awe of God."[480] Dreams are portrayed as another vanity. They are not seen as a means of communication from God but as meaningless experiences.

- One of Job's friend, Zophar, saw the dream as a picture of voidness. He said, "Like a dream he flies away, no more to be found, banished like a vision of the night."[481]

- Psalm 73:20 pictures the dream as a nightmare from which one awakes despising the fantasies. "In Psalm 126:1 the dream is likened to the wish that has been fulfilled."[482]

- Jeremiah saw lying prophets prophesying "the delusions of their own minds."[483]

- Daniel speaks of Nebuchadnezzar's dream as what "passed through your mind"[484] and "that you may understand what went through your mind."[485] Rabbi Yonathan has characterized this kind of dream saying: "'A man is not shown in his dream anything that he did not think about while awake.' It is notable that this type of dream is illustrated in the Talmud by the (sic!) Daniel's words"[486] quoted above. These dreams usually have their source in the

---

[477] "In the very same way, these dreamers pollute their own bodies, reject authority and slander celestial beings."

[478] Cf. Gerhard Maier, Martin Holland, *Jakobusbrief. Judasbrief* (Neuhausen-Stuttgart: Hänssler-Verlag, 1996), 137. Bräumer comments: "Only Jude knows to report of dreamers who pollute their own bodies in dreams." Bräumer, 127.

[479] John B.F. Miller, 53. In other Bible versions it is not Eccl 5:2 but verse 3, as for example in the NIV.

[480] Ecclesiastes 5:7.

[481] Job 20:8.

[482] Kelsey, 47.

[483] Jeremiah 23:26.

[484] Daniel 2:28.

[485] Daniel 2:30. Other versions: "that you may know the thoughts of your mind."

[486] Aron Pinker, "A Dream of a Dream in Daniel 2." *Jewish Bible Quarterly* 33 no 4 (2005), 235.

desires, fears and cravings of the human heart. Dreams of fear and desires as well as sexual dreams fall under this category.

Moreover, in the Bible we find dreams which are a reflection of the human heart. Their direct source is usually neither in God nor in his adversary. Some writers see them negatively and without value, but when we look into the book of Daniel the dreams have value in "that you may know the thoughts of your mind." The dream of Nebuchadnezzar with the great tree mirrors his own life and it was sent by God. Actually, modern psychology sees the value of dreams exactly in this, so that we may know our subconscious desires and thoughts. Even though many dreams may have their source in man's own soul, this does not mean they are worthless. Behind dreaming we will still find God who created man so that we are dreaming every night. As we have already noted, scientific studies show that dreaming is necessary for good health.

3.6 What Kind of Dreams Do We Find in the Bible?

3.6.1 Message Dreams versus Symbolic Dreams

Basically, we can distinguish between **message dreams** and **symbolic dreams**. "This classification was first conceived by Artimedorus of Daldis."[487] Husser thinks, "this typology seems on the whole to be well suited to the task of defining the various dream accounts we find in the Old Testament."[488]

3.6.2 Types of Dreams Taken from Cultural Dream Theory

Of the six types of dreams which Lohmann presents from cultural dream theory[489] we can identify four types in the Bible.

○ We find the **nonsense type** as in Ecclesiastes 5:7 or Isaiah 29:8. Dreams are meaningless and not useful.

○ When dreaming entails an enhanced capacity for thought it is the **discernment** type of dream. This we meet in several parable dreams, like the ones with the servants of the Pharaoh and with Pharaoh himself, as well as with Nebuchadnezzar.

○ The **message type** is very common in the Bible. As we have seen, God has often sent his messages through dreams. God has spoken in dreams.

○ We also find the **visitation type** of dream, when a messenger comes to meet a person, causing a genuine experience with an external agent. Among others, Joseph's dreams[490] fall into this category as the angel visited him in his dreams.

---

[487] Jean-Marie Husser, *Dreams and Dream Narratives in the Biblical World* (Sheffield, UK: Sheffield Academic Press, 1999), 99.
[488] Ibid.
[489] See under point 2.3.3.2.
[490] Matthew 2.

Do we find any biblical dreams in connection with the **Soul Travel Theory**? Maybe we could count the experiences which Paul tells us in 2Corinthians 12:1-5 in this category. Paul says, "Whether it was in the body or out of the body I do not know – God knows. And I know that this man – ... – was caught up to paradise."[491] Though in this context Paul does not speak of a dream experience but of "visions and revelations from the Lord,"[492] which is also different from a classic animist soul travel experience. Yet in some other respects the similarities cannot be overlooked. However, Husser concludes in his studies about dreams in the biblical world: "As in all the other neighbouring cultures of the ancient Near East, there is never any mention of a voyage undertaken by the dreamer to a land of dreams."[493]

3.6.3 Types of Dreams Applied to Life Situations

We find dreams from false prophets which were **lies and empty promises**. Jeremiah warned the people of Israel against these (Jer 27:9-10). They spoke what people wanted to hear and thereby led God's people astray. It is a clear misuse of dreams because dreams are a personal experience and cannot be checked whether they really have been seen as the dreamer was telling.

Some dreams caused great **fear** or were **nightmare**s. Pharaoh is troubled. Nebuchadnezzar said, "I had a dream that made me afraid."[494] Job spoke of suffering under terrible nightmares as we have noted. Pilate's wife said, "I have suffered a great deal today in a dream."[495]

"In Psalm 126:1 the dream is likened to the **wish** that has been fulfilled."[496] A dream has come true, as the Jews returned from exile in jubilation.

In the Bible we will find different kinds of message dreams. Most message dreams are **warnings** like the one when God appeared to Abimelech (Gen 20:7) or to Laban. The Magi are warned as well as Joseph. The dream of Pilate's wife is a warning to her husband. Some message dreams are straight **instructions** as the dream to Joseph to take his family out of Egypt (Mt 2:19f). Other dreams are **encouragements** and give comfort in difficult circumstances like Solomon's dream at Gibeon or Paul's vision at night in Corinth. Jacob's dream in Bethel was an encouragement for long term, while the other two dreams heartened him and **gave direction** to his life.

Through some dreams God gives **a look into the future**. Jacob received many promises for his future on the level of salvation history. On the other hand, Gideon knew the immediate future, that he will win the upcoming battle, through the

---

[491] 2Corinthians 12:3-4.
[492] 2Corinthians 12:1.
[493] Husser, 101.
[494] Daniel 4:5.
[495] Matthew 27:19.
[496] Kelsey, 47.

dream of a Midianite.[497] The dream is a **confirmation** of God's promise to him personally.

Daniel received a dream from God on an **apocalyptic** level which showed what will happen at the end of the days.[498] He also interpreted Nebuchadnezzar's dream in this way.[499] These dreams were given for comfort and instruction of God's people in future times.

We can summarize that dreams from God are for warning or confirmation, encouragement and instruction, guidance and the revelation of the future salvation of God. They can have meaning on a personal or more universal level.

3.7 Interpretation of Dreams

"Rabbi Chisda (died 309) said: A dream which is not interpreted is like an unread letter."[500]

We do not find any dream in the Bible which is kept unclear as to its meaning. Message dreams are very clear in their meaning while parable dreams are always interpreted if they were unclear. "Dreams needing interpretation are almost always experienced by non-Israelites, although the dream is sent by the God of Israel."[501] In almost every case a Jew had to be there to properly interpret that revelation because, from Genesis 12 on, the Jew became the custodian of divine revelation.[502]

3.7.1 Who Was Interpreting Dreams?

The Bible is very clear that interpretation belongs to the living God.[503] Joseph and Daniel testified to this truth to the respective kings in the middle of heathen surroundings.

Of Daniel it is said that he "could understand visions and dreams of all kinds."[504] This is written in the context of his learning experience in Babylon. According to dream expert Gaby Pfeil it means, "The ability to understand dreams through studying the Scriptures and science, and gain experience in it."[505] Whether and

---

[497] Judges 7:13-14.

[498] Daniel 7.

[499] Daniel 2.

[500] "Rab Chisda (gest. 309) hat gesagt: Ein Traum den man nicht deutet, ist wie ein Brief, den man nicht liest." (Translation into English by the author). Hermann L. Strack und Paul Billerbeck, *Das Evangelium des Matthäus erläutert aus Talmud und Midrasch* (München, Germany: C.H. Beck'sche Verlagsbuchhandlung Oskar Beck, 1922), 60.

[501] Ottoson, "chalam," *TDOT* 4:430. (In John B.F. Miller, 42).

[502] The one exception is a Midianite interpreting the dream of his friend (Judges 7:14).

[503] Genesis 40:8; 41:16; Daniel 2:27.

[504] Daniel 1:17.

[505] "Träume verstehen können durch das Studium der Schrift und der Wissenschaft, und darin Erfahrung sammeln.!" (Translation by the author). "Unseren Träumen auf der Spur." Notes given out on a Seminar on Dreams in Amden, CH, 25th-29th September 2014, 2. I attended the seminar at the

how much Daniel learned from the Babylonian magicians is not reported. But when he interpreted the two main dreams of Nebuchadnezzar, it is very clear that the magicians were unable to know and interpret the king's dream. Daniel however was enabled by God who revealed the dream and its interpretation to him. Daniel had received the gift of interpretation from God. It is open to discussion whether he also learned to interpret dreams. When Daniel dreamed himself, he was troubled by it and he could not understand part of his dream. Still in the dream he therefore "approached one of those standing there and asked him the true meaning of all this."[506] The celestial being gave him a clear and detailed interpretation. It is the only dream in the Bible which is interpreted by a heavenly being. C.L. Seow observes: "Indeed, the solution to the mystery of dream visions will come not from a gifted earthly sage, which is how Daniel is portrayed in chapter 1-6, but from a celestial intermediary."[507] The other well-known interpreter of dreams is Joseph in the Old Testament. "Just as Joseph was said to have been a man 'who a spirit of God was in him' (so the Hebrew of Gen 41:38), Daniel is regarded as one 'who a spirit of the holy God was in him' (so the Aramaic of Daniel 4:8)."[508]

Both men were filled with the Spirit of God. So we come back to the statement that the interpretation belongs to God. God's Spirit can reveal the meaning of a parable dream.[509]

When Joseph dreamed as a young lad, his brothers and his father respectively interpreted his dreams. It was kind of like discussing dreams in the family but this does not mean that Joseph had not first understood the dream himself.

In Judges 7:14 a Midianite soldier dreamed and his friend interpreted it for him. The interpretation was obviously given by God so that Gideon would be encouraged by it.

When Paul had the dream vision in Troas about the man from Macedonia who called them over, he told it to his companions and they together decided that this was God's call to leave for Europe. It becomes clear that they unanimously agreed on the meaning of the vision which Paul had had at night.[510]

False prophets used dreams as a manipulative tool against which God speaks through the prophet Jeremiah. There were prophets at the king's court. They were more committed to the earthly king than to God. They were politically motivated to speak what the king wanted to hear.[511] The misuse of dreams serves those who are skeptical about dreams to warn against the danger of dreaming. Warnings against taking dreams seriously often have to do with a possible misuse of dreams.

---

prayer house which was led by Gaby Pfeil.
[506] Daniel 7:16.
[507] Choon Leong Seow, *Daniel* (Louisville, KY: Westminster John Knox, 2003), 101.
[508] Seow, 67.
[509] John 16:13; 1Corinthians 2:10ff.
[510] Acts 16:10.
[511] 1Kings 22:1-28. Even though the story does not refer explicitly to a dream it gives us a picture of how these prophets functioned.

But when God poured out His Spirit, He promised that all people will have dreams and visions.[512] We may expect that the same Spirit will interpret the dreams where this is necessary. The interpretation of dream-visions can be counted as the gift of the Holy Spirit.[513] Gerhard Dautzenberg provides evidence that ever since Plato, the Greek word family of διακρίνω means the interpretation of dreams and riddles.[514] He argues that the gift of "distinguishing between spirits" (1Cor 12:10) means "interpreting the revelations of the Spirit" referring also to 1Cor 14:29. This gift is mentioned after the gift of prophecy. He connects the two gifts in which case it would mean to interpret pictures, visions or dreams of prophecies.[515] We do not need to take Dautzenberg's stand that 1Cor 12:10 exclusively refers to "interpreting the revelations of the Spirit" but we can conclude safely that διακρίνω was commonly used for "interpreting" dreams and therefore διάκρισις πνευμάτων could include the gift of interpreting. Then the word διακρίνω in 1Cor 14:29 also makes sense.[516] If the interpretation of dreams belongs to God, it makes sense that God's Spirit will give the gift of interpretation not only to Joseph and Daniel but also to spirit-filled believers in our New Testament times.

On the other hand, most of the dreams reported in the Bible were clear in their meanings to the dreamer or his family and friends, without outside interpretation. Only one dream is interpreted by a celestial being, but many prophets asked God to give the interpretation of visions they had received.

3.7.2 Reasons and Purposes of Dreams in the Bible

We find several different reasons and purposes of dreams. This is a summary of how God uses dreams to reach his goals, as we can observe in the Bible.

To Communicate With People

God is a creative God and He uses many means to communicate with people. For example, He speaks to people through His Word, His Spirit, through circumstanc-

---

[512] Joel 2:28; Acts 2:17.

[513] Cf. Rüegg and Rieser, Abs. 50.

[514] Gerhard Dautzenberg, "Zum religionsgeschichtlichen Hintergrund der διακρισις πνευματον 1Ko 12,10." In *Biblische Zeitschrift* 15 (Paderborn, Germany: 1971), 93-104.

[515] Rüegg and Rieser take the arguments of Dautzenberg when they explain: Verstehen wir dagegen die „Unterscheidung" als Gabe des Deutens, dann fügt sich alles sehr treffend: Eingebung + Deutung, Sprachenrede + Auslegung.", Abs.55. („When we understand 'distinguishing' as the gift of interpretation, then everything falls into its place: Prophecy + giving meaning, speaking in tongues + interpretation." Translation by the author). But Grudem in his response to Dautzenberg shows that the word διακρινω is used only once for interpreting prophecies otherwise other words are used. Grudem comes to the conclusion that "the more common translation, 'distinguishing between the spirits', is still to be preferred." W. Grudem, "A Response to Gerhard Dautzenberg on 1 Cor 12:10." *Biblische Zeitschrift* 2 (Paderborn, Germany: 1978), 270. On the other hand, Grudem has to admit that διακρινω was often used for interpreting dreams. He writes: "It is certainly safe to conclude from this evidence that διακρινω and διάκρισις could be used as technical terms to refer to the interpretation of dreams." Ibid, 259-260.

[516] NIV translates 1Corinthians 14:29 "Two or three prophets should speak, and the others should weigh carefully what is said." "Should weigh carefully" then could be translated "should interpret" what is said.

es in life and in dreams and visions. To communicate with the Magi, God showed his care towards them in using a star and a dream – means of communication with which these men were familiar. During dreams, when we are asleep and our senses are not under our control, God's access to our minds is more free and immediate.

To Know Our Innermost Being Better

Dreams which rise up out of our soul help us to know our innermost being better.[517] They can play an important role in psychology and pastoral care.

To Test God's People

Dreams from spirits are a test from God, not to listen to them, but to love God wholeheartedly.[518]

To Preserve God's People

God has given dreams to preserve God's covenant people and people in the world through times of disaster.[519]

To Know God

One of the main purposes of dreams is that people will come to know God better.[520] How could Abimelech have come to know God without the dream that brought him into deeper contact with Abraham? Abraham prayed for him and he and his family were healed.[521] God wants people and even kings and world rulers to worship Him and acknowledge Him as the Most High God.[522] Dreams and the gift of interpretation has been given in order to open doors for witnessing to the Highest God. He is eager to see people turn from their wicked ways and seek Him.[523] God even used a dream to install Jacob as the agent of His promise, which He had given to Abraham and Isaac before him.[524]

To Warn and Protect People

God spoke a stern warning to Abimelech should he not give Sarah back to Abraham, he would die.[525] After Solomon had well established his kingdom, God

---

[517] Daniel 2:28.

[518] Deuteronomy 13:3.

[519] As through the dreams to Pharaoh, or the dreams to Joseph to rescue God's son.

[520] The dreams of the cupbearer and baker gave Joseph opportunity to testify to the living God (Genesis 40:8). See also Genesis 41:16; Daniel 2:28.

[521] Genesis 20:3ff.

[522] For example Pharaoh (Genesis 41) and Nebuchadnezzar (Daniel 2:28; 4:25).

[523] Job 33:15ff. Daniel 4:27.

[524] Genesis 28:12-15.

[525] Genesis 20:7.

warned him not to turn away from Him.[526] The Magi were warned in a dream not to go back to King Herod. God warned Joseph about the plans of Herod to kill Jesus.[527] God used dreams to protect people, like Sarah and Jacob and they were not even aware of it.[528] God wants to protect people from destruction[529] – even His own son.[530]

To Encourage God's People

But as often as there are warnings, there is also encouragement for the dreamer. God's promises to Jacob that God would be with him and that He would not leave him[531] must have been a great encouragement for Jacob. The dream Joseph dreamed twice[532] had the capacity to encourage him when he was down in the cistern and in the dungeon. Gideon and his servant were encouraged by the interpretation of the dream by the Midianite which they overheard and which God had prepared for them.[533] God encouraged King Solomon in his dreams.[534] In the New Testament we find Paul being encouraged by a vision at night, not to fear but to preach, because God was with him and He had many people in the city of Corinth.[535]

To Reveal the Future

Through dreams God has revealed future events.[536] With Joseph, it was on a personal level, while with Jacob, it was on the level of salvation history to come. "God has shown to Pharaoh what he is about to do."[537] Through Nebuchadnezzar's two dreams and the interpretations of Daniel, as well as Daniel's dream and the interpretation of the celestial being, the apocalyptic future was revealed.[538]

To Instruct and Lead People

God sent dreams in order to instruct and lead people, like the angel who told Jacob in a dream to leave the country and go back to his father's house.[539] Or God in-

---

[526] 1Kings 9:6ff.
[527] Matthew 2:13.
[528] Genesis 20:3ff; 31:24.
[529] Therefore the Pharaoh had his dream – and surely God was preparing his saving operation for Jacob and his family. Genesis 41. Job 33:15ff.
[530] Matthew 2:12.13.
[531] Genesis 28:15.
[532] Genesis 37:5-11.
[533] Judges 7:11.
[534] 1Kings 3:5-15; 9:1-9.
[535] Acts 18:9-10.
[536] Genesis 28:13-14; 37:5-11;
[537] Genesis 41:28.
[538] Daniel 2:29; 4:24-27; 7:17-27.
[539] Genesis 31:13.

structed Solomon to walk with the Lord.[540] He also led Joseph to marry Mary and he led him back from Egypt to Nazareth.[541] When Paul and his team were stuck in Troas, God was leading them by a vision of the night which Paul had received.[542] And one purpose of Nebuchadnezzar's dream was, "that you may understand what went through your mind."[543] This means that God can use dreams to teach people about their attitude and thinking which they would not be aware of otherwise.

To Stay Healthy

This reason is not given explicitly in the Bible but dreams are part of God's creation. Research has shown that through dreaming, impressions of the day are processed in order to stay healthy. "When people are hindered consistently to dream, their psyche and body will get sick."[544]

3.8 Summary

The Bible tells us that God has spoken through dreams to all sorts of people, young and old, men and women. Some were his covenant people, others were from heathen nations. For the present time, after the Holy Spirit has been poured out on all flesh, Joel prophesied that young and old, servants and maidservants will have dreams and visions. In confirming this truth at Pentecost, Peter gives significance to this fact.

We have seen that the source of dreams can be God, evil spirits, they can originate in our own souls revealing the subconscious, or they may be a reflection of daily cares. They also could be made up by men.[545] Dreams which have their origin in "soul travel" are foreign to the biblical accounts.

When the meaning of a symbolic dream was unclear, heathen kings like Pharaoh and Nebuchadnezzar asked magicians, clairvoyants and dream readers for help.[546] When they could not help, Joseph and Daniel respectively, were consulted. Both of these men of God made it very clear that interpretation of dreams belongs to God.

When God promised that in the age of the Holy Spirit people without regard to their gender, status and race will have dreams, God has also given the gift of interpretation. We have seen that the gift of "diakrisis pneumaton" includes the gift of interpreting.

---

[540] 1Kings 9:4-5.
[541] Matthew 1:20; 2:19-23.
[542] Acts 16:6-10.
[543] Daniel 2:30.
[544] "Wenn man Menschen konsequent am Träumen hindert, werden sie psychisch und physisch krank." (Translation by the author). Grün, 65. Cf. Samuel Pfeifer in his booklet.
[545] Jeremiah 23:25-26. See 35N who asked: "Who knows what he really dreamed?"
[546] This was true of ordinary people as well as the account of the dreams of the cupbearer and the baker suggests.

Does the Bible tell us of any one dream which contains an evil message to God's people? Does any dream reveal and accuse other people of evil deeds? None of this is found there. God does not give evil dreams to his people. He gives dreams of warning in order to help and to save people.

God has revealed significant events through dreams. Salvation history has been partly revealed through dreams. Jacob's dream at Bethel was much more than a personal encouragement. In the same way the dreams of Pharaoh, Daniel and Nebuchadnezzar have played significant roles in revealing God's plan of salvation for his own people. In the book of Daniel we see how God uses a dream to predict the ultimate triumph of the kingdom of God. Even though King Solomon did not speak very highly of dreams in one place,[547] one of the most significant moments in his own life was his dream at Gibeon. It was the initiation of his successful kingship. The dream made an immediate impact on his life. Solomon returned from the "high place" to Jerusalem offering sacrifices before the ark of the Lord's covenant. It seems that this wise move, in obedience to God's Word, was sparked by his wonderful dream.

Dreams in the Bible have great significance in people's lives. All three dreams which are reported of Jacob came to him in crisis situations. The same is true when Paul speaks of his four dream visions at night. Dreams have helped the Joseph of the Old Testament as well as the Joseph of the New Testament to master the crises of their lives. God spoke to these men of God and gave them promises and directions which were of great significance to them. This can still be the case for Christians today.

---

[547] Ecclesiastes 1:1; 5:2. The same is true of the prophet Jeremiah, who was very skeptical of dreams, yet he still received dreams from God. Cf. Jeremiah 31:26.

4. Methodology and Procedure

This study has been carried out in the context of more than twenty years of participant observation among the Sgaw Karen people. I have become aware of the significance which dreams play in many of the Karen people's lives. These observations led me to start asking people purposefully about their dream experiences. Dreams, by their very nature, cannot be observed from the outside but need to be talked about. Many Karen talk quite freely about them and through the years I have overheard many talks about dreams.

4.1 Qualitative Research

The research design of the study is a qualitative study of dreams. This has become the common research method in social science.[548] "While quantitative research only tests for variables that have been predetermined by the researcher, qualitative research methodology is flexible enough to discover previously unknown variables."[549] This widens the pool of knowledge in the respective area. The aim in interviews is as Spradley put it: *"Both questions and answers must be discovered from informants."*[550]

The study will take an *emic* approach which investigates how local people feel and think, whereby the researcher takes the following attitude: "I want to understand the world from your point of view ... to walk in your shoes ... Will you become my teacher and help me understand?"[551]

4.2 Cultural Issues

Because of the high illiteracy rate among Karen who are middle-aged and older in the area in which the research is done, any study involving a written questionnaire would not succeed. Even asking a set of direct questions would not be helpful, since it is a culturally inappropriate way to gather data for informational purposes. Rather such questioning signifies the desire to make a point or even to accuse. Therefore, guided oral interviews are a more practical research method in a traditional culture such as the Karen. The validity and worth of an interview rests on the extent that the interviewee's idea has been truly reflected. In order to achieve this goal, semi-structured questioning has been used as the appropriate method, because there is leverage to comment and talk around and about until the main information is given.

---

[548] Margaret D. LeCompte & Jean J. Schensul, *Analyzing and Interpreting Ethnographic Data* (Walnut Creek, CA: AltaMira Press, 1999). Nicholas Walliman, *Social Research Methods* (London, UK: Sage Publications, 2006), 129.

[549] Kenneth Robert Nehrbass, *Christianity and Animism in a South Pacific Society. Four Ecclesiastical Approaches Toward "Kastom"*. A Dissertation for the Doctor of Philosophy. (La Mirada, CA: Intercultural Studies Biola University, 2010), 190.

[550] James P. Spradley, *The Ethnographic Interview* (Belmont, CA: Wadsworth Group, 1979), 84.

[551] Spradley, 34.

Mainly middle-aged and older people were interviewed. Young people in the city have been under many other influences and may think in different ways while young people in the village are impressed by their parents and village culture but do not have the experience and influence of the older.

4.3 Interviewing

The researcher has interviewed Karen from all sorts of life situations about their dream experiences. Interviews have been recorded and transcribed except for parts which did not relate to dreams. Many of these interviews were quite unstructured. I tried to follow the lead the interviewee was taking when he was talking about a dream. Quite a number of times these interviews were done with several people present, most of them sharing some of their experiences with dreams.

I have designed an interview guide with key questions. These were grouped along the areas about which I wanted to research (see under 4.6.), at the same time being open to new strings of information. Even though I have written the questions down beforehand they were not meant to all be asked of all interviewees, however they were used spontaneously in the interview without referring to it explicitly all the time. The aim was to find out the world view on dreams among Karen people and the impact dreams have in their daily life. Questions asked were not so specific "that alternative avenues of enquiry that might arise during the collection of fieldwork data are closed off."[552] Premature closing would have been detrimental to the process of qualitative research.

Since many of the interview partners had never had the opportunity to attend any official school, I used questions which draw descriptions of the experiences and then built on the information gathered to try to find out more regarding how Karen think and feel about their dreams.

Since Karen people in the mountains are used to talk in groups together, I carried out some of the interviews in small groups where people were open to share. This kind of talk in small groups facilitated the process of the interview. Those participating easily forgot about the character of an interview and shared their experiences more freely. I have made the same experience as Joll has observed: "Group interviews were marked by an increased synergy in which everyone appeared to enjoy themselves more, often yielding data of higher quality."[553]

I have known many of the participants personally over a longer period of time, a good rapport and trust had been established. I did many of the interviews myself in the local Sgaw Karen language. One to one interviews were possible with some people. In one area where people knew of me but I had not yet established a rapport with them, a local young man, who studies in Chiang Mai, accompanied me

---

[552] *Interviewing in qualitative research, chapter 15,* 317. (no author). http://www.comp.dit.ie/dgordon/ Courses/ResearchMethods/Lectures/ Week4/Chap15-Interviews.pdf (21.5.2014).

[553] Chris Joll, *What Muslims in Cabangtiga Mean by Merit: Merit Making Rhetoric, Islamic Discourse and the Thai Milieu.* A Dissertation for the Doctor of Philosophy (Bangi, Malaysia: University Kebangsaan, 2009) 108.

and helped with the interviews. He was also able to give me the background of the interview partners.

In an attempt to find out ways concerning how the experience of dreams among Christians can be redeemed, I have asked a few of the main Christian leaders in depth, how they deal with Christians who are in fear because they have had bad dreams.

The whole process is comparable to a spiral. It starts in broad circles and comes back to similar questions and answers, yet this new information leads to further questioning. The spiral has a direction, coming from the more open-ended questions to the semi-structure question guide and from there to the in depth interviews. If the interviews went in circles instead of spiraling it meant that the information which was available was given so that a new string of questions could be talked about.

4.4 Limitations to the Validity of Research

I am aware that I am known to people in my roles of Bible teaching missionary, social development helper and friend. There was the danger that some may want to please me with answers that may reflect what they conceive to be "the biblical view of dreams." Therefore I informed people about the purpose of these talks, and especially that I am a learner who wants to better understand their dream world and the influence it has on their lives.

I have been aware of another limitation to the validity of this kind of interview, namely leading questions as well as my preconceived ideas after having read on the topic extensively. I may not have always avoided leading questions in spontaneous talks. "However this same vulnerability and complexity produces a richness and depth to data worth many of the risks."[554]

4.5 Ethical Issues

"Among the most serious harms that anthropologists should seek to avoid are harm to dignity, and to bodily and material well-being."[555] "Due regard should be given to the dignity, integrity and privacy of those involved at any level."[556] The semi-structured interviews allowed respondents to share private matters even to a deep level. The persons who did that have been aware of the fact that the interviews were not for use on a private level only. They have given consent to share the stories publicly.

---

[554] Nigel Newton, "The use of semi-structured interviews in qualitative research: strengths and weaknesses." (2010), 4f. https://www.academia.edu/1561689 Accessed 21st May 2014, 4-5

[555] American Anthropological Association, „Statement of Ethics" http://ethics.aaanet.org/ethics-statement-1-do-no-harm/ Accessed 22nd May 2014.

[556] Nicholas Walliman, *Social Research Methods* (London, UK: Sage Publications, 2006), 39.

4.6 Data Analysis

With the help of two young Karen men, I transcribed the approximate 70 interviews from Sgaw Karen language into English. This arduous work had the effect that I have become very familiar with the contents of all the interviews. I have not used specific qualitative analysis software. The X Mind 6 program has been a help to gain a quick and better overview of the material to a certain theme or code. The main codes for my *thematic analysis*[557] were

- Spread and popularity of dreams among the Karen
- Areas of life which Karen mainly dream about
- Categories of different kinds of dreams
- Understanding the origin of dreams
- Interpretation of dreams
- Meanings of dreams
- Beneficial impact of dreams
- Detrimental impact of dreams
- Redeeming the dreams – approaches taken by Karen

I read the interviews several times and put the same material together to the different themes. For the content analysis I used the advanced finding key, eliciting more important code terms, like "elephant", '*lo ta*', '*plü kau*' or '*k'la*'. This kind of manual tools are time consuming, but on the other hand in reading and working through the interviews in depth I could link the same or similar content together not only by code words but by actual meanings. This has brought to light results which go beyond what I could have managed by using a computer program which is not able to understand the meaning of the text.

4.7 Biblical Critique

Firstly, I did my own exegesis on the basis that the Bible – Old and New Testament together – is God's Word in which God has revealed himself and his plan of salvation to humanity. I have taken into consideration literacy critique but did not follow the historical-critical method.

Following the exegesis, I took into consideration commentaries and other literature on the different dream passages in the Bible. I have taken a short look on how Christians have viewed dreams in the past and present, as well as how theologians from different backgrounds think about them.

Even though "visions and dreams" are often mentioned together and cannot always be kept separate from each other, my examination is focused on the instanc-

---

[557] I learned about thematic, comparative and content analysis from Catherine Dawson's discussion in chapter 11 "How to Analyze Your Data" in her book *Introduction to Research Methods* (Oxford, UK: How To Books, 2009), 114-133.

Methodology and Procedure

es where the term "dream" is explicitly mentioned in the Bible, including the term "vision in the night."

On these biblical findings the research compares Karen dreams with the biblical view of dreams. Similarities and differences are exposed. Lastly, a biblical critique is given on the Karen Christian experience of dreams as well as on the Karen Animist-Buddhist view of dreams. The critique closes with a biblical perspective on redeeming the dreams.

5. Results, Findings and Evaluation

5.1 Animist-Buddhist Compared to Christian Karen Views

5.1.1 Spread and Popularity of Dreams Among the Karen

Dreams among the Karen are talked about in everyday life. I was amazed how easy it is to talk about dreams with Karen from all sorts of life. Non-Christians as well as Christians are ready to share their dream experiences. From the simple farmer to the spirit priest, from the housewife to the headman, from a new Christian to the pastor, all have to share some stories about dreams. There is a basic knowledge about dream interpretation. They talk about dreams in the family or ask friends if they are not sure what a dream means. In some cases they may even ask the spirit priest about the meaning.

Therefore, it surprised me that nearly all Karen – Christians as well as non-Christians – who I asked whether they like to dream, answered, "No, I do not like to dream."[558] "If I could stop it, I would."[559] Or "How can we like dreams?"[560] Or "If I could, I would not like to dream at all."[561] Or "Dreaming is not nice."[562] Hardly anybody desires to dream. Only Jae said, "I do not want to dream bad dreams. But good dreams, I really want to dream them."[563] Probably, most of the other interviewees would agree on that, too.

Why Do Karen Not Like to Dream?

Some explained why they do not like to dream. The spirit priest S and his companion agreed, "Bad dreams occur more often. Good dreams are less."[564] The same spirit priest said, "If I do not dream at night I go wherever I want (during the day), but when I dream it is different."[565] After a bad dream many Karen feel restricted in what they can do the next day. Others are worried after dreaming[566] or feel tired.[567] Several Christians said that dreams are a temptation.[568] What that exactly

---

[558] 52Ch; 47P; 23P; 34R; 50Phi; 67BR. These references refer to the interviews in Appendix B. It is the interview number and the letters are the abbreviation for the name of the person who was interviewed.
[559] 50Phi.
[560] 45S; 45G; 50Phue.
[561] 42Mo.
[562] 28Kri.
[563] 63Jae.
[564] 45S; 45G.
[565] 45S.
[566] 42Mo; 67BR.
[567] 34R.
[568] 23P; 47P.

means is explained later on. Grandfather P mentioned what many have said in other contexts that "If you dream a lot, you are not well."[569] Without specifically asking, two middle aged men gave their advice on how dreaming can be stopped. Mr Buka said, "I wash my hair with 'bu chi sa'[570] which is dried and then add seven beans into the water and boil it. If you do this you will dream less! You will be happy."[571] Notice, how he equals happiness with not having any dreams. Another man suggested, "When you dream a lot you need to put a knife under your pillow so you will not dream so much anymore."[572]

Comparison Between Animist-Buddhist and Christian Views

Generally, I could not find a big difference in the popularity of dreaming between the two groups. Karen from both groups do not like to dream.

Christians have mentioned that to non-Christians dreams are more important.[573] Or a man who has become a Christian four years ago, mentioned that as a Christian "I hardly dream now."[574] Some Christians consciously ignore dreams. They only want to trust in God's Word. One of the leading Christians in the Omkoi area has put it this way, "I do not think about dreams very much. Whether I have a good dream or a bad one, I do not think about it. My life is in God's hand. Some dream a lot but they do not understand the meaning. I believe that the bad things do not come through dreams."[575]

When Do Dreams Occur Most?

According to some Karen, dreams occur most when you are not well. Many see it the other way round, "If you dream a lot, you are not well."[576] Others commented that if you are healthy, you do not dream a lot.[577]

5.1.2 Main Areas of Life Which Karen Dream About

I did not specifically ask many questions about this but categorizing what has been mentioned in the interviews gives us some interesting insights. There is no claim that the mentioned areas or details within, are complete, far from it. But it gives us some ideas about how culture, life experiences and dreams are connected with each other.

---

[569] 50Phue.
[570] 'bu chi sa' is the fruit of the acacia tree. The Thai call it 'som poi'.
[571] 43B.
[572] 48HP.
[573] 44T.
[574] 23P.
[575] 67BR.
[576] 50Phue.
[577] 63Jae.

Dreams About Animals

At least 17 different animals have been mentioned by Karen in the dreams I listened to. Fish[578] is often mentioned, generally known as a good dream. Some have dreamed about big animals like elephants,[579] buffaloes[580] or cows[581] haunting them. Since dreaming about elephants has different meanings, I asked more about them. Therefore elephants have been mentioned the most out of all the animals. Snakes,[582] dogs,[583] cats,[584] tigers[585] or bears[586] can bite, while a bee,[587] a 'da bo'[588] can sting or leeches[589] are sucking your blood in bad dreams, but if you can beat them off you are okay. Others have dreamed about killing deer,[590] pigs,[591] birds,[592] a turtle[593] or an ape.[594] Karen have also dreamed about termite hills[595] and bees.[596]

Dreams About What Karen Do

I have not heard of anybody dreaming about planting rice or vegetables, but if they are about to plant or harvest rice, many watch their dreams.[597] Harvesting rice occurs in their dreams.[598] Cooking food,[599] looking for food,[600] looking for 'choemiti',[601] going up or downhill,[602] going up a tree,[603] walking up or down a river,[604]

---

[578] 10S; 11T; 12J; 25M; 30Ch; 31DM; 40M; 43B; 57Ti; 58N.

[579] 24E; 25M; 28Ch; 31DM; 32BR; 33P; 38P; 43B; 45S; 47P; 50Phi; 54Ch; 64Ch.

[580] 31DM; 32BR; 45G; 47P; 50Phue; 52Ch.

[581] 42Mo; 44T; 47P; 52Ch; 63Jae.

[582] 38Luwa; 57Ti; 58N; 63Jae.

[583] 28Ch; 31DM; 33P; 34R; 37M; 38P; 50Phue; 58N.

[584] 25M; 33P; 43B; 50Phi.

[585] 33P.

[586] 33P; 40M in a 'hta'.

[587] 33P.

[588] 56G.

[589] 10S.

[590] 57A; 59N; 33P; 39M; 45S; 50Phue.

[591] 38P; 39M; 40M; 57A.

[592] 14P; 31P; 32BR.

[593] 34R.

[594] 31DM.

[595] 43B; 57A.

[596] 38P.

[597] 28Kri; 31DM; 33P; 38M; 38P; 54Ch; 58N; 65HT.

[598] 56G.

[599] 34R; 62ST. Cf. Supomo giving testimony on her illness on 5th Aug. 2012 in Thibokhi, Tak Province. See under 2.4.2.

[600] 57A.

[601] 42Mo. 'Choemiti' is a root they dig out and sell for cash.

[602] 12J; 21H; 50Phue; 51D; 53Ch; 63W; 65HT; 67BR.

[603] 63Jae.

drawing water,[605] crossing the river in water or going over a bridge,[606] riding an elephant[607] or coming back home[608] have been mentioned. Fishing[609] and hunting,[610] killing animals[611] or people[612], a gun[613] or a trap[614] are other dream motives. Eating rice,[615] pepper,[616] meat,[617] melons,[618] cucumbers,[619] bananas,[620] salt[621] and drinking water[622] or alcohol[623] belongs to their dream life, too. Bowel movement, going to the toilet or urinating is not taboo in dreams.[624] One older man said, that he has dreamed about singing '*hta*'.[625] Some have dreamed about flying[626] and planes landing.[627] Money[628] plays its role.

Elements of nature like fire,[629] water,[630] storms,[631] rain[632] and floods,[633] light[634] and darkness,[635] sun[636] and moon[637] or trees[638] are not missing either.

---

[604] 12J.
[605] 55G.
[606] 12J; 13Oe; 16N; 31P.
[607] 64Ch.
[608] 37M; 43B.
[609] 25M; 28Kri; 32DM.
[610] 25M; 31P; 45S; 46P; 57A.
[611] 25M; 31DM; 33P; 39M; 44T; 50Phue.
[612] 19S; 33P; 39M; 40M.
[613] 31P; 31D.
[614] 48HP.
[615] 31DM; 42Mo; 43B.
[616] 12J; 22H; 25M; 28Ch; 30Ch; 38M; 53Ch; 55G; 67BR.
[617] 12J; 13Oe; 45S; 45G; 57A; 58N; 62ST; 65HT.
[618] 31P; 40M; 45S; 45G; 50Phue; 50Phi; 55G.
[619] 28Ch; 29D; 33P; 34R; 45S.
[620] 18P; 34R; 45S.
[621] 37M.
[622] 46P.
[623] 70Ch.
[624] 25M; 49H; 51D.
[625] 50Phue.
[626] 28D; 33P; 45S; 54Ch.
[627] 32BR; 40M; 44T.
[628] 18Chra; 25M; 33P; 42Mo.
[629] 12J; 24E; 26E; 28Ch; 30Ch; 34R; 38MM; 42Mo; 43B; 44T; 45S; 46P; 58N; 59N; 67BR.
[630] 19S; 31P; 31DM; 38M; 43N; 44T; 45G; 46P; 50Phue; 51D; 55G; 59N.
[631] 12J; 31P; 34R; 66Somu.
[632] 12J; 26Kri; 26Ch; 26D; 31P; 44T; 54Ch.
[633] 12J.
[634] 12J; 43B; 57A.
[635] 21H; 37M; 43B; 57A.

Dreams About Family and Relationships

Very common are dreams and their interpretation about expecting a baby[639] and about the gender of the child.[640] Some have dreamed about their child being reborn.[641] Many fear the dream about carrying (*'pü'*) a child.[642] Some were bold enough to tell that they dreamed about the other gender or were sexually tempted in dreams.[643]

Dreams About Their Faith

Animist-Buddhist Karen often tell dreams about the Hades called *'plü kau'*.[644] Their *'k'la'* may encounter spirits and may even be caught by them which will require "a calling back the *'k'la'* ceremony". They believe, if a person dreams that someone is giving meat to another person, that the giver cast a spell of death (*'lo ta'*) on the receiving person.[645]

Many Karen Christians still dream in the same old ways as described above. Their old beliefs of the afterworld (*'plü kau'*) or the cursing, *'lo ta'*, are still deeply anchored and through dreaming it, are reinforced again. But many Christians think like Oelopa who said, "If they really believe in God, they do not believe that anymore."[646] Another Christian said, "Sometimes when I dream about ancestor worship or spirit doctors, then I may not feel well. When I go and pray nothing bad is going to happen."[647]

Some Christians have started to dream new dreams and have been encouraged by it. Dreaming about singing or worshiping God or seeing many people come together to meet on a hill.[648] During an awakening time around 2007 some children had visions and dreams "of heaven, hell, and the crucifixion of Jesus."[649] One older Christian commented: "Nowadays the Holy Spirit talks to people in dreams."[650]

---

[636] 34R; 40M.

[637] 40M.

[638] 12J; 14P; 25M; 28Ch; 32BR; 40M; 43B; 45G; 58N; 63Jae.

[639] 34R; 40G; 45S; 55G. Cf. Noh Chila's phone call on New Year 2009. See under 2.4.2.

[640] 28Ch; 31D; 31P; 33P; 34R; 45G; 50Phi.

[641] 14P; 38MM.

[642] 27M; 48HP; 50Phi; 66Somu. Cf. Supomo giving testimony on her illness on 5th Aug. 2012 in Thibokhi, Tak Province. See under 2.4.2.

[643] 14P; 18P; 38P; 39Ch; 45S; 57A; 57Ti; 58N.

[644] 25M; 28Kri; 30Ch; 31P; 38P; 45S; 45G; 47P; 53Ch; 54Ch; 57A; 62Pue; 63Jae; 65HT.

[645] 12J; 23P; 45S; 58N; 62ST; 65HT.

[646] 13Oe.

[647] 64Ch.

[648] 28D; 31D; 33P; 58N; 68S; 69P.

[649] Worapong Jariyaphruttipong (Sidney). "Transformation in Omkoi, Thailand." www.Sentinelgroup.org/fire-quest/asia/Thailand/introduction/. Accessed 29th July 2015.

[650] 31P.

5.1.3 Categorizing Different Kinds of Dreams

One basic differentiation of dreams is often made – **message versus symbolic dreams**. Among the Karen symbolic dreams predominate. The proportion between message and symbolic dreams may be about 10% to 90%. Besides this basic distinction I will give another three types of categorizing.

Types of Cultural Dream Theory

I have mentioned "a paradigm of the six types of cultural dream theory known from the ethnographic record,"[651] to which Lohmann refers.

Three of them are clearly existent among the Karen. These are the "message type", the "visitation type" and the "soul travel theory type". The "none-sense type" occurs in a different mode.

Message type

A twenty year old mother heard a message in a dream while she was pregnant. She said, "In a dream, a person came to tell me 'this house will not be established, a girl will not get up in this house. But if it were a boy it does not matter, but a girl cannot get up.' ... It was not a spirit or a deceased person. It just spoke like a person and I did not fear when it spoke."[652] Then she gave birth to a girl who had cleft palates and the mother did not have any milk for her.

Besides hearing a message without any pictures, some have seen the person who spoke.[653] One man said, "Before my wife died, I dreamed that my wife entrusted the children to me and she went off."[654] Somu who comes from this village, explains: His wife had cancer and after he had dreamed, his wife died two or three days later.

Another woman did not see the speaker (God), but besides the message she also received pictures.[655]

Visitation type of dream

Three people have given me accounts of a visitation type of dream. One lady was healed by someone visiting her in the dream.[656] A longstanding Christian and elder of a church said, "The Holy Spirit came to me and I was so happy. I was really glad. It was like the angel coming to Mary – and she was happy. I dreamed this way once."[657] Before a Karen Christian leader started his own foundation he was visited by his grandfather who was a Christian leader and had died 20 years earlier.[658]

---

[651] Lohmann, *Evaluating Dreams*, 230.
[652] 41NG.
[653] 29A.
[654] 36L.
[655] 16N.
[656] 17N.
[657] 31D.
[658] 29A.

Soul travel theory type

The "soul travel theory type" of dream was mentioned several times.[659] An Animist-Buddhist headman told me

There was one (*'k'la'*) who went there – I dreamed that my *'k'la'* went off to the realm of the dead (*'plü kau'*). It went to a village and it was with friends and it was so nice. It was marvelous. Then I (*'k'la'*) came back, but I could not overcome a fallen tree. Then I awoke and I was like dead from morning until midday. Then I got ill for over two months and I nearly died. I was ill for two months because I had gone into the realm of the dead. There was only one tree who hindered me.[660]

This type of dream is there but many others do not make the connection between dreaming and the *'k'la'* wandering.

None-sense type

The "none-sense type" of dream as it is outlined by Lohmann, did not come up in my research. But for a certain type of dream, Karen speak of *'plo so'*. **'Plo so'** means to dream about things you were doing or thinking during the day. This kind of dream is thought to be trivial. Such dreams become significant only, if there is something unusual in it. This type of dream corresponds closely to what Hollan found among the Toraja. These dreams have to do with the activities of the previous day, and are not taken as important and not much thought is given to them.[661]

Good and Bad Dreams

The most popular distinction among the Karen is between "good" and "bad" dreams. Whether it is a good or a bad dream depends on its interpretation. Karen interpret their dreams analogous to a set of known interpretations – it is like a dream book passed down orally.[662] Very often people will not tell you the dream but they may just comment, "I had a bad dream" or "I had a good dream." To know whether a dream is good or bad is important in order to know whether to take action or not, and in addition, what kind of action to take. To say, "I had a bad dream", is excuse enough not to join in work or any other activity. "The bad dreams occur more often."[663] I have come to the same conclusion as Pertony who did research among the Aboriginals in Australia[664], that bad dreams outweigh the good ones by far.

Different Types of Dreams Derived From Their Interpretation

The following eight types of dreams, I found among the Karen, has a lot to do with the interpretation of dreams by the people. They are dreams as warning, en-

---

[659] 42Mo; 47P; 62P; 65HT.
[660] 25M.
[661] Hollan, The Personal Use, 168ff. The Cultural, 175.
[662] We find a parallel to this among the Toraja. See under 2.3.3.1.
[663] 45S; 45G.
[664] B. Pertony, "Dreams and Dream Beliefs in North Western Australia" in *Oceania*, Vol. 32, No. 2 (Dec., 1961), 149.

couragement, accusation, instruction, wish fulfilling, confirmation, fear/nightmare and seeing things happen (revelation).

Warning

One Christian lady said, "Often dreams are like a warning." And she gives the following example: "When we were going to build this house I dreamed. A big fire was spreading. The fire destroyed our house. Sometimes we are warned in dreams about problems that may arise and we need to pray. These are dreams of warning to us."[665]

Another lady told me, "We wanted to plant tomatoes in the paddy fields. We prayed in the evening. But at night I dreamed about stinky fish. The fish had no water, dried. We had no water, so we did not plant, otherwise we would have lost it all. The dream was a warning."[666]

In many ways Karen understand most bad dreams as a warning, therefore they do not go out. The dilemma with this kind of warning is that you may have to stay home when it would be time to plant. The dreamer loses his freedom. He is kept captive by all the "warnings".[667]

Accusation

Quite often people see in a dream who has caused the illness by '*lo ta*'. A Christian headman complained, "Sometimes people accuse another person that he/she has seen in a dream one person giving meat to another and then this creates great problems."[668]

Instruction

This is the message type of dream we have already examined.

Encouragement

All Karen are encouraged by good dreams, like going uphill or seeing a lot of fish. But remarkably all the reports of specific dreams by which they were encouraged came from Christians.[669]

Wishful dreams

"I dreamed about getting a car. I was so happy. But when I woke up, I did not have one."[670]

---

[665] 58N.
[666] 31DM.
[667] 45S. Cf. 32BR.
[668] 65HT. Cf. 58N.
[669] 31D; 44T; 50Phue; 58N; 68S.
[670] 43B.

Confirmation

When Karen have to make important decisions, some are looking for an auspicious dream. "Some when they want to marry and think whether they should marry a certain girl, they say if I have good dreams, then I will marry her; if my dream is not nice I will not marry her. My brother Johapa (12J) did it that way."[671] When I asked Mr. B whether dreams ever helped him, he answered, "Yes. If we are going to do fields: If we have good dreams we go and do it – if we have a bad dream we are not going to do it."[672]

Fear/nightmare

Karen experience the same kind of dream you will find all over the world, namely that you are haunted by an animal[673] or by a spirit[674] thereby experiencing horrible fear. When I asked Mr R whether he remembers a very bad dream, he gave the following account, "Yes, I do. Dreaming about 'pa te qa'. I saw it and it ran after me. I feared it but I could not escape. I tried to overcome it but could not overcome it. After dreaming like this I felt very tired."[675]

Seeing things happen (revelation)

Somu's father said, if he dreams of his son in Chiang Mai and he is sitting, then he does not come home but if he is rising he will come back. He welcomed us in his village with the words, "I dreamed that my son carried salt to our house, we had no salt anymore."[676] He had dreamed this the night before we came up. Hayami reports that she often was welcomed with the words, "I have dreamed last night that you were coming."[677] So much so that he suspected it to be a social nicety. Mr. P said, "Sometimes I dream they (children) are not well, and when I phone them they are not well."[678] Mrs. N, a Christian leader and teacher, has dreamed very specifically, she said,

Sometimes we do not know the meaning of a dream, we have to ask the Holy Spirit. E.g. The pastor of our church – his wife dreamed that a snake bit her. The poison went to her heart. She did not understand so she came to me, and told me that the snake bit her and the poison went to her heart. Then I went to prayer. Then I dreamed that the pastor was in prison. When I asked him why he is in prison, he said, 'I do not know why they caught me, I have done nothing wrong.' When I rose in the morning I saw the pastor. I said to him, 'Last night we prayed for you and at night God revealed that you are having problems.' A month later it had

---

[671] 28Ch.

[672] 43B. Cf. 31DM.

[673] 45G; 63Jae.

[674] 31DM; 34R; 39Ch; 42Mo.

[675] 34R.

[676] 37M. Salt is very important, because it is one of the few essentials Karen always had to import from outside.

[677] Hayami, *Between Hills*, 29.

[678] 38P.

become obvious that he lived in adultery. The problem was now open and so it would be possible to solve the problem. We gave him a chance to repent. Now he is divorced and has married another woman and has a new child.[679]

This is the kind of dream many Karen Christians would like to see happen more often in order to bring clarity into dark affairs. It would replace the practice of the spirit doctors more effectively.

All these kind of dreams are found among Animist-Buddhists and Christians alike. From my many interviews I can conclude that message dreams and dreams of specific encouragement happen more often among Christians.

5.1.4 Understanding the Origin of Dreams

Of the thirty people I asked the question, "Where do dreams come from?" fourteen answered, "I do not know." Another two avoided answering and one said, "I just dream."[680] Christians and non-Christians alike gave this answer. That means that about half of the Karen I asked could not explain the origin of dreams. A few of those who answered, "I do not know," when I asked directly,[681] later gave some hints of what they thought.[682]

The second most popular answer, given by twelve people, was that dreams come from an evil source, the spirits, the devil or it is a temptation (by the devil).[683] Again, Animist-Buddhist and Christians answered alike. The answer that dreams are a temptation was only given by Christians.[684] One Christian mother defined, what that means. "When I have bad dreams, I know the devil comes to do evil."[685] For others, it is a temptation to be drawn back into the old faith and make sacrifices. That so many see the source of dreams as the devil and evil spirits underlines our observation that the majority of the Karen have a negative understanding of dreams, and that bad dreams outweigh good dreams.

Five answered or implied that dreams come from God or the Holy Spirit.[686] These were answers of Christians. P14 is referring to the fact that non-Christian Karen speak about dreams coming from '*Ywa*' (God) even though they do not worship '*Ywa*'. This is due to the fact that the Bible uses the traditional word '*Ywa*' for God. Karen Christians who have been taught in the Christian faith understand the word '*Ywa*' differently than those who only know the traditional stories about '*Ywa*'.

---

[679] 58N.
[680] 12J; 18Chra; 19S; 22M; 25M; 27M; 31D; 42Pa; 45S; 47P; 48HP; 56G; 57Ti; 64Ch; 65HT.
[681] As mentioned before, expecting answers to direct questions does not work very well among those Karen who did not have any formal education.
[682] 22M; 25M; 27M; 31D.
[683] 13Oe; 27M; 31P; 18P; 19E; 22M; 23P; 28Ch; 31D; 51D; 58N; 64Ch.
[684] 18P; 19E; 23P; 31D.
[685] 51D.
[686] 13Oe; 14P; 28D; 31P; 58N.

Four persons brought dreaming in direct connection with the *'k'la'* wandering.[687] "When the *'k'la'* wander you can see many things."[688] You see these things in dreams. Still, it is an amazingly low figure. It means that the *'k'la'* wandering is not always seen as the source or reason for dreaming. While set in the context of talks it has come out very clearly that dreams and *'k'la'* wandering are clearly connected. It can be concluded that the *'k'la'* wandering is a reason for dreaming.

Another reason for dreaming mentioned, is one's work or one's thinking during the day which they experience in a dream (*'plo so'*) again. "If we think a lot about something, we may dream about it."[689] One educated Karen lady explained more. She said, "Some dreams come from seeing dirty things or experiencing evil. Some watch too much TV and then they dream about that. Some keep bad experiences in their heart, so they dream bad dreams."[690] Otherwise, the psychological interpretation that dreams have their source deep in our subconscious was not given by anybody.

In summary, it can be said that many Karen are unsure or do not know where dreams come from. The other half of the Karen I interviewed, think that dreams come from evil spirits, from God, the *'k'la'* wandering or they are just an expression of what you have done and thought during the day. The latter they call *'plo so'*.

5.1.5 Meanings and Interpretation of Dreams

Even though my questions were not geared to draw out meanings of dreams from people, I was given over one hundred different meanings.[691] Thirteen are about the meaning of the gender of the child to be born. Of the rest, about one third are good dreams. Bad dreams make up two thirds of the meanings given.[692] This is another indicator of the overwhelming negative meanings dreams are given in Karen culture.

From the number of references, you can see which meanings of dreams are well-known and probably often dreamed.[693] Uphill/downhill with its variations is the most mentioned meaning, followed by seeing a lot of fish. Then follow the bad meanings of fire, pepper and giving meat. On the positive side is the theme of pregnancy and gender and dreaming about a female elephant during harvest time. Some meanings are so well-known that one could speak of an oral dreambook.

---

[687] 13Oe; 25M; 31P; 42Mo.

[688] 42Mo.

[689] 44T. 58N.

[690] 58N. This was her own experience. This influential leader gave me a book about dreaming, written by an American woman. The book was translated into Thai. This and other teaching of Christian psychologists (e.g. Larry Crabb) has widened her horizon on dreams.

[691] See Appendix A. Dreams and their meanings given by the interviewees.

[692] Pentony recorded 80 different dreams in the Northern Kimberley region from three different tribes. "Thirty of the eighty dreams recorded were regarded by the dreamer as being 'bad' dreams. Three of the eighty were pronounced 'good'. The remainder are neutral in tone." B. Pentony, "Dreams and Dream Beliefs in North Western Australia" in *Oceania*, Vol. 32, No. 2 (Dec., 1961), 149.

[693] See Appendix A.

Who Interprets Dreams?

Usually dreams are told in the family or wider family in the village. This is the main body of interpretation. "If people think it is a good dream you go out, if not, you stay home."[694] A dream may be told to someone who is trusted and may know more about it. If an Animist-Buddhist is disturbed by a dream, he may go and ask a spirit doctor about the meaning.[695] This will happen frequently, when someone after he has dreamed, is not well. He then wants to know the meaning and what he can do about it.

Christians who are still anchored strongly in animism may do the same.[696] If their faith in Christ is strong, they will pray about and ask God for protection. Some Christians go and ask a pastor. As one pastor said, "Many people have come and asked me about the meaning of dreams. I do not know. I tell them to leave it in God's hand."[697] A very few may ask God to show what a dream means. A charismatic leader in the women's work said: "Sometimes we do not know the meaning of a dream, we have to ask the Holy Spirit."[698] Once she then dreamed another dream which threw light on the first one. Another time she knew the meaning after she had prayed. She felt that God had been the interpreter.

Since there are only a very few Christians interpreting dreams or who have the gift of interpreting dreams, many Christians are tempted to go to the spirit priest with their questions.

How Are Dreams Interpreted?

Some dreams are clear because of the commonly known meaning which I call the "oral dreambook."[699] Quite often Karen did not tell a specific meaning to a dream but say, this is a bad dream or a good dream.[700] "Good" or "bad" is then applied to their family or to their present work and plans. This means that dream interpretation has a subjective meaning in the person's circumstances. For example, if someone plans to plant tomatoes but he has a bad or good dream the night before, the meaning is applied to that planned activity. Either the planting is expected to succeed or it will be a loss. In the latter case, it is probably not being planted at all – at least not on that present day.

In addition, many interpretations given, have a subjective touch. Someone dreams about a subject and then he observes what will happen. As one thoughtful man said, "Dreams show what is going to happen. 'Hey, I have dreamed and now it has

---

[694] 12J.

[695] 14P; 25M.

[696] 13Oe; 32BR.

[697] 67BR.

[698] 58N.

[699] Among the Karen, I have made the same observation as Hollan among the Toraja that many dreams are interpreted by lay people according to widely known symbols, a kind of "dreambook" interpretation. See under 2.3.3.1. Toraja.

[700] See Appendix A.

come about' – that is how it happens most of the time."[701] That means, after something has happened they remember the dream. Or as his brother explained, "When I have had a certain dream, I remember what happened. If I dream about raining, dried trees or a storm coming and then the children get sick – we then remember that."[702] He thinks, in this way, the meanings of dreams have been formed – that is, the common meaning is reinforced or it may be questioned. For example, a man remembers, when he still was not a Christian, "When I was still single I dreamed – when my mother was ill – the sun was blinding me and in the evening my mother died."[703] He is not saying, the meaning of "the sun blinding", means that someone dies. But he still makes that connection between his dream and the sadness of that day. He still wonders whether that dream was a bad omen. He also said, "I dreamed about an uncle in M. who killed two pigs. Not long after, two of his children died. These two children were already married."[704] Killing pigs is generally speaking a bad dream. He then brought that bad dream in connection to the death of two of his relatives even though that particular dream is usually not thought of an omen of death. When I asked a woman what her best dream ever was, she replied, "I dreamed that a single girl came to visit. Then I got money. If I dream about doing mountain rice fields and the rice looks good, then I am healthy. If I dream about a single girl, I get money."[705] This looks like she making her own experience into a general meaning which she believes is true for her. Among the Karen it is very true of what Pentony observed among the Australian Aboriginals, "There is a marked tendency to relate the dream closely to the material realities of the moment. Should the person be feeling ill, then the dream becomes a potent factor in the situation."[706]

From their own experience some Karen question the common meaning or relativise it. As one man put it, "When I dream of fish my money goes away. I do not like to dream about fish. Money goes off."[707] Another commented, "I dreamed about fish and I thought I would make a good deal. Someone from Lampang came to sell pans and I bought them for 1000 Baht. They were bad pans, we could not really use them. They got rusty."[708] Or another said, "My older brother was planting and he was dreaming about going uphill, but in the end he did not earn anything. Afterwards he thought this is not always true!"[709] All these critical comments and observations were reported by Christians.

---

[701] 28Ch.

[702] 12J. This is in accordance with animistic thinking. This happens in other areas of life as well. In the early days when people have newly believed in Christ, there was a double wedding of two Christian couples. After a year both these couples each had a disabled baby. Their logic was, not to have any double weddings anymore, because they had observed what had happened to them.

[703] 40M.

[704] 40M.

[705] 42Mo.

[706] Pentony, 148.

[707] 28Kri. 12J.

[708] 57Ti.

[709] 67BR.

Karen are aware that dreams do not have the same meaning for everybody all the time. Therefore, they observe what happens and what the experiences of other people are. Therefore they like to talk about it in order to understand more about it.

When people go and ask a spirit doctor about the meaning of a dream, he does not interpret and give meaning into a vacuum, because people usually have an issue. The spirit doctor may '*uu hti*' (blow into the water) or look at chicken bones or at a skirt of a woman in order to give advice and direction. Firm Christians usually do not do this kind of asking spirits.

Opposite Meaning of What Has Been Seen in A Dream

Conspicuously, the meaning of what you dream is often the opposite of what you have seen in the dream. "Dreams often show the opposite."[710] For example, going up the mountain is hard, but has a positive meaning. To be part of a wedding[711] is wonderful but the meaning is devastating, someone is going to die. When the gun is defective you succeed in hunting.[712] And if you dream about killing a person you will find food or succeed in hunting.[713] "If you dream that somebody has cursed you, it means that that person has blessed you!"[714]

Could it be that these opposite meanings have a connection with the traditional belief that in the '*plü kau*' everything is working the opposite way?[715] It could well be, since for traditional Karen, dreams often convey pictures of the afterworld, the '*plü kau*'.

Dreams with Ambiguous Meanings

Dreams about the dead and the afterworld ('*plü*' and '*plü kau*') are ambiguous which means they can be good, bad or neutral.[716] It depends a lot on the circumstances and what people think. One animist said, "If I dream about my (deceased) father, I cannot do anything good afterwards. ... If I dream about a dead person I am going to succeed. But if I see my father, we will have fights."[717] If you see a deceased person ('*plü*') who was happy and working well, it is a good dream, but if you dream of a lazy person, it is a bad dream. "Each person is different."[718] "If you dream about eating with a dead person ('*plü*'), it is a bad dream. If you have cut your fields and you dream about '*plü*', the fire will burn the fields very

---

[710] 14P.
[711] 62ST; 66Somu.
[712] 31P.
[713] 39M; 33P.
[714] 39Ch.
[715] For more details see page 33ff.
[716] An old influential man who was one of the early Christians in the area says, he went to the '*plü kau*'. Asked whether he feared, he answered, "Why fear? I did not fear." 31P.
[717] 43B.
[718] 42Pa.

well."[719] "If you dream about the '*plü*', there are some good dreams and some bad dreams.[720] If I dream about a friend who has died, I always get sick."[721] Some enjoy a meal in the '*plü kau*'[722] but others fear dreadfully when father and/or mother appear. They may come to call one of their children which could mean death.[723]

> *I dreamed my father came to me and asked me to go with him. I nearly died and they did a ceremony to cut me off from my father (not a Christian then). He had come twice. And since I have become a Christian he came again and asked me to go with him but God did not give me to him. I have just recently dreamed this again and then I got very sick!*[724]

When we interviewed this woman she was just recovering from the illness.

Dreams about elephants are ambiguous as well. It depends on which season you dream about it, and whether it is a cow or a bull. With the elephants, it is much clearer under which circumstances it is a good or a bad dream than with the '*plü*' and the '*plü kau*'.

When you dream about a snake biting you, it is a bad dream,[725] but when you see a big snake it means you will have a long life.[726]

Crossing a bridge over a river can predict the death of a relative,[727] while to someone else to get across a river means that he can do anything.[728]

To dream about bananas means sickness,[729] but when the wife is pregnant it means the child will be a boy.[730]

"Interpretations are never without some ambiguity since the relationship between dream symbols and the object they represent may be variable."[731] Hollan's observation applies to the dreaming of the Karen, too.

The ambiguity of the meaning of a dream shows clearly that Karen do not interpret dreams according to a set of meanings only, but that the circumstances and

---

[719] 45S.

[720] One man said about good and bad dreams in connection with the afterworld, "It is about fifty-fifty." 57A.

[721] 45G.

[722] 31P; 54Ch.

[723] 28Ch; 38MM. Larchronja gives an example where grandparents came to beg a child. Larchronja, 94.

[724] 38MM.

[725] 58N.

[726] 38P; 38Luwa.

[727] 12J; 16N.

[728] 38P.

[729] 45S.

[730] 34R.

[731] Hollan, The Personal Use, 170.

the personality of the dreamer play their role, too.[732] Especially dreams about the afterworld may need the interpretation of a specialist.

Same Dreams And / Or Meanings in Different Cultures

Dreams of being haunted are common all over the world, also with the Karen.[733] Of course they fear when an elephant is after them. While the dream is the same or very similar to dreams in other cultures, the interpretation may be different. For the Karen, it means spirits are at work. "If you see an elephant – its *'k'la'* is a demon."[734]

The Jesuit priest M.M.J. Kemlin[735] was working among the Reungao people of Kontum province in Vietnam. "One of the interpretations that Kemlin discovered was that if one dreams of going downstream in a canoe, then that person can expect that his current enterprise will not go smoothly, but will encounter problems. If one dreams of going upstream in a canoe, then he can expect that his current enterprise will go smoothly."[736] This is the same interpretation the Karen give, "If you want to go out to plant and you dream about going uphill or walking up a river that is a good dream, that is what people say."[737]

While Pentony reports of the Australian Aboriginals, "Fire is always bad to dream about,"[738] Hollan found that among the Toraja in Indonesia, the meaning of dreaming about fire is to lose wealth and become poor.[739] Both statements are true for the Karen, as well.[740] But while the Australian Aboriginals relate fire to black magic, I could not find this particular meaning among the Karen.

In the old Asabano tradition, killing a man indicated that hunting success would follow soon.[741] The same meaning is found among the Karen.[742] Dreaming of the dead in the Asabano pre-Christian state meant fear that someone will die. We find the same fear among the Karen when they dream of the deceased mother or father

---

[732] My summary given about dream interpretation among the Toraja can be applied to the Karen as well. "From the Toraja it becomes clear that dreams in animistic culture may not only have a set of commonly known interpretations that have to be rigidly applied, but that a dream may be seen ambiguously and that gives room for personalization, reinterpretation or even manipulation of the dream." See last paragraph of 2.3.3.1.

[733] 25M; 38P; 32BR.

[734] 45S.

[735] M. M. J. Kemlin, "Les songes et leurs interprétation chez les Reungao." *Bulletin de l'Ecole Française d'Extrême Orient* 10:507-538.

[736] Marilyn Gregerson, fishnet-bounces+jldeal=comcast.net@lists.bethel.edu [mailto:fishnet-bounces+jldeal=comcast.net@lists.bethel.edu] On Behalf Of Marilyn Gregerson. March 28, 2014.

[737] 12J.

[738] Pentony, 147.

[739] Hollan, The Personal Use, 171. Except for this one meaning which is the same among the Karen, I could not discover any other identical meanings in his list.

[740] 12J; 28Ch; 38MM; 42Mo; 44T; 59N; 67BR.

[741] Lohmann, Evaluating, 234.

[742] 39M; 33P.

appearing.[743] With the Christian Asabano those dreams of fear have been replaced by more positive ones.

From our observations, we conclude that there are some amazing analogies of dreams and their interpretation occurring in different cultures. There are similarities in how animistic cultures handle dreams and their ambiguity. There are lessons to be learnt, how people groups with an animistic background interpret and give meaning or even change interpretations of dreams. Yet, the unique interpretation and meaning of dreams in each culture must not be ignored either.

Difference Between Animist-Buddhists and Christians

The most obvious difference between Animist-Buddhist and Christian Karen concerning dream interpretation is that Animists and Buddhists will consult a spirit doctor if they are worried about a dream, while firm Christians will not take refuge in this practice anymore. Many Christians coming from an animistic background feel a vacuum in this respect. They may want to ask a Christian specialist, an evangelist, a pastor or a missionary, but only a few of them are able or willing to help them interpret dreams. They may want to avoid playing the role of a "Christian spirit doctor" or they feel that dreams should not be given much significance. Therefore, some Christians cannot withstand the temptation to consult the spirit doctor.

Another difference between the two groups above is how they look at dreams. While Animist-Buddhists usually take dreams very seriously and do not openly challenge the commonly known meaning of a dream, Christians start to look at dreams more critically. They seem to have a more distant attitude towards dreams, because dreams have lost some of their absolute truth against the Word of God. I have found the questioning of dreams and their meanings among Christians but not among Animist-Buddhists.[744]

A third difference I have observed is that some Christians start to give meaning or new meanings to special dreams. One pastor could see how his dreams applied to an unfortunate church split. One Christian wondered whether "fire" could be a more positive symbol when interpreted from its meaning in the Bible.[745] Another Christian woman discovered that a serpent may have a positive meaning as well.[746] An elder was encouraged when his dream of being nailed to a cross was given a new meaning of suffering, not just of judgment.[747] The student, Somu, reinterpreted his father's dream in a sensitive, significant and helpful way.[748]

These examples show a hopeful new approach Christians could take.

---

[743] 28Ch; 38MM.
[744] See under point 4.1.5.2.
[745] 54R.
[746] 58N.
[747] 69P.
[748] 66Somu.

5.1.6 Beneficial and Detrimental Impact of Dreams

Dreams often lead to some religious activity. In this section, I will look at the impact of dreams apart from doing prayers and ceremonies in order to be protected from bad dreams. We will look at that more closely under section 5.1.7.

Beneficial Impact

For some Karen, dreams are a help in **making the right decision**.[749] If you have a good dream, you go for it. If you have a bad dream, you will not do what you would have liked to do. Atipa decided to become a Christian against the opposition of his mother because he had such a good dream when the evangelist stayed at his house.[750] Chilapa's brother decided to marry the girl he had in mind after he had dreamed a good dream.[751]

Among the Karen, dreams are often seen as a confirmation of what they intended to do. Or they dream and then they wait until the dream is confirmed in a life situation.

A former spirit priest who had become a Christian said that he **gained knowledge through dreams**.[752] Another commented that dreams show **what is going to happen**.[753]

Many Karen are **encouraged** by good dreams. "When I have a good dream, I have good thoughts."[754] If they dream about a lot of fish or going uphill, they gladly go out to plant.[755] A non-Christian headman has been encouraged to buy a lot of lottery tickets after he has had good dreams.[756] But he has not won yet![757]

Some Christians were **encouraged by specific dreams**. One leader who was going to start a business, saw his father-in-law who had been a prominent leader among the Karen Christians in a dream. His appearances and giving his consent to the plans were a tremendous encouragement to him.[758] This dream came very close to what the Toraja experience in dreams when the ancestors give advice concerning what they should do.[759]

---

[749] 43B
[750] See under 2.4.2. Cf. 57A.
[751] 28Ch.
[752] 14P.
[753] 28Ch.
[754] 47P.
[755] 47P.
[756] This happens in other cultures also. E.g. in Italy dreaming is important before you buy lottery tickets.
[757] 25M.
[758] 29A.
[759] Douglas Hollan, "To the Afterworld and Back: Mourning and Dreams of the Dead among the Toraja." *Ethos,* Vol. 23, No. 4 (Dec. 1995): 431.

One older Christian lady who suffered from a noise in her ear, was healed through a dream. She said, "I dreamed that somebody came to check on me. My 'k'la' waited gladly. I had a noise in my ear. He came to look at one ear. And afterwards the noise was gone."[760]

A farmer, who is an evangelist and pastor at the same time, had a dream that impressed him. He was sure that the dream came from God. In the dream, he saw a large house which was built on a mountain. A stream of people were moving to the house. His interpretation is that this is a picture for revival. Many will come to worship God. The dream has been an encouragement to him and it has caused him to expect more of God working among the Karen people. It has also encouraged him to visit other villages. He has seen a lot of fruit since.[761] When Grandmother N was a young Christian, she heard God's voice in a dream and then she saw into hell and into heaven. This dream has been a great encouragement to her over the many years since she dreamed it.[762] A village leader said, "When I have a good dream, I have good thoughts."[763]

One Christian lady was threatened by men in dreams and sometimes tempted sexually. These bad dreams which bothered her greatly, led her to search for freedom. In the end, a dream played a significant role in gaining it. She testified,

> Then I was thinking, do my problems come from my ancestors? I started to fast. And I asked God to help me because I did not understand the problem. I did not want this kind of life. I fasted three days. After three days I dreamed, I was on a rock and there was a tree up there and on one side it was a cliff, on the other side stones as well. At that time I held onto the tree. Then I remembered the hymn 'God sets us on a rock.' I dreamed about an older woman who was single – they usually wear a white dress – and the white dress was dirty and she was climbing up the rock and reached it. She tried to throw me off the rock. But I held fast to the tree with one hand – the woman tried to tear away my other hand but then the woman fell down. I went to see, but I could not see her anymore, it was so deep. Then I woke up and God had given me freedom! God had freed me from the sin of my ancestors. Then I fasted seven days. I knew I was pure. The Holy Spirit came into my thinking. Since then I have not dreamed any bad, dirty dreams. I have overcome, I have victory in this area. God has given me freedom.[764]

Karen dream positive and good dreams but it seems that they do not occur very often. The special dreams which I have been told, all have been dreamed by Christians who have been greatly encouraged by them.

---

[760] 17N.
[761] 68S.
[762] 16N.
[763] 47P.
[764] 58N.

Detrimental Impact

Very often dreams are seen as the cause or the starting point for troubles, sickness, hurts or even death, even though it is not always clear whether the bad dream was first or the sickness or whether "dreams show what is going to happen."[765] Especially **sickness** is brought into relation to dreaming. As one farmer stated the thoughts of many, "If you dream a lot, you will get sick."[766] One grandmother who has become a Christian recently said, "I dreamed a lot and lost six children."[767] She was implying that dreaming a lot played a role in these fatalities. Dreams may not always concern the one dreaming, but it could be about their spouse or one of their children who will not be well.[768] Bad dreams may lead to hurts if precautions are not taken. [769]

A former spirit doctor turned Christian gives an example:

You are with your wife. And another woman wants you to marry and marries you and really loves you. And then you realize it is a dream. Formerly, the people said the devil has come to marry you. If you dream like that, people think the wife or the children will get sick and you have to 'ki cü'. You have to 'ki cü' very quickly and the spirit doctor has to go and do sacrifices.[770]

I was told the following dream in connection with the death of a child:

I went to sleep in the field. I dreamed about two hills of termites. One was destroyed, the other was intact. I had two children and one got sick. I carried the sick child back to the village, it lost consciousness and it had already died when I arrived here. There must have been a power from Satan. I dreamed about this, then I became a Christian. Then these problems were solved. This was my dream about the termite hills.[771]

One non-Christian Karen expressed succinctly how dreams, sickness and the wandering of the *'k'la'* are related to each other: "If you are not well, you sleep and you dream a lot. The *'k'la'* wander a lot. But if you are healthy, you do not dream, the *'k'la'* do not wander."[772]

The connection between dreaming and sickness, hurts and troubles is the reason why many **fear**[773] and **worry**[774] when they have had a bad dream. One of the

---

[765] 28Ch.
[766] 56G. Cf. 20S; 21M; 23P; 25M; 54Ch.
[767] 38MM.
[768] 12J. 54Ch.
[769] 54C; Cf. 12P; 64Ch; 65HT.
[770] 14P.
[771] 57A.
[772] 63Jae. Cf. 38Luwa.
[773] 12J; 28D.
[774] 42Mo; 47P; 67BR.

evangelists stated, "Dreams can cause lots of thinking and a heavy heart."[775] Or another, "If we have bad dreams our hearts are not well."[776]

The consequences of fear and worry, make a real impact on their lives. Generally, Animist-Buddhist Karen **do not go out to work**[777] after they have had a bad dream. They usually stay at home. If they still go out they will take other precautionary measures. Many Christians said that they still will go out to work while trusting in God's protection.[778] When asked specifically about whether they still go to plant rice or tomatoes after having had a bad dream the night before, some Christians hesitated to answer or said, this could be a warning not to go and plant.[779] Some think like the Christian headman of a hill village who said, "Actually, if you plan to plant rice and you have a bad dream, you will not eat, so you better wait one or two days until you go to plant."[780]

After having had a look at the detrimental effects of dreaming generally, we will now give our attention to one specific negative impact of dreams among the Karen. It is the connection between

Dreaming and '*lo ta*'

Over the years I have heard about people doing '*lo ta*'.[781] I did not give much attention to it. I thought this is a practice Christians would not do anymore. A young pastor told me, '*lo ta*' is the one thing Karen fear most.[782] But then, a few years ago, in a mainly Christian village, a whole clan of five families were expelled from the village, including the lay pastor. We knew most of the Christian families personally. Behind the drama was the accusation that the head of the extended family, Grandfather S had done '*lo ta*'.[783] It was said that because of him, three people in the village had already died. The accusers were part of the Christian community, too. [784] When I started to ask questions about it, especially how they would know that this particular man was the culprit, the answers always came down to the fact that people had dreamed about him, and in addition they had asked a spirit doctor who confirmed the findings.[785] This story has been one of the reasons that made me curious to know more about dreams among the Karen. By investigating into this sensitive area I was told more stories about '*lo ta*' which have happened. Most of the time one point was the same, somebody had dreamed

---

[775] 64Ch.

[776] 28Kri.

[777] 11T; 20S; 25M; 35Ch; 42Mo; 43B; 45S; 49H.

[778] 31D; 24E; 31P; 48HP; 57Ti.

[779] 14P; 31DM.

[780] 65HT; 33P.

[781] To bewitch, to cast a death spell, sorcery, to curse someone to death.

[782] 12G.

[783] The interviews 12J; 13Oe; 32BR and 35N relate to this case.

[784] 12J; 13Oe.

[785] The spirit doctor "blows water" ('*uu hti*'), a ritual which should show who is guilty. Or they may perform an oracle in which the accused person has to drink water which will destroy him, if he is guilty. See N58.

about a person giving meat to another.[786] That means the one who gives the pork or other meat to a person, is the one who '*lo ta*' the one who ate of it. This dream is often seen by the victim of the supposed witchcraft. In the above case, even two people had dreamed this dream. It holds true what Pentony observed, "The victim becomes beware of the fact that he has been the object of black magic by the content of his dreams."[787] If there is suspicion that somebody was '*lo ta*' and has died, the people do want to know whether this really was the case. Therefore, they do not bury the dead person but they want to burn them. If, after the cremation, a lot of meat is left, the case is confirmed. After one man had died, Grandfather S did not want the village people to burn the man but to bury him. His son-in-law said, because he thought it is not right to burn a body of a Christian.[788] But this drew more suspicion on Grandfather S because this was seen as a cover up of his evil deeds. Then another young man died of cancer. In practically all the cases I have heard of '*lo ta*', the medical doctors in the hospitals had diagnosed the illness as cancer.[789] Anyway, Grandfather S was accused again of '*lo ta*', because there had been a disagreement between grandfather S and this young man before he got ill. This time the body was burned and there was lots of meat left afterwards.[790] This confirmed the verdict, that he was '*lo ta*'. People in the village accused another son-in-law who was the lay pastor in the village that he had taken Grandfather S to a Buddhist temple.[791] All this added up to the verdict that he must be the evil man. But because Grandfather S' extended family was convinced that he was not guilty and accused without reason, all of them were thrown out of the village. They went to live in the lowlands. After Grandfather S had exhorted his descendants to stay faithful to Jesus, he disappeared and has not been seen since. Many think that he has committed suicide. In other cases, the suspected witch was killed.[792]

Later, I asked his son-in-law[793] what he thought of the accusation. He said, "One man, Mr. P, was an enemy of my father-in-law. Because he had bad thoughts he had bad dreams. It's '*plo so*'.[794] Who knows what he really dreamed? He wanted to destroy my father-in-law. But in the meantime he has died himself." This statement reveals how questionable dreams about giving meat, respectively eating the received meat are. While most Karen believe that '*lo ta*' really happens, I have heard of two other cases in the area where the dreams have been questioned and

---

[786] 58N; 45S; 62PenY about ST. 65HT.

[787] Pentony, 145.

[788] 35N.

[789] See also 58N.

[790] 12J. The young man who died was a nephew of 12J.

[791] 12J, an elder of the Christian church in the village asked me, "For a Christian, is it right to go there?"

[792] See under 2.4.2. footnote 251. Interview with Supopa in the village of Thibokhi, 3rd Aug. 2012, on MP3. This is in accordance with what Lohmann reports about the Asabano when they were not yet Christians. Roger Ivar Lohmann, "The Role of Dreams in Religious Enculturation among the Asabano of Papua New Guinea" in *Ethos,* 28 (1) (2000), 88.

[793] 35N.

[794] To dream about things you were doing or thinking during the day. This kind of dream is thought to be trivial.

some influential people in the villages were able to defuse the situations, so that at least no revenge would be taken. But still, a lot of hurt and suspicion is left.[795]

The impact of '*lo ta*' and the significant part dreams play in these dramas has stunned me. So many lives destroyed, so many relationships ruined, so much quarrel, suspicion and fear,[796] as well as deep sadness are the fruit of it. Therefore, the theme "Redeeming the Experience of Dreams in the Omkoi Karen Christian Context" is right on target. Before I turn to this theme, I will compare the impact dreams have on Animist-Buddhist and Christian Karen respectively.

Impact of Dreams on Animist-Buddhist and Christian Karen

It is striking that among Animist-Buddhist Karen dreams are seen as authoritative and very important. To avoid troubles from so called bad dreams, Animist-Buddhists usually stay at home or they do a ceremony if they have to go out. A very few said that they sometimes ignore their dreams and go out anyway. Most of them fear and worry when they have had a bad dream.

Several Karen who have become Christians testified that their dream life or their attitude towards dreams has changed.[797] Here are some of the statements:

"When we dreamed about bad things, while we did not know God well, we feared,"[798] implying that this is not the case anymore.

"Since I have become a Christian I always go out when I have dreamed. God is watching. I do not think about it. It does not matter. I believe. I do not follow the dreams. I believe in God the highest."[799]

"No matter what I have dreamed, I always go out. I pray before. If I could not pray to God, I often would not dare to go out."[800]

"Formerly, before I was a Christian, when I had a bad dream it came about. But since I worship God it does not matter anymore."[801]

"Since we worship God we dream less and better."[802]

For many Christians the experience of dreams have become more positive, but on the other hand many still are stuck with good or bad dreams just like the Animist-Buddhist Karen.

In summary: Dreams influence people strongly. Outsiders easily underestimate the impact of dreams on the lives of the majority of the Karen. It is encouraging that some Christians have found a more positive experience of dreams, or are giving

---

[795] 32BR.
[796] Even the spirit doctors are in fear of the ones they accuse of '*lo ta*'. See 45S.
[797] 64Ch.
[798] 28D.
[799] 18P.
[800] 14E.
[801] 18P.
[802] 20W.

less significance to bad dreams because they have found a new faith. Dreams are less seen as a fate you cannot escape. Yet it cannot be ignored that far too many Karen – Animist-Buddhists or Animists who have become Christians – are in fear of bad dreams or are believing in dreams that are given a very destructive meaning.

5.1.7 Redeeming the Experience of Dreams – Approaches by Karen

The many bad dreams with their expected evil results cause a lot of fear. This challenges the Karen to find ways to abate or if possible to revoke the impact of bad dreams. They want to be saved from them. This is the same with Animist-Buddhists as well as Christians. The way they hope to achieve this, though, varies.

Animistic Practices

The most common practice, after an animist has had a bad dream, is to stay at home[803] for a day in order not to endanger his life. It is a kind of taboo.[804] But this is not always practical or possible. Therefore, if an animist has to go out, he will '*yo hpe yo blo*' or '*yo hpe hoko*' that is he will stamp the ashes or stamp the earth so that the spirits will not see where his feet go.[805] In addition, others will pray[806] to '*Ywa*' (God)[807] or pray in front of the Buddha shelf[808] in order to gain protection from the unseen world. If a dream is very worrying, animists consult a spirit doctor. As a non-Christian headman put it, "If you have bad dreams, you ask the spirit doctor to help perform ceremonies, so the bad spirit will go away so that you are redeemed of the bad spirit. The spirit doctor will '*ki cü*'."[809] Different ceremonies and sacrifices[810] can be part of the practices, depending on the dream and the present circumstances of the dreamer. If you have a dream that means someone has '*lo ta*' a person that person will go to the spirit doctor who then will find out whether the person seen in the dream has really done it. This is often done by 'ba aw hti' (drinking water) or '*uu hti*' (blowing water).[811]

One grandfather told me that when he was young and not a Christian yet, "I dreamed and things were about to happen that way. Then my father told me I should curse the dreams so that they do not happen. If I dreamed a person would die, they died. If I dreamed that I killed a deer, I was going to kill a deer."[812] The curse worked. Afterwards his dreams were not predictions anymore.

---

[803] 12J; 19S; 25M; 31P; 33P; 37M; 39Ch; 42Mo; 49H; 53Ch; 57Ti; 61PenY.
[804] Literal meaning of the Karen expression '*ta dü ta htoo*' which is used for this practice.
[805] 14P; 20S; 39Ch; 42Pa; 62PenY; 63Jae.
[806] 42Mo; 63Jae. Without specifying to whom they pray.
[807] 39Ch. For animists '*Ywa*' is the High God, it is the word which is used for God in the Bible.
[808] 21M; 39Ch; 51D.
[809] 25M; 52Ch; 57A.
[810] Especially after someone has dreamed about spirits. 20S; 25M.
[811] 43B; 51D; 58N.
[812] 50Phue.

Two men revealed how they fight dreaming a lot. One said that it helps when you sleep on a knife.[813] The other explained that he washes his hair with acacia water in order to dream less.[814]

Christian Practices

When Christians experience a bad dream they usually pray[815] and commit the dream into God's hand.[816] They ask God to redeem[817] them from the bad or evil the dream may predict. Leaders in the Christian community also go to pray with other Christians who have had a bad dream.[818] One Christian mother said that she dreams less when people come to pray with her.[819] Christians pray that God will protect them. While some pray not to dream bad dreams,[820] one thoughtful evangelist asked God to change his bad dream,[821] and God did. He said, "Pray that God will even give blessing through the dream."[822] "We must remember that God is bigger than anything, God can change evil into good."[823] The same lady sometimes refuses to accept a bad dream in the name of Jesus.[824] She also has fasted to get rid of her evil and disturbing dreams.[825] Or when she and her husband had built a new house she got involved in spiritual warfare. She said,

> *I took oil and declared God's reign and drew crosses on the wall and I prayed, 'In the name of Jesus Christ, devil disappear!' I drew crosses in each room. I asked that the blood of Jesus would come to reign. If there were any gods or any fornication, I asked God for forgiveness. Then when I prayed, there was a noise. I got a chicken skin and it was exactly midday. Then I*

---

[813] 48HP.

[814] 43B.

[815] Animist-Buddhists pray too, as we have seen, even though it is not always clear to whom they pray. In Jewish tradition prayers played a big role. The following prayer in the Talmud which was said during the priestly benediction, could similarly be used by Christians as well. "Sovereign of the Universe, I am Thine and my dreams are Thine. I have dreamed a dream and do not know what it is. Whether I have dreamed about myself, or my companions have dreamed about me, or I have dreamed about others, if they are good dreams, confirm and reinforce them like the dreams of Joseph, and if they require a remedy, heal them, as the waters of Marah were healed by Moses our teacher, and as Miriam was healed of her leprosy and Hezekiah of his sickness, and the waters of Jericho by Elisha. As Thou didst turn the curse of the wicked Balaam into a blessing, so turn all my dreams into something beneficial for me." Abraham Arzi, „Dreams. In the Talmud," *Encyclopaedia Judaica* Vol. 6 (Jerusalem, Israel: Keter Publishing House, 1971), 210.

[816] 33P; 12J; 24E; 28Ch; 28D; 28Kri; 31D; 31P; 34R; 50Phi; 50Phue; 58N; 61P; 67BR.

[817] 26E; 28D; 31D; 33P.

[818] 12J; 31P.

[819] 51D.

[820] 28D.

[821] 28Ch.

[822] 28Ch.

[823] 58N.

[824] 58N.

[825] The Jewish Rabbi Rab (died 247) recommended fasting as the best remedy against bad dreams. Strack, Billerbeck, 55.

> knew that the devil still had had a stronghold. ... Then I dreamed at night. I saw the devil leaving through the curtain. Afterwards I was freed from the bad dreams.[826]

Another wife of a leading Christian pastor was accused of 'lo ta'. In traditional Karen culture she had every reason to fear. But she decided not to fear but trust God and go out to work. She said, "I have a clear conscience and I am in God's hand." After her father had died, a Christian woman dreamed that her father did not live in a nice house in the 'plü kau'. But she refused to accept that view, instead she hold fast to the promise of God that her father is in the kingdom of God and not in the 'plü kau' as animists believe. She then added, "If you dream that the person does not have a nice house to live in, it makes your heart sad. I think we need to trust completely in God."[827]

A few Christians have started to question some traditional interpretation of dreams.[828] One example is the re-interpretation of an already mentioned dream of suffering.[829] The other is the experience of Somu with his father.

> My father dreamed that his newly built house needed to be lowered and that he needed to improve the foundation. Then he saw a big storm coming. My father interpreted the dream that his life would be shorter. But I told him that was not the right interpretation, it meant that he needed to be humble. He needed to strengthen his foundation in Christ. Then a storm came – the headman got very unhappy about me – and the father had to be humble so that the storm did not damage our house/family.[830]

A young Christian leader said that he does not tell bad dreams to people but to God alone. When I asked him, "Why?" He answered, "If I tell people, they will advise me to do things which are not according to God's Word. If we tell our bad dreams to people, we give too much attention to the devil's work!"[831]

Comparison between Animistic and Christian Practices

There are two practices which are neither animistic nor Christian but done by both.

Firstly, some animists and many Christians try to ignore dreams. Typically, they say, do not think about it, nothing will happen.[832] Or, do not believe in or follow dreams.[833] Christians may say, do not believe in dreams, but in the Word of God. Or

---

[826] 58N.
[827] 30Ch.
[828] 34R asked whether 'fire' would not have a positive meaning in the Bible. Or 58N discovered that a serpent could have a good meaning in certain circumstances because it is also a symbol for healing.
[829] 69P.
[830] 66Somu.
[831] 60E.
[832] 19S; 47P.
[833] 18P; 31P; 42Mo; 67BR.

as a lay evangelist testified, "I learnt from evangelists, fear God and do not give significance to dreams."[834] There are more Christians who think like this than animists.

Secondly, both Christians and non-Christians see some bad dreams as a warning and they want to be careful and attentive about what they do and say.[835]

While animists usually stay at home after having had a bad dream or doing '*yo hpe*' if they need to go out, Christians usually pray and go out, but many would not do a very important work on that day, like planting rice or vegetables.

When a dream is worrying and/or the meaning not known, animists will consult a spirit doctor and perform ceremonies and sacrifices. Some Christians will consciously trust their Lord to protect them while a few may engage in spiritual warfare with prayer and fasting. Many Christians do not know good alternatives to the animistic practices and are tempted to go back to the old rituals.[836] I asked one of the main leaders what should be done about this. He said, "We have to teach people and to talk to people."[837] But he also said, "I have done this many times, but still Christians are consulting the spirit doctors."[838]

Here are the beginnings of some Christians questioning the traditional negative meanings and starting to re-interpret dreams from a Christian perspective as well as expecting new dreams from God. This may give hope for a change for the better.

5.2 Biblical Critique on the Karen View of Dreams

5.2.1 Similarities between A Biblical and A Karen View of Dreams

In Karen culture as well as in the biblical view dreams are a source of revelation of the unseen world.

Receivers of significant dreams are God's own people as well as heathen people. Karen Christians as well as non-Christians receive dreams which they think are significant.

As in the Bible,[839] Karen do know of dreams which are insignificant. They call them '*plo so*', which is dreaming about daily work and chores or things you have been thinking about.

---

[834] 64Ch.

[835] 12J; 31DM; 43B; 45S; 53Ch.

[836] It holds true for the Karen Christians in the Omkoi area what Hollan wrote about the Toraja that "their religious and existential beliefs are still influenced by traditional ideas." Douglas Hollan, "The Cultural and Intersubjective Context of Dream Remembrance and Reporting." In *Dream Travelers. Sleep Experiences and Culture in the Western Pacific*, ed. Roger Ivar Lohmann (New York, NY: Palgrave Macmillan, 2003), 171.

[837] 32BR.

[838] To me it shows that the vacuum has not been filled by common Christian practices.

[839] Ecclesiastes 5:2.

Dreams in the Bible are often very clear messages and do not need interpretation, though in some instances an interpreter was necessary. The same is true in Karen culture. Karen usually understand the message of a dream, but on certain occasions they may ask a specialist to interpret the dream.

Dreams very often ask for the receiver to take a certain action. This is true in God's Word[840] as well as with the Karen.

One reaction to dreams is fear. We find this in the Bible[841] and it is strong among the Karen. A Karen evangelist commented on fear: "If great kings like Pharaoh and Nebuchadnezzar feared after they had dreamed – what about normal people?"[842]

5.2.2 Biblical Critique on the Animist-Buddhist View of Dreams

Karen Animist-Buddhists either do not know where dreams come from or they think that spirits may be the source of dreams. The "Highest God" ('*Ywa*') has not been mentioned to me by Animist-Buddhists as a source.[843] Some think that dreams are what their '*k'la*' sees when wandering during sleep. Many are aware of mundane dreams which may reflect the thoughts and activities of the day.

In contrast, the Bible uses the following sentences: "God came to Abimelech in a dream" (Gen 20:3). "The angel of God said to me in the dream" (Gen 31:11). "Then Joseph said to Pharaoh, ... "God has revealed to Pharaoh what he is about to do" (Gen 41:25). "I (God) speak to him (prophet) in dreams" (Nu 12:6). "The Lord appeared to Solomon during the night in a dream" (1Kings 3:5). Daniel makes it clear to Nebuchadnezzar that his dreams came from God (Dan 2:28; 4:24). "An angel of the Lord appeared to him in a dream (Mt 1:20; 2:19). In the dreams from God, God is active. He is going out to the one to whom he gives his revelation while, with the animistic Karen part of their soul ('*k'la*') is active and "sees" things.

For Karen it is important to distinguish between good or bad dreams. They make no distinction about the source of dreams. The Bible, on the other hand, warns about sources of dreams other than God. If the dream does not have its origin in God, people should not take heed of it. They should not listen to it.[844] Therefore, it is much more important to know the source of the dream than to listen to what people say, whether a dream is good or bad. Because if the dream comes from

---

[840] Gen 20:3; 31:24; 41:1-36; Mt 1:20; 2:12.13.19.22.

[841] Gen 23:8 "They were very much afraid". Gen 41:8 "In the morning his mind was troubled". Dan 2 "had dreams, his mind was troubled". Dan 4 "I had a dream that made me afraid ... terrified me". Gen 28:16 "He was afraid and said, 'How awesome is this place'". In contrast to Pharaoh's or Nebuchadnezzar's fear, Jacob's was a fear of God.

[842] Ch70.

[843] Except one Christian mentioned that some Animist-Buddhist Karen say that they receive dreams from 'Ywa', even though they do not worship him. See 14P.

[844] Deuteronomy 13:3.

God it is a good dream for the dreamer. It may be an encouragement or it may be a warning. God never gives evil dreams.

For Animist-Buddhist Karen dreams are very important and are usually taken as a truth revealed. In believing dreams this way they put themselves under a power they do not really know. Bad dreams are like a taboo. If you trespass upon them, you will encounter problems. They are caught in this and for that reason they do not like to dream. In contrast, God gives us freedom. The truth of a dream has to be checked in light of the Word of God and whether the dream will draw people to God or away from Him. The Bible also speaks of false prophets who made up their own dream stories or misused dreams to their own end. Knowing this, it helps those who take God's Word seriously to discern dreams against the revealed truth of the Bible. There is an authority higher than the dreams themselves.

If the meaning of a dream is unknown and bothers Animist-Buddhist Karen, they will consult a spirit doctor similar to what the heathen kings Pharaoh and Nebuchadnezzar have done. In this connection the Bible states very clearly that the interpretation of dreams belongs to God. Since the spirit doctors do not know God, their interpretation does not come from God. Therefore, the Animist-Buddhist Karen are held captive in their fear of bad dreams.

We have said that fear after dreaming is common for Karen as well as for people mentioned in the Bible. But at a closer look there is a marked difference. Interestingly, in the Bible we find that those who were outside the covenant of God feared after they had dreamed. This is true for Abimelech, the chief cupbearer and the chief baker, for Pharaoh, the Midianite soldiers, Nebuchadnezzar and Pilate's wife. On the other hand, Jacob was filled with awe and was encouraged by the dreams he had. Joseph had no fear after his dream. Solomon sacrificed to the Lord and "gave a feast to all his court" (1King 3:15). Prophets could be troubled by their visions, like Daniel (7:15), not because they feared something bad for themselves personally but because of the awesome message God had entrusted to them. Joseph in the NT and the Magi who believed, obeyed what God had revealed to them in dreams. They had no fear about them, but acted as they were told. From this it becomes clear that God's people do not need to fear dreams, though dreams may cause them to stand in awe of God.

Animist-Buddhist Karen think that spirits have caused the dream or that some of their own 'k'la' have encountered what they have dreamed. It is very real and very personal. Therefore dreaming causes a lot of fear among them! This fear does not always disappear automatically when those people become Christians.

In God's Word we do not find any dreams in which other people are accused of doing evil like sorcery or black magic as is the case with 'lo ta'. But God's Word calls Satan the accuser of the brethren,[845] and a liar[846] who knows how to bedevil a community. Therefore, we know that those dreams do not come from God and must not be trusted or obeyed.

---

[845] Revelation 12:10.
[846] John 8:44.

In the Bible we do not find any given general meaning to dreams. Something like a dreambook is foreign to God's Word. Dreams are often in the form of a message, some are given in symbols or in a mixture of both. Where the meaning of the dream is not clear by itself, each one has its own interpretation. The question can be asked, how seriously should the commonly known meanings of dreams be taken? Does God give dreams to the Karen which correspond to their "oral dreambook"? As we have seen earlier, many meanings of dreams are exactly the opposite of what they dream which corresponds with their world view on the '*plü kau*'. Therefore, the question is, whether some of their symbols which have a negative interpretation,[847] should be re-interpreted by what these symbols mean in the biblical and Christian context.

The main themes of the traditional animistic religion of the Karen are mainly negative. Karen are primarily concerned with protecting their own small positive sphere of life against dangers from the outside. Rituals are done against threats or against sickness. But the conveyance of a positive perspective in life through their traditional religion is missing.[848] This coincides with my observation and corresponds with their dream life. As we have seen, Karen dreams are mainly negative and discussions about dreams are often about how to ward off the ill-effects of a bad dream. The religious specialists are more asked for help on this than actually to find out the meaning of a dream. In contrast, the dreams from God reported in the Bible are positive and helpful, because the Christian faith is constructive and gives positive perspectives for life. It can be expected that a change to the Christian faith will ultimately lead to a change of their dreams, as has happened among the Asabano.

5.2.3 Biblical Critique on Some Karen Christians' Views of Dreams

What has been said in the last section basically holds true for the Karen Christians as well. There are a few points which I want to address – some specific problems encountered with Christians.

Some Karen Christians try to ignore dreams, explaining that they have no significance anymore, since we believe in the Word of God. Sometimes they have been taught by missionaries[849] of what the prophet Jeremiah said, "Let the prophet who has a dream tell his dream, but let the one who has my word speak it faithfully. For what has straw to do with grain? declares the LORD."[850] But we have seen

---

[847] Some examples of negative symbols are fire; carrying a child; going to a wedding.

[848] Roland Mischung summarizes his research on traditional Karen religion with the following words: "Demgegenüber ist die religiöse Vorstellungswelt der Karen überwiegend von *negativen* Themen, von einer Grundhaltung der Reserve und Selbstabgrenzung bestimmt." Und: "Das Spezifische der traditionellen Karen-Religion besteht nicht in ihren Vorstellungsinhalten, sondern in der Tatsache, dass der überwiegende Teil ihrer rituellen Praxis der Bewältigung einer negativ strukturierten Wirklichkeit gewidmet ist, ohne dass dem ein entsprechend elaborierter positiver Sinnkomplex gegenüberstünde." Mischung, 227+228.

[849] "I learnt from evangelists, fear God, do not give significance to dreams. They said, 'Fear God and do not trust in dreams.'" 64Ch.

[850] Jeremiah 23:28.

that these words of Jeremiah were mainly geared against the false prophets who misused dreams or set dreams above God's Word. If dreams were to be ignored because we have the Word of God, why should God have spoken to Joseph and the Magi in the New Testament or why should He have promised that when the Holy Spirit comes people will dream and see visions? Dreams are one of the vehicles God uses to speak to people, therefore Christians should not ignore or deny them. In addition, we know that all people dream. Actually, to ignore dreams does not work. It only leads people back to their old ways, because they feel that they are not understood.

On the other side of the spectrum, we will find Christians who believe in their (traditional) dreams more than the promises of God in His Word. If they experience a bad dream or dream of '*lo ta*' they fear so much that they look for help anywhere they can, often ending up with a spirit doctor. It is as an experienced senior missionary among the Karen in Tak province has written: "Put simply, bad dreams seem to be a form of taboo (…) that can have power over Karen if they choose to believe that these dreams (…) will come true."[851] But God wants his children to trust him for help and protection. He wants them to know that they are safe in His good hands, and that the devil has no ultimate power over them. "Again and again, we need to confront our dreams with the reality of our life and with the Word of God in the Bible."[852] When Karen do this, bad dreams lose their power over them.

Some Karen Christians go and consult the spirit doctor because they think that they did not get an answer or the help they hoped for. As I have shown before, some Karen feel that there is a vacuum among Christians whom they should ask if they have experienced an exceptional dream and none of the Christian leaders is able to interpret it or take it seriously. As we have seen in the Old Testament, God gave the gift of interpretation to Joseph and Daniel. In dependence on God – because God is the interpreter of dreams – they could give the right interpretation, and by doing it they saved many people. In New Testament times we can expect that God gives the gift of interpretation and distinguishing between spirits[853] to some Christians in His church. Surely, it is not in God's will that we leave the interpretation of dreams to spirit doctors, magicians or dream readers, instead he wants us to seek Him earnestly.

The gift of distinguishing between spirits is necessary, too, when Karen Christians dream a so-called bad dream. Some do not go out ('*dü ta*'), do not plant fields on that day, because they believe it is a warning from God. In the Bible we have seen that some dreams are warnings from God, but those warnings are spoken very clearly. While with the Karen there are so many bad dreams, if the Christians are going to heed each time they have had a bad dream and take it as a warning, they will be bound into their old faith and fear again. Therefore, it is important to know

---

[851] Keith Hale, E-mail to me on 18th May 2014.
[852] Anselm Grün, *Träume auf dem geistlichen Weg*. (Münsterschwarzach, DE: Vier-Türme-Verlag, 1989/2001), 12. "Wir müssen die Träume immer wieder konfrontieren mit der Realität unseres Lebens und mit dem Wort Gottes in der Bibel. "
[853] 1Corinthians 12:10.

when a dream is a warning from God or whether it is just another dream from a spirit who wants to draw them back into their old beliefs.

As the interviews have shown, some Christians have dreamed some very encouraging new dreams[854] or have been released from old disturbing dreams.[855] I am convinced that the more the Karen Christians are influenced by God's Word and the Holy Spirit working in them, the more people will receive dreams which will be helpful to them. Praying for a new dream will be a better way to experience this than ignoring or denying dreams. God wants us to be open to Him, accept all the ways of He is communicating to us and yet be discerning about the source of dreams.

5.2.4 Biblical Perspective on Redeeming the Experience of Dreams

Scientifically it is proven that all people dream every night. Therefore, dreams can be seen as a vehicle of communication from the unseen world or the subconscious. God has used dreams – his own creation – to communicate with people. But since we live in a fallen world, other forces have taken hold of this vehicle as well. Therefore, the gift of "distinguishing the spirits" and with it the gift of interpretation of dreams is necessary in some instances in order to know whether a dream is a message from God, a revelation of the subconscious, a vanity or whether a dream has its origin with an evil spirit.[856]

Following are some criteria which can help to discern a dream's source among people with an animistic background:

Dreams which accuse other people of doing evil (*'lo ta'*) are not from God but have their origin in evil spirits. They are a temptation from the devil. Christians are not to listen to such dreams. Some Christians may want to dismiss the dream in the name of Jesus of Nazareth who came in the flesh.[857] If Christians believe the accuser, who is the devil, they will come under his power. If they are going to accuse the person which has been seen in the dream, they sin against that person. If they are going to inquire with the spirit doctor, they are doing what God has forbidden them to do.[858] Instead they are called to take shelter in Jesus Christ. They are bought by the blood of Jesus and are protected by it.[859] God is the One in

---

[854] 58N; 68S; 69P.

[855] "Formerly I dreamed about the *'plü'* and it rained. I prayed to God about the bad dream, 'Please do not let me dream or give me better dreams.' So later I dreamed about the *'plü'*, but there was no rain, but all dry. It really changed!" 28Ch.

[856] "According to Evagrius many dreams we experience are prompted by demons. They want to weaken and sicken us." (Translation by the author). Grün, 32. Evagrius Ponticus was an early Christian monk (died 399) and spiritual writer who has written the Praktikos. He engaged himself intensely with dreams.

[857] 1John 4:2.

[858] Deuteronomy 18:10-15.

[859] Acts 20:28; 1Peter 1:18-19; Romans 5:9.

whose hand their lives dwell,[860] and when someone is ill, he shall trust God in life or in death. '*Lo ta*' has no power over him.

And how should the one react who is accused of '*lo ta*', because someone has seen him in a dream? He should take shelter with God as the Christian lady did who was accused of '*lo ta*', but did not fear and went out to work, trusting in the name of Jesus. Her husband also went to talk with the family who accused her. He said that they must go and talk with the accusers, otherwise as time goes by, they will think more and more that the wife is guilty. In case of an accusation of '*lo ta*', the elders of the church need to offer their prayer and they need to talk with all involved. Spiritual warfare may be necessary in order to set people free from fear and believing lies, giving encouragement and protection in prayer to the one who feels that he is a victim. Mature Christians also need to talk to the one who is accused and pray with him. Sometimes there is an unsolved conflict on which the accusation of '*lo ta*' has grown. Spiritually minded people who have a standing in the village need to help to solve these conflicts.

Dreams which lead Christians away from God, e.g. that they should go to a spirit priest in order to perform ceremonies,[861] are given by evil spirits. They have to be dealt with spiritually. Often teaching from the Bible, visiting and praying with the person is enough. Sometimes spiritual warfare with fasting and praying is important in order to set an oppressed person free.

How should Christians handle "bad dreams"? As we have seen from the Bible, there are no bad dreams from God. God always wants the best for us. The question is whether what is interpreted as a bad dream among Karen, is really a bad dream. Or could there be some other interpretation from a Christian point of view, like the example of Somu[862] has shown? As we have seen with the dreams of Joseph – his brothers gave a bad interpretation but he himself was most likely thinking in a different way. I think there could be a place to talk about dreams in the church and give – where appropriate – a more spiritual positive interpretation. The symbols seen in the dream may have a positive meaning in the Bible which could be applied.

Instead of heeding the taboo and staying at home for the day, Christians can be encouraged to pray and trust God to watch over them and to exercise faith against bad dreams. And still, perhaps a bad dream is not that negative, if it causes people to pray to God to watch their steps[863] and reminds them to be careful in their words and actions that day.

If somebody is convinced that the dream is a warning from God, he has to consider taking appropriate action, but most likely it should not be to heed of the traditional taboo ('*ta dü ta htü*'). Because if he starts to heed the taboo again, he will put himself under that power and he will be caught in it again.

---

[860] John 10:28-29.

[861] One Christian lady told me that after the death of her husband who had been an opium addict, she was bothered by him. In dreams he came to her again and again and told her to do '*ki cü*'.

[862] 66Somu.

[863] Grün writes that for Evagrius "Negative dreams are an incentive to turn to Jesus so that he will heal our sick soul and so that he will give us his peace." (Translation by the author). Grün, 32.

Because God is above all dreams, a person who often dreams bad dreams may want to pray to God to receive a different kind of dream as one Karen evangelist has successfully done it. "It can be a help to ask God in the evening to send us good dreams and that we also may notice what he wants to tell us."[864]

As we have seen, people often dream about what occupies their mind at present or has occupied it in the past. It is important that the lives of Christians are more and more influenced by the Word of God and by its promises and hopes, as well as by the work of the Holy Spirit. In the context of a Christian community with intentional discipleship, Christians are likely to receive different dreams from God, as has been the case with some children and adults in the Omkoi area.

The Karen in the researched area are not much aware of the possibility that dreams can be an expression of their subconscious, as Daniel explained to Nebuchadnezzar when God wanted him to know "what went through your mind."[865] "It is exactly what the interpretation of the dream does for us: It reveals to us the thoughts of our unconscious mind."[866] In Daniel 4, Nebuchadnezzar's dream about the big tree is also about his own life.

According to most western psychological dream interpretations, dreams are thought to work in this way. They reveal the subconscious of the dreamer. The question is what message it holds for him. Many Christian counselors[867] use the dreams of the counselees to help them to understand what is going on in their lives. Grün gives the following advice: Write down your dreams. Take dreams seriously and start a conversation with them which can lead into a prayer. Discuss the dreams with others, your pastor.[868] The counselor should ask questions[869] so that the counselee can discover the meaning of the dream for himself. In addition, Grün gives the dreamer a Bible passage to meditate on, not the dream.[870]

Could this approach towards dreams work among the Karen? I think on a personal level it may help some people who are open for something new. It would widen their horizon and take away the fear of bad dreams.

A similar approach would be to take the dream before God in prayerful listening and reflect it on a passage of God's Word.

---

[864] "Eine Hilfe kann auch sein, abends Gott darum zu bitten, dass er uns gute Träume schicke und dass wir auch beachten mögen, was er uns sagt." (Translation by the author). Grün, 67.

[865] Daniel 2:30.

[866] Sanford, *God's forgotten*, 90.

[867] Among many others, Kelsey, Sanford, Ruthe or Grün.

[868] Grün, 67-72.

[869] "From where do you know some of the dream elements? Do you know persons, places, stations of your life – do they remind you of anything? Do you discover any cues about your present situation – an encouragement, an order or a warning?" "Does the dream address any (spiritual) challenge?" Gaby Pfeil. "When you awoke what was the main feeling the dream reflected? Which problems in your life and in your relationships are raised in the dream?" Ruthe, *Traumbotschaften*, 143. (Translation by the author).

[870] "Deshalb gebe ich immer einen Bibeltext zur Meditation und nicht den Traum." Grün, 74.

Many of the above remarks regarding a biblical view for redeeming the experience of dreams have already seen some beginnings with some Karen Christians. Therefore, it is important to encourage and strengthen these hopeful beginnings and teach from the Bible regarding how to encounter bad dreams which are a temptation to many Christians.

6. Conclusion

6.1 Appraisal

Research findings reveal some clear answers pertaining to the main research questions and their sub-questions which we have asked in the Introduction. As assumed, the research has shown high significance and popularity of dreams among the Karen. Dreams are imbedded into the respective culture and often reveal the feelings and thinking of the people. Therefore, it does not surprise that the main issues in dreams of the Karen are spirits and their work, illness and death including the realm of the dead, family – especially pregnancy, relationships as well as their agricultural work. Half of the people asked did not have an answer to the question, "Where do dreams come from?" Most of the others answered that dreams are a work of evil spirits (bad dreams) or that they are what their 'k'la' has seen. A few Christians answered that God is the source of (good) dreams. As the majority of dreams reported were "bad dreams", their impact is accordingly. For Animist-Buddhists bad dreams are a taboo ('ta dü ta htü') not to be broken. Especially dreams about seeing the person who has 'lo ta' someone. On the other hand, for many Christians, a "bad dream" is a reason to pray and still go out to work which then breaks the old taboo. Animist-Buddhists who are not able to heed the taboo (to stay home), will 'yo hpe' in order to skirt around the taboo. If the dream shows the reason for their problems, e.g. illness, they will consult a spirit doctor and if necessary, perform a ceremony. If Animist-Buddhists have an extraordinary dream, but do not know the meaning, they will ask for help from their traditional experts, while some Christians feel a vacuum of spiritual leadership in these circumstances and therefore are tempted to go for help to a spirit doctor again. Another significant difference between Animist-Buddhists and Christians we found pertains to the interpretation of dreams. While Animist-Buddhists take the traditional meaning to be absolute, Christians have started to challenge some meanings in the light of their faith. For them, dreams have to be checked against the Word of God and have therefore lost their unchallenged meanings. The biblical perspective on dreams, given in this research, gives Christians some specific benchmarks in order to locate the source of the dream and how to deal with it.

The research has shown some interesting differences between Christians and Animist-Buddhists, yet at the same time, it also has revealed strong animistic undercurrents among Christians which have to be addressed. Could it be that dreams mirror how deeply the new Christian faith has taken root? The research has shown that this is the case to a certain degree. However, it is not only the dreams themselves, but also how Christians handle their dreams which sheds light on their faith.

The other main question we have asked is, "Can the experience of dreams among the Karen be redeemed?" We have seen that Animist-Buddhists and Christians are looking for different ways to be redeemed from "bad dreams".

Faith/world view and dreams influence each other remarkably.

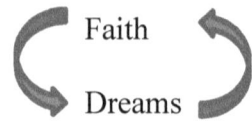

If people's faith is changing it can be expected that their dream world will change, too.[871] The research has shown that Christians, even children, who have been affected by a revival, started to have new dreams. And the other way around, we have discovered that many Christians view "old dreams" as a temptation to be drawn back into the traditional animistic faith. Therefore, some Christians try to ignore dreams. For Christians to experience new dreams is obviously a work of God. When change happens, usually God involves people to do their part. In the following "Recommendations" section I will show how this research can help to redeem the dreams in the Omkoi Karen Christian Context.

6.2 Recommendations

6.2.1 To the Karen Christian Community

Do not ignore dreams nor talk dreams down. Dreams are like a vehicle which can be used by different sources to communicate from the unseen world. God has used them for his purposes even until today. Therefore, take dreams seriously, but do not give them the place of absolute truth.

Dreams and their interpretation need to be checked against the revealed will of God in His Word. Dreams from God do not accuse others. The devil is the accuser.

If you experience bad dreams and nightmares that recur, they may well be demonic. Pray to God in the name of the Lord Jesus Christ to set you free.[872]

Dreams from evil spirits or the devil are not to be trusted. Dreams interpreted by spirit doctors are not to be trusted either. Do not believe in them otherwise you will become a slave to them. "In the name of Jesus of Nazareth who came in the flesh", refuse those dreams and under His protection go out to do your work. If you are fearful, ask someone else to pray with you.

Dreams from God may give warning, but often they are messages of encouragement.

Pray – not only not to have a dream or a bad dream – but pray for good dreams from God. Pray that God will speak to you clearly through dreams.[873]

---

[871] See the example of the Asabano, under point 2.3.3.2.

[872] Mark Bubeck advises the following prayer before sleep each night in order to eliminate this problem: "In the name of the Lord Jesus Christ, I submit my mind and my dream activities only to the work of the Holy Spirit. I bind up all powers of darkness and forbid them to work in my dream abilities or any part of my subconscious while I sleep." Mark I. Bubeck, *The Adversary. The Christian Versus Demon Activity* (Chicago, IL: Moody Press, 1975), 145.

6.2.2 To Missionaries, Karen Evangelists and Pastors

As we have seen, there is a connection between faith and dreams. Therefore it is important to teach God's Word and disciple Christians to become followers of Jesus in all aspects of their lives. If God's Word and the Holy Spirit penetrate and fill the Christians' lives, we can expect dreams to change as well.

Do not ignore dreams. Take the dreamer and his dream seriously by listening to his dream story.

In or after church, spend time where dreams can be told and discerned together, as well as giving the opportunity to pray about them.

Together with the dreamer discern the source of the dream on the basis of God's Word. Take a time of listening prayer. God may give the dreamer or yourself an impression. If not, entrust the dreamer in prayer into God's hand. Encourage him to go about his work in faith.

Show to the dreamer the limits of dreams. God's promises are more important and trustworthy than dreams.

In cases of accusing '*lo ta*', go and talk with the parties involved. If they are Christians, biblical teaching and a close spiritual walk with them is of utmost importance. You may have to get involved in spiritual warfare.

Ask yourself whether there is a spiritual person in the church who has the gift of interpreting dreams? If there is, work together with that person in order to build up the church of God.

Start to interpret dreams from a biblical perspective. What meaning do different dream symbols have in the Bible? Start with your own dreams.

Start to ask yourself about your feelings when you were dreaming. Are they a familiar part of your life? When? Where? Does the dream reveal a truth about yourself? If you find it helpful for yourself, then you may start to ask others when they talk about their dreams.

6.2.3 To Theological Education Institutions and Training Centers

Since dreams are not only important to Karen but to many other peoples, theological education institutions should think about how they can equip their trainees regarding dreams so that they will not be helpless when they are confronted with dreams in their community. Could a special seminar on dreams be planned?

---

[873] Richard Foster writes into a western evangelical context which is more skeptical towards dreams: „If we are convinced that dreams can be a key to unlocking the door to the inner world, ... we can specifically pray, inviting God to inform us through our dreams. We should tell Him of our willingness to allow Him to speak to us in this way. At the same time it is wise to pray a prayer of protection, since to open ourselves to spiritual influence can be dangerous as well as profitable. We simply ask God to surround us with the light of His protection as He ministers to our spirit." Richard Foster, *Celebration of Discipline. The path to spiritual growth* (London, UK: Hodder & Stoughton, 1980), 23.

Another approach could be to integrate interpretation of dreams into a class concerning pastoral care or as a special time the first half hour in the morning once per week. A dream could be told and discerned together – giving a practical lesson in contextualized theology – and providing an example concerning how dreams can be dealt with.

In summary, it is crucial that the animistic mindset, which is infested with lies by evil spirits who also use dreams to hold people captive or draw them back, be replaced continually with the truth from God. The negative thoughts coming from their old beliefs and dreams have to be continuously challenged with the fact that God is their loving Father and His intention is to bless and redeem them and not harm them. As their relationship with God deepens, the power of evil dreams on their lives will loosen. The more the Christians understand the love, holiness and power of God and the more they learn to trust HIM fully, the more freedom they will experience, and the better they will know the voice of God, even through dreams.

6.3 Further Research

The present research only touches a little on the understanding that dreams reveal our subconscious and that they are an expression of our innermost being. More research on this kind of psychological and pastoral interpretation of dreams should be done. How this would impact people with an animistic background could be researched – until present a foreign approach to the Karen in the researched area.

We have seen how dreams and the *'k'la'* concept are intertwined. The *'k'la'* concept is part of the (traditional) Karen world view and it is part and parcel of their (Christian) faith. Because *'k'la'* are not mentioned in the Bible they are ignored by the Christian teaching. But they have to be addressed, because the widespread belief of reincarnation even among Christians has its foundation in the *'k'la'* concept.

Research needs to be done on how the *'k'la'* concept can be addressed and whether ways could be found to change and integrate it into a Christian world view. Another area of contextualized theology among the Karen which needs research is the traditional concept of the *'plü kau'* in comparison to Sheol, Hades or Paradise in the Bible.

Appendix A: Dreams and their meanings given by the interviewees

Good dreams	
Dream	Meaning
A lot of fish[874]	Earn or receive money
Going uphill or upriver[875]	What you plant will bring its fruit. You will succeed in what you do. Things are going well
Going up a tree[876]	Good dream
Water flowing upwards[877]	Good dream
Able to get across water[878]	Can do anything. Weed the field easily
Killing a person[879]	Find food, succeed in hunting
Seeing a near relative come to visit[880] Seeing him sitting[881]	That person comes That person stays where it is
A corpse, dead relative [882]	Succeed, succeed in hunting
Gun is defective[883]	Succed in hunting
Someone cursed you[884]	The person has blessed you
Woman giving you a pipe out of banana leaves[885]	Hunt a deer

---

[874] 10S; 11T; 31DM; 40M; 43B; 54Ch; 58N; 59N; 67BR; 70Ch. These references refer to Appendix B.
[875] 12J; 23P; 31DM; 43B; 50Phue; 67BR.
[876] 63Jae.
[877] 43N.
[878] 38P.
[879] 39M; 33P.
[880] 28Kri; 37M.
[881] 37M.
[882] 12J; 31P.
[883] 31P.
[884] 39Ch.
[885] 18P.

Pure or small water[886] Lots of pure water[887] Broad place in the river[888]	Good dream The dream is about the heart/spirit Good to plant, earn well.
Washing myself[889]	Being healthy
'*plü kau*' without rain[890] '*plü*' during the cutting field season[891] '*plü*' who was happy and working well[892]	Eat, succeed Fields burn well Good dream
Female elephant (and its baby) during harvest and threshing time[893]	More to eat, lots of rice, full granary
Big snake[894]	To get very old
Bees coming to the house[895]	'*k'la*' of rice coming into the house
Mountain rice looks good[896]	Being healthy
Keeping each other hands[897]	Working together well
Coming home[898]	Being healthy
Light[899]	Being healthy
Person in light (angel)[900]	Like God's kingdom
Holding a stone in the hand[901]	Cure against curse; Christians: Bible
Three doves[902]	Father, Son, Holy Spirit – revival

---

[886] 19S; 20S (same person). 43B.
[887] 59N.
[888] 38M.
[889] 42Mo; 63W. 34R dreamed about 'washing myself in the river' and his child and he himself got a cold.
[890] 31P.
[891] 45S.
[892] 42Pa.
[893] 28Ch; 31DM; 38P; 38M; 43B; 45S; 45G.
[894] 38P; 38Luwa.
[895] 38P.
[896] 42Mo.
[897] 43N; 43B.
[898] 43B.
[899] 43B.
[900] 12J.
[901] 62ST.
[902] 28D.

Appendix A

People moving into a big house on the mountain[903]	Revival
Seeing a godly person (when you are ill)[904]	Being healed
Becoming pregnant or during pregnancy:	
Clean Water[905]	Child will be healthy
Water coming out of a bamboo cane[906]	Boy
A well[907]	Girl
Female or male melon[908]	Get pregnant. Girl or boy respectively
Eating melon (or other fruit)[909]	Getting pregnant. Girl
Cucumber, bean or banana[910]	Boy
Turtle[911]	Girl
Water coming from a tap.[912]	Boy
River[913]	Girl
Big river[914]	Boy
Dead mother appears[915]	Girl
Going over a bridge[916]	Boy
Going through the water[917]	Girl

---

[903] 68S.
[904] 64Ch.
[905] 45G
[906] 31D; 45G.
[907] 31D; 45G; 50Phue.
[908] 31P; 45S; 45G; 56G.
[909] 40M; 50Phi.
[910] 28D; 34R; 45S; 50Phi.
[911] 34R.
[912] 38M.
[913] 38M.
[914] 50Phue.
[915] 28Ch.
[916] 45G.
[917] 45G.

Bad dreams	
Dream	**Meaning**
Stinky fish[918]	Lose money
Cutting fields[919]	Buffaloes and cows go into the field eating the rice
Flood/river/bridge not able to cross[920]	Sickness occurs or somebody is going to die. Encounter problems.
Crossing a bridge over river[921]	Somebody near to you is going to die
Going downhill; going downriver, not making it up the mountain[922]	Lose money, animals or fields; not succeed, no strength
Killing a pig or a deer; shooting an animal[923]	Not shooting anything when you go hunting
Male elephant – during harvest time[924] Elephant (running, riding it)[925]	Not enough rice, rice granary not full Chills, shivering, shaking. Fell from a tree
Elephants or buffaloes haunting[926]	Spirits are at work. Elephant's *'k'la'* is a demon[927]
Someone gives you money[928] Nice dream about a person[929]	You will get sick or other problems arise Problems with that person.
Dirty water. High waters[930]	Hindrances and problems. Anger and hate
Darkness[931]	Bad dream

---

[918] 12G; 31DM.
[919] 12J.
[920] 12J; 13Oe; 32BR; 38P.
[921] 12J; 16N.
[922] 12J; 28Ch; 33P; 37M; 38P; 50Phue; 51D; 63Jae; 65HT; 67BR.
[923] 33P; 40M; 45S; 57A.
[924] 38P; 38M; 54Ch.
[925] 24E; 25M; 50Phi; 64Ch.
[926] 25M; 38P; 32BR; 54Ch.
[927] 45S.
[928] 18Chra.
[929] 44T.
[930] 19S; 20S; 31P; 59N.
[931] 21M; 43P.

Hunting[932]	Bad dream
Trap[933]	Sickness
Coming back not into your house[934]	Bad dream
Moon coming up[935]	Bad dream
Buffaloes[936]	Plantations are not good
Killing a bear,[937] (big animals generally, except female elephant in harvesting season)	Someone will die (Bad dream)
Deer[938]	Earn no money
Carry a child (*'pü'*)[939]	Sickness
Seeing your child who is away, not well[940]	The child is not well
Peppers, eating or pounding[941]	Quarreling/fighting in the family or with friends. Suffering. Your heart is not well. (*'ta he sa'*)
Raining[942]	A heavy heart
Drinking alcohol[943]	It is going to rain
Fire[944]	Illness to come. Problems. Hot heart, leads to quarrels What is not good will happen to you.
Flying[945]	Lose hair
Plane landing[946]	Catch people, people die

---

[932] 25M.
[933] 48HP.
[934] 43B.
[935] 40M.
[936] 31DM.
[937] 40M.
[938] 59N.
[939] 25M; 27M; 66Somu.
[940] 38P
[941] 22M; 25M; 28Ch; 38M; 53Ch; 67BR; 70Ch.
[942] 28Kri.
[943] 70Ch.
[944] 12J; 28Ch; 38MM; 42Mo; 44T; 59N; 67BR.
[945] 28Ch. (He has not much hair left!)
[946] 32BR; 40M; 44T.

'*plü*' and rain[947] '*plü*'[948] Father and/or mother's '*k'la*' appear[949] Eat with a '*plü*'.[950] Deceased person who was lazy[951]	Big rain destroyed plants Hatred. Being hurt. Heart will be broken Fear that the child will die (called by parents to return) Bad dream You will not succeed
'*plü kau*'[952] Not having a nice house in the '*plü kau*'[953] '*plü kau*' when already ill[954] Hell[955]	Difficulties. Quarreling.[956] Bad for the dead person Going to die Suffering
A storm coming[957]	Quarreling at hand
Stung by a bee[958]	Get sick
Animal biting Cat, dog or wolf biting[959] (if you can beat it off – no harm)	Causes illness. Shivering It stands for the '*ta yo*', strong evil spirit
Hearing a cat behind you[960]	Evil spirits ('*ta yo*')
Leeches sucking your blood[961]	No strength, tired
Snake which is cut up[962] Snake[963]	Short life Devil

---

[947] 28Kri.
[948] 12J; 42Mo; 65HT.
[949] 28Ch; 38MM.
[950] 45S.
[951] 42Pa.
[952] 54Ch; 61ST.
[953] 30Ch.
[954] 38P.
[955] 61ST.
[956] Dreaming about the '*plü kau*' is ambiguous in its meaning. It can be a good or a bad. It depends on the situation and on the people. See 54Ch; 57A.
[957] 31P.
[958] 33P.
[959] 33P; 38P; 50Phi; 58N.
[960] 25M.
[961] 10S.
[962] 38Luwa; 38P.
[963] 58N.

Appendix A

Marrying – a woman wants to marry me[964] Wedding[965]	Wife or children getting sick. Spirit of the water ('*na hti*') comes to harm Person will die soon
Taking milk from a woman[966]	'*na hti*' comes to people
A woman keeping a mirror in front[967]	A splinter into the eye
Losing shoes[968]	Lost the love of your spouse
Tree, dried or broken[969] Carrying it or part of it[970] A fallen tree preventing you to come back[971]	Old person dies Carrying a corpse Hindrances ahead, sickness
People depart from each other[972]	Not working well together
Honey or wax[973]	Get a cold
Singing with a teenaged girl[974]	Man's child got sick[975]
During conception or pregnancy: Well is dry[976] Bent cucumber[977]	Child will die Child unhealthy
Bananas[978]	Sickness
Bowel movement[979]	Sickness through divination/sorcery
Harvesting rice[980]	Buffaloes or cows went into the rice

---

[964] 14P; 39Ch; 53Ch; 57A; 57Ti. In Karen culture in the given area, it is usually the women who ask the men to marry them.
[965] 66Somu.
[966] 45S.
[967] 57A.
[968] Story under 2.4.2.
[969] 12J; 40M.
[970] 12J; 14P.
[971] 25M.
[972] 43B.
[973] 43B.
[974] 48HP.
[975] 48P.
[976] 45G; 56G.
[977] 34R.
[978] 45S.
[979] 51D.
[980] 56G.

	field to feed
Snake biting[981]	Unfaithfulness in marriage
Giving meat[982]	'lo ta'

---

[981] 58N.
[982] 12J; 13Oe; 32BR; 35N; 45G; 58N; 65HT.

Appendix B:
Interviews with Karen about dreams

10:

2013-11-29. Dreams interview with Somu (S) in the car from Omkoi to Chiang Mai. For details see 66Somu.

Once Somu dreamed about lots of fish which meant he would get money. A few days later, a teacher gave him some money unexpectedly.

He explains another meaning of dreams. "If you dream about many leeches sucking your blood that means you will become tired and be without strength."

11:

2013-12-21. Man of Thibokhi (T) above village. Non-Christian, 40 years.

T: When I dream I do not go out. I fast. I stay in the house.

HB: What do you dream?

T: If I dream that a person has died, I do not go out. If I have a bad dream I do not go out.

HB: Have you ever dreamed something that happened afterwards?

T: No. I do not go out for a day and then it is okay.

HB: Do you know the meaning?

T: I do not know.

HB: But if you dream about fish?

T: Oh, if you dream about fish you will make money.

Mr. Gula, who helped with the transcription explains (2014-06-25): "If you dream about stinky fish – you will lose money."

12:

2014-02-24. Johapa (J). A longstanding Christian. Brother of 28Ch. 60 years. Lives in Maeleakhi, a village far up in the mountains which has turned mainly Christian, but has persistently kept to some of their old animistic traditions and beliefs. Mr Gula, (G) young pastor who helped me with transcribing the interviews.

J: If Karen, non-Christians, are to go out to work fields but have a bad dream the night before, they do not go out.

HB: What kind of a bad dream?

J: If you dream about dead people, about your grandfather or grandmother, the Karen call it dreams of the afterworld (*'plü kau'*) – then you do not go out. If you dream about broken trees or about a fire spreading, you do not go out to work. If you dream about peppers – '*ta he sa*' your heart is not well – if you dream about the afterworld your heart will be broken, that is no good. If you dream about a tree which has fallen/broken - it means somebody is going to die, maybe a child or your wife. If you dream about crossing a bridge over the river ('*we to*'), it has the same meaning. If you dream about somebody carrying a tree or part of it, somebody will die. You will have to carry a corpse.

HB: Then you will fear?

Yes, then you do not go to work.

HB: Have you ever had good dreams about the '*plü*'?

J: Yes, if you dream about dead relatives you will go out and succeed. There are two kinds of dreams about the afterworld: It depends on the dream and what people say. If people think it is a good dream you go out, if not, you stay at home.

J: Formerly, in the Bible there were dreams – like Joseph. God made him aware of a danger. So if you are not a Christian, and you dream that there is a danger, you do not go out.

HB: Are most dreams bad or good?

J: There are good dreams. If you want to go out to plant and you dream about going uphill or walking up a river that is a good dream that is what people say. If you dream about going downhill, it is a bad dream. You are not going out to work. As Christians, we pray to God and if you then have a good dream, we go out. If you dream about walking down a river it is a bad dream.

J: Is it this way with foreigners?

HB: Some.

J: Some say, if you dream about fish you do not always make money. If you dream about '*plü*', your heart will be broken. If you will work and not eat, you may not have strength to work. You will get sick.

HB: What do you think: Where do dreams come from? Those who do not worship God, what do they think?

J: (no answer)

HB: Non-Christians think the '*k'la*' wander?

J: If you are afraid, the '*k'la*' wander. If you do not fear anything, the '*k'la*' do not wander. If non-Christians go to the graves, the '*k'la*' wander. You have to go back and '*ki cü*' and call the '*k'la*' back. That is those who do not know God yet. If you are Christians and you go to the graves and you fear, you pray.

HB: Is it true that some go to that place where something happened and pray there?

Sometimes, if somebody goes out to the forest and he gets sick. Then we go and pray with him. If he does not get better, he wants us to go to the place where he started to get sick and pray there. Is this okay?

HB: Why does he want you to go there?

J: Because he was afraid there, therefore he wants to go there. Actually in the Bible we are told to pray – but many have come and asked me to go and pray with them at that certain place.

HB: Do they think that there are certain spirits there?

J: Yes, they think there are spirits there. Like *'po xa'* spirits, they want us to go there. Have you ever gone to pray like that?

HB: I think I have gone once.

J: Some get better after we have prayed in their house, others want us to go out to the place and pray there. I have gone many times. Non-Christians go out to call their *'k'la'* back at that place. But we do not do that.

HB: If you go out to pray only that is okay ... .

J: We only go out to pray – we do not anything else.

J: I would like missionaries to come and explain it again more clearly.

HB: Asking about the story which occurred in Maeleakhi.

J: If we are Christians, we should not go to the Buddhist temple. But Suva [former lay pastor] he did.

HB: Did he go alone or with people?

J: Suva went for his father-in-law. He led the uncle (father-in-law) and he did it. He should not have done it. This was the problem, then they went out of the village. Nebluethupa said he could stay anywhere, in Maeleakhi or Tarolekhi or anywhere. But actually his parent-in-law gave him a place in Maeleakhi. But then he followed his father-in-law and went off with him. If he had said that he was sorry and wanted to stay – that would have been different, but he said he could go anywhere. But he was proud ... After his father-in-law disappeared, Nebluethupa came to ask for money for him. But we had nothing to do with him. We did not kill him, we do not know where he is.

HB: Did his father-in-law have problems in the village before?

J: He had problems many times. People say he could *'lo ta'*, do sorcery, to people.

G: *'lo ta'* – "this is the one thing Karen fear most!" It occurred many times, people said he could *'lo ta'*. That happened many times.

HB: How does this happen?

J: I do not understand. If people got sick, they dreamed that his father-in-law gave them meat. Pusopa dreamed that he gave him meat. He was an enemy with the father-in-law. Then his stomach grew big and he died. He had gone to the doctor and the doctor said he had cancer. At that time he was healed but later on his tummy grew big again. Somuphue [father-in-law of Nebluethupa] did not want him to be cremated. He came to me to ask them not to burn him, but to bury him. The village wanted him to be cremated, but he did not want it. So they did not cremate him. Then another person died. And they thought: What is Somuphue doing? Later, my nephew was asked by Somuphue to go and buy chemicals for planting peppers. On the way back someone asked my nephew for the chemicals and he did not bring them to Somuphue. Then he got sick - his belly grew big and he died. And then they cremated him and they saw that his belly was full of meat! [that means he was '*lo ta*']. It was like that. But how it came about nobody knows really. Then they went to see the spirit doctor and he said it was sorcery ('*lo ta*'). Many people have died because of sorcery. Two or three people.

J: In your country, do people dream and then get sick?

HB: Mmm, among the Christians, not many. I explain the psychological meaning of dreams.

HB: Where do dreams come from? Are they coming from God or the devil or through the '*k'la*' which wander?

J: When I have had a certain dream, I remember what happened. – If I dream about raining, dried trees or a storm coming and then the children get sick - we then remember that. If we dream about cutting the fields ('*pä qü*'), we think the buffaloes and cows come into the field and eat the rice. If we dream about floods, then sickness will occur. If we can cross the floods, it is okay, it does not matter. If we cannot cross and are taken away, we think someone will get ill or is going to die.

HB: Dreams about sickness or death, or sowing rice, planting rice – do you have any?

J: If we are going to plant rice and dream about '*plü*' or about going down river – oh we will not eat [bad harvest, not earn any money]. If you go uphill or up-river, then it is a good dream. That is what each one remembers. Do you have those dreams among foreigners?

HB: I do not really know. Do you think that during a dream, spirits come or the '*k'la*' wander? What do you think?

J: Dream about going out [does not know].

HB: An angel came to Joseph.

J: God was warning him. It was a dream. And Jacob knew that God was there when he dreamed about the angels going up and down. Dreams can be a warning – sometimes about good things we should do or bad things we should not do.

HB: But I see people that if they dream, they believe in dreams.

J: I can see in our village that people believe in dreams. If they have bad dreams, we go and pray with them. Sometimes if they dream the child may get sick, we go and pray.

HB: (I explain what I do when I dream...)

J: Actually we see in the Bible that if we encounter problems, we should tell God in prayer.

HB: Have you ever dreamed about God and Heaven?

J: Some people have seen a person in light (angel) and if you compare with the Bible it may be like God's kingdom. Like Mary, she saw an angel coming to her.

13:

2014-02-25. Oelopa (Oe), 50 years, my former language informant. Lives in Sop Lahn, his wife is from Maeleakhi. Interview at the Karen center in Omkoi.

Oe: During the time I was not well [depression], I dreamed about a bridge I could not cross. I could not cross. When I tried to cross I fell from it. I fell from it. Then I prayed to God. I had problems. I could not make the experience [solve the problem – to cross], until I killed myself [attempt of suicide – shot himself in the ear]. I could not solve the problem until I made a fool of myself.

HB: Asked about the throwing out of a clan in his wife's village (see 12 above). Dreams played a role, didn't they?

Oe: I have heard that people say that. The one who was ill said, Nebluethupa's father-in-law gave him meat. Yeah, the one who was ill said that. Then another person dreamed that Nebluethupa's father in law gave the meat. [which means he cast a spell on him – '*lo ta*'].

HB: To do it this way, is that right? What do you think about it?

Oe: To do it this way is not easy. It leads to broken relationships and quarrelling. Illness often comes with many different things together. But Karen today believe that way and because they believe that way, it comes that way. If they would not believe it, it would not come about. Because they believe it is so, it happens. If they dream something they believe that the person involved can do it. And the person who is ill believes that the other person is doing the evil thing to him. And when the person does it according to the dream, the ill person believes it more and more that it is that way.

HB: Were those Christians?

Oe: Yes, they were Christians. Also the one who dreamed was a Christian.

HB: How do they know for sure?

Oe: They know because they went to the spirit doctor. They asked the spirit doctor and he told them. They believe they know for sure in this way.

HB: Did they go to the spirit doctor to ask about the dream?

Oe: Yes, and he told them. They believe him. But the spirit doctor does not come from God but from the devil. The devil does these things.

HB: I heard that people believe while they dream that their '*k'la*' is wandering and they see into the afterworld, and it comes back – do they believe it?

Oe: There are, this happens. Many think so. This belief is there. Most are non-Christians or those who do not know God for sure. They believe this. If they really believe in God, they do not believe that anymore.

Oe: If a dream comes from God, you are not bothered – you will be glad, you will be happy. If it comes from an evil source, your heart is not glad, it will make you doubt.

14:

2014-02-26. Patupa (P) from Sop Lahn. 60 years old. Older brother of 13Oe. He was a spirit doctor, but now has been a Christian for many years.

P: Dreams often show the opposite. I once went to sleep in the forest to Prinjapa. I could not sleep and I saw an old person coming out of the stump. I could not sleep – I was frightened. He looked like one with big teeth over his face. When I rose I went to hunt birds and I got them. The fear became happiness.

P: Tells about dreams in the Bible:

If we look at the tradition (*'mo'le pa'la'*) like the village of Glocki[983], they use dreams. If you have a bad dream, you have to stay at home otherwise you will be hurt. If you go out, you have to be careful not to be hurt. You had better stay at home – but go out the next day. If you still go out, you have '*yo hpe yo blo*' [to stamp into the ashes so dust will come up in order to make the spirit not see your feet]. and then you pray to the spirits so that the different spirits will not see you. Then no harm happens.

An uncle said you have to pray so nothing will happen. When I dream and I get problems I pray that God will protect me. This is our duty.

HB: What do you think or what do Karen think, who are not Christians, where do dreams come from?

P: 'ta bo ba' – through knowledge. It is like before Christ was born and the angel went to Mary to tell her. Formerly when you dreamed about a fallen tree that meant it is a corpse. Someone died and they were going to bury him. Therefore, they would call the spirit doctor so that he will '*ki cü*' and bring a sacrifice and pray. Sometimes they will get knowledge through dreams.

HB: Who causes dreams?

P: They say it comes from God. They use the name of God for it. If we look at people who 'uu ta', they say it comes from God (*Ywa*).[984] But they do not worship God.

God gives dreams they say. They say, children and grandchildren, if you have bad dreams, do not go out. If you go and ask them why they do not go out, they may answer my father has had a bad dream. But as Christians we still go out because God is with us.

P: e.g. You are with your wife. And another woman wants you to marry and marries you and really loves you. And then you realize it is a dream. Formerly, the people said the devil has come to marry you. If you dream like that, people think the wife or the children will get sick and you have to '*ki cü*'. You have to '*ki cü*' very quickly and the spirit doctor has to go and do sacrifices.

HB: Is it like that, the '*k'la*' go?

P: Yes. The '*k'la*' go. Our ancestors said there are 33. There is one behind each ear and one on the fontanel. During the night they wander, they say. They go out

---

[983] A village in the Omkoi district where no Christians live. They have resisted the gospel until today.

[984] Karen animists use the same word for God as the Christians but with other connotations.

to other houses, to the fields and they go and eat what is left there. But the three main *'k'la'* do not wander away. If those three go away, then the person dies. They pray and *'ki cü'* and they call the *'k'la'* back. The 33 *'k'la'* have to come back. If they have come back, they give them 'me to' [rice cooked in leaves which are bound together]. As if they would see them.

HB: Do dreams come from *'k'la'* ha'?

P: Formerly, I was a spirit doctor, too. An uncle – he made people afraid with spirits but now we do not fear anymore. Formerly, we had to pay the spirit doctor. If you were not going to pay, he would come and get the money. They had no love. But now, if Maripa[985] goes to pray with people, you do not ask for money.

HB: If people died, formerly where did Karen think they went?

P: They went to heaven. Others had to show the sun (where the sun comes up or goes down). *'Hta'* [poem] about the belief that everything is in the opposite way in the *'plü kau'*.

HB: Do people from the *'plü kau'* come up in dreams?

P: Formerly they said they could.

P: e.g. Your father has died and you dream that the father comes to you and asks you to come to him as well. That is when your father has already died. And then your wife gets pregnant. That meant that your father had come back in the womb of your wife. That is a good dream. If the child then is born and has a same mark as your father, then it is confirmed that this is the case. Many people in the church will say the devil has brought you back.

P: Formerly, if people were 'born again' they would die soon. But nowadays as they are born to Christians, they stay. They marry and have children. They have many children. They are God's creation. They do not die because they do not belong to the devil anymore, they are God's creation. The Bible says death and life is in God's hand. Two of my children have died. God has given and God has taken them. God curses and God blesses. Do not take revenge. It belongs to God. God helps, wait for God and he will help and wait for God and he will bless you. Do not worry.

HB: The three *'k'la'* do not wander?

P: They do not wander.

About being „born again" – P. explains:

P: Some say that the ancestors are born as Christians now. (Another man who stands there, agrees.) But if we were born in the old way, that would be bad!

15:

2014-02-26. Patupa (P). See 14P. Interviewed at the Karen center in Omkoi.

P: Formerly I was a *'mo'le pa'la'* – 'spirit doctor'.

---

[985] My Karen name.

HB: Where do people go when they die?

P: To heaven.

16:

2014-03-04. Nasephi (N), village of Bakkha, grandmother, 60years. The interview was done at the Karen center in Omkoi, during a Bible training seminar she was part of.

N: I have dreamed that I have to do God's work. He said, I will have to trust Him and honor Him. Give your heart fully even if problems arise. You have to go with me and I will rescue you. You have to do God's work and I will work for you. I will be with you and your children. God's Word says, if you honor me, I will honor you.

HB: Did he tell you to use medicine?

N: No, he said trust me. For God nothing is impossible, I can do anything. If you get into problems do not look for any other gods. God can do anything. I told him I will not go and look for any other god. If I die, I will die for you.

HB: Did you dream this dream a long time ago?

N: I have dreamed this a long time ago. I was still in Maelan.

HB: But you were already a Christian?

N: Of course.

HB: When you dreamed did you see God or how do you know that it was God?

N: God showed me that there are two ways. God asked me: Which way do you want to go the way into heaven or hell? I want to go to heaven. I went to see hell and saw the suffering. It was not nice to look at. I said, 'if in hell is more suffering than on this earth, I want to go to heaven.' If you do not want to go to hell you have to do righteous works. If you are a righteous person, Jesus will receive you.

HB: When you were not a Christian yet, did you ever dream?

N: I dreamed so many bad dreams. It was mostly bad. But once when I fasted (as a Christian) and prayed, I saw a light twinkle three times before me. I went to worship in the church three evenings. Then a temptation came while I was praying – somebody or something made a noise (*gra gra*). I went alone. I thought, what is this? Is it the devil?

I once went up early in the morning and the Holy Spirit said, 'If you pray, I will be with you.' He said, 'If you fear, it is not good. You have to have a firm heart. I will go with you and be with you.' I went to water the field. Nobody was there. I went to sleep for 8 days.

HB: Since you have become a Christian have you ever had bad dreams?

N: No, never. Praise God.

I dreamed one, two or three times after I had become a Christian for one or two days (*'lo so'*). I got very sick. And once I was crossing a bridge. If we love God, God loves us.

17:

2014-03-04. Na's mother (N) in Thigekhi, 50 years. Christian.

N: I dreamed that somebody came to check on me. My *'k'la'* waited gladly. I had a noise in my ear. He came to look at one ear. And afterwards the noise was gone.

18:

2014-03-16. Pathi Mujupü from Chroeta (P), 63 years, Christian. Chra, spirit doctor from Thibokhi.

P: Since I have become a Christian I always go out when I have dreamed. God is watching. I do not think about it. It does not matter. I believe. I do not follow the dreams. I believe in God the Highest.

HB: Have you ever dreamed?

P: Formerly, before I was a Christian and I had a bad dream it came about. But since I worship God it does not matter anymore.

HB: I would like to know how dreams come about?

P: If you dream, do you fear sometimes? [He asks another man who sits there.]

Chra: Sometimes I cry out in a dream.

HB: Where do Karen think dreams come from?

Chra: I do not know.

P: It is a temptation.

HB: Are there any good dreams?

P: If you dream that a woman gives you a pipe made out of banana leaves – then you will hunt a deer.

Chra: If you dream that someone gives you money, you will get sick.

19:

2014-03-17. DioSutongPuindoi (S), 65 years. Genaechoetha, and his wife (W). He is the former headman, the only Christian couple in the village. I was visiting with the housefather of the children's hostel in Thibokhi, Mr. Ela (E), 25 years.

HB: Have you ever dreamed?

S: The first time I remember I dreamed [after becoming a Christian] I was in Mae Sot. Why did I dream, I do not know. I dreamed a dream which made me fear as somebody was going to kill me. I told him, "I have done nothing wrong. Why do you want to kill me?" He did not answer. It was kind of a teenager. I called the child but he did not answer. What this meant I did not know.

HB: Were you a Christian then?

W: Yes.

S: I got very ill.

HB: What did you do afterwards?

S: Afterwards I did not dream anymore. When I dreamed afterwards they were always good dreams. I dreamed that the water was gone. I dreamed that I went up a mountain. There was still a little water. The water was pure.

HB: What does that mean?

S: Pure water is good. Dirty water is bad.

W: Sometimes he is well, sometimes he is ill. In the evening he has a headache.

S: In the evening it comes up to my head and aches.

HB : Where do dreams come from, what do people think?

S: I don't know where dreams come from.

E: It is a temptation.

S: Yes, it must be that way, that it is a temptation.

HB: What do you think, formerly, did dreams come through 'k'la ha' or did spirits come to visit? What do you think?

W: I do not think anything.

S: I do not think anything. We worship God and, if our heart is with God, we do not need to think about dreams.

20:

2014-03-18. DioSutongPuindoi Genaechoetha (60yrs) and his wife (W) and Ela (E) talking about how he became a Christian. He has been a Christian for about 4 years.

HB: Formerly, when you were not Christians yet, did you ever dream?

S: When we were still doing ancestor worship, when we had a bad dream, we did not go out, we had to stay at home. If we wanted to go out, we had to *'yo pi hoko'* – stamp the earth. [similar to *'yo hpe'*]. This was the tradition.

HB: If you dreamed did you know the meaning or did you have to go to see the spirit doctor?

S: Sometimes when we had dreamed and went out we got sick or were hurt. This was when we had bad dreams.

W: Since we worship God we dream less and better. Last night I could not sleep. I was sleeping and woke up again.

HB: Do you have good dreams, too?

S: There are good dreams. Mostly I have good dreams. I dream about water, pure water, just a little water. When I was not a Christian I dreamed about lots of water and dirty water. That is a bad dream. Walking in dirty water is a bad dream. Since I worship God I do not dream such dreams anymore. I have never dreamed about this. I dreamed, as I said yesterday, I went to Mae Jo and I got sick. I got a bad headache and it made me fear that I would have to die. [See the interview Nr. 19].

S: While I was a Buddhist I dreamed that bad spirits came to me. We had to go and give sacrifices. That was the case then. Sometimes I did not know the meaning of it. As Buddhists we had to go and consult a spirit doctor. But since we worship we do not think about it. But when I got sick (as told) it gave me a lot to think about. Why did I get sick? But I think we do not sacrifice. I prayed.

21:

2014-03-18. Young couple in Plelu. He (H) comes from an Animist-Buddhist home but was brought up in a Catholic school. His wife (W) comes from a Christian home but her father is an opium smoker. She is the daughter of 51D. She has not had much Christian input.

H: I had a bad dream. I was up and downhill. I had a bad dream. Bad spirits. We will have hindrances.

HB: What evil dreams have you seen?

H: I have seen darkness. I was in the forest and it got dark.

HB: If you dream like this, what do you do?

H: You will not be well!

W: If we have bad dreams, sometimes we are not able to work. You get so tired and sometimes you get sick.

H/W: If you dream about going downhill, you will not eat. You may go out for a day's work for someone and you do not eat. Or you have to repair the car.

HB: If you were not a Christian, what would you do?

H: I do not know – if you are Buddhist you go to worship the Phra [Buddhist monk or Buddha statue].

HB: What do you do when you dream like this?

W: I do not know.

HB: Do you pray?

W: Yes, just do it like that. If I go back to the village and I go to church I am not courageous enough to tell. [That people should pray for her].

HB: Explains what they can do.

W: I cannot pray.

HB: Explains more – you have to believe more in God's Word than dreams!

HB: Do you often dream?

W: I dream a lot.

HB explains what they can do.

H: Can I be baptized?

22:

2014-03-18. The same couple in Plelu

HB: Where do dreams come from?

H: I do not know, it is like the devil does it, when it is a bad dream. If you dream about peppers, people say you will get angry at friends.

23:

2014-03-23. Pathi (P) in Toepopu, 45 years. He has been the first Christian in his village for four years now.

P: I do not like to dream. The devil comes to tempt me. When I dreamed my leg was aching. When we were not Christians yet, we had to feed the pigs. But now we do not do that anymore.

HB: Now do you still dream?

P: I hardly dream now.

HB: How do you know a dream is special?

P: When I dream I am not well. Bad dreams, cursing ('*lo ta*'), being unwell, that's it.

HB: Do you sometimes have good dreams?

P: Yes, when I dream about going uphill, it is going well.

24:

2014-04-02. Mr. Eta (E), Christian leader in Thibokhi, 48 years. No children. His wife has been ill for many months. She then went to Buddhist relatives to Pabako and did ceremonies. Later, she repented but has still not been very well – physically as well as spiritually.

HB: Do you often dream?

E: Yes, every night.

HB: What do you dream?

E: I dream about elephants and fire.

HB: Does it make you fear?

E: In the body I do not fear.

HB: But dreaming about fire is not nice, is it?

E: No, it is not nice.

HB: Dreaming about elephants, what does it mean?

E: It is a temptation. It causes cold heart and body [chills and shivering].

HB: We are going to pray that the bad dreams do not come again, would you like that?

E: I pray every morning and every evening.

HB: If you were not a Christian yet, what would you do, when you dream like this?

E: I would go and look for a spirit doctor for help, but we who worship God, we pray.

HB: explains what he does when he has had a bad dream.

E: No matter what I have dreamed, I always go out. I pray before. If I could not pray to God, I often would not dare to go out.

HB: What would you do then?

E: Just be in the house. But now we always go. Jesus has given us freedom and redemption, so I go out all the time, even if I did not have a nice dream, I still go.

25:

2014-04-03. Muene (M), headman, 38 years. Thibokhi, non-Christian. I went to see him with Ela (E) who is the housefather of the Christian hostel in the village.

HB: Have you ever dreamed?

M: What dream? Yes, I dream.

HB: Are they mainly good dreams?

M: I dreamed about having caught a big fish at least one kilo. I went to buy lottery tickets but I did not win. I bought lottery tickets for 150 Baht. Sometimes I have bought for 500 or 600 Baht. Once 670 Baht. Each month, I buy for about 2000 Baht or for over 1000 Baht. I buy each month about twice. This time I nearly got the right number.

HB: Have you ever won?

M: No, never.

[Another man who stands by says, If you have dreamed about one big fish you will not win.]

M: Another time I saw in a dream many fish in a well and I was going to catch them. I dreamed that somebody gave me money, then my car was broken and I had to pay 12-15.000 Baht. When I was eating fish after two or three days I received money. I once dreamed about a fish which was about six kilos and I killed it with a knife and then I took it and it was only one kilo. I went to buy lottery – I bought 807 but the winning number was 866. I bought many numbers. Some do win, others not.

[E – this is like a game].

HB: If you have bad dreams, what do you do?

M: If I have bad dreams – you have to stay home and wait, you do not go out. If you have good dreams, then you have to go and do things and you will receive. If you dream that you are hunting or if you dream that you carry a child and it urinates on you, it is a bad dream. If you dream about peppers, eating peppers, quarreling occurs in the family or between husband and wife.

HB: Have you ever dreamed about peppers?

M: I have dreamed about peppers often. I then quarrel with my wife. There is a kind of dream which is about the *'plü'*. If you dream that your *'k'la'* is eating with the ancestors/deceased then it is a good dream, you will eat [will be successful]. Some do eat, others do not eat.

HB: If you dream about *'plü'*, does some good come of it?

M: Yes, there are some good things. Some eat, others not.

HB: Where do dreams come from?

M: I cannot say.

HB: Do spirits come to you or does your *'k'la'* wander?

M: They do not come to you. The *'k'la'* ha'. Your own *'k'la'* is wandering.

HB: Do they go to the *'plü kau'*?

M: There was one (*'k'la'*) who went there – I dreamed that my *'k'la'* went off to the realm of the dead (*'plü kau'*). It went to a village and it was with friends and it was so nice. It was marvelous. Then I (*'k'la'*) came back, but I could not overcome a fallen tree. Then I awoke and I was like dead from morning until midday. Then I got ill for over two months and I nearly died. I was ill for two months because I had gone into the realm of the dead. There was only one tree who hindered me.

HB: When was that?

M: I had this dream after I was married for one year. My hair fell out. I had only very little hair. Now I am married for 12 years.

HB: If you dream about the *'plü kau'* and you awake, do you have to consult a spirit doctor or does it not matter?

M: It does not matter, it depends on the person. If you have bad dreams, you ask the spirit doctor to help perform ceremonies, so the bad spirit will go away so that you are redeemed of the bad spirit. The spirit doctor will *'ki cü'*.

E: The Christians will pray.

M: Once we had to do *'lä'*, a sacrifice ceremony, when I nearly died. The sacrifice you may see on the way. We used seven *'swae la'* – wooden splinter which were sooty so that you could write on, a little rice, cooked rice (the first taken from the pan) and a kernel of salt, one pepper, rice husk and some threads. All these we had to sacrifice. I had such a bad backache I could not sit. I slept day and night. My father said we had to go *'ga'* [predict, clairvoyance]. Afterwards I could get up. He prepared a sacrifice. The grandmother and the father had done everything. I was getting better. The *'ta mü qa'* [demons] have power.

E: The devil has power, only God is bigger.

M: Formerly, I did *'au qai'*. My grandparents *'au qai'*. [Explains what he did.] It was not in vain.

HB: When the (Karen) Buddhists dream, do they do the same things as the Karen did formerly?

M: Yes. When you had a bad dream you stayed at home. I once dreamed an elephant was after me. It was on a mountain. It was a nice place – I was fleeing and the elephant coming behind. Then I could flee into a cave. On the evening of that day I was not well, I was shivering and shaking. I had to (*'lä ta'*) make a sacrifice. When you dream about an elephant you have to stay in the house. You just wait. If you go out, the spirits will wait on the way and they will meet you.

E: The spirits are all over. They watch us.

HB: If the *'k'la ha'*, is it the important *'k'la'* or others?

M: The *'k'la'* go off if there is a big noise and fear. And then evil spirits will catch it. Sometimes you will get ill or even die. Once I saw a cat when I was driving in the car. The cat was behaving strangely. I thought it must be a *'ta yo'* bad spirit. I feared so much that I shook. Will this *'ta yo'* come up to me? When I came back home, nothing bad happened.

M: If you walk around does a cat sometimes follow you?

HB: I have not seen it.

M: Have you heard a cat behind you?

HB: What does it mean?

M: It is not a cat it is evil spirits!

26:

2014-04-05. Eliamo (E) Chogepuh, Christian.

E: When we dream about pepper, fire and going downhill, then the people fast and do not go out. But now we believe in God. We ask God to save us that we do not fall into difficulties. God gives us strength.

[She wants prayer for her and her family – her husband who is an OPT. OPT is a local official who is responsible for the money of government projects].

HB: What do you do when you have bad dreams?

E: I cannot do anything. We pray to God when we see problems arise. We have to pray. Sometimes I go to sleep and forget to pray. We need to pray so when the devil comes to tempt us during the night [through dreams].

HB: I explain what I do when I have a bad dream.

27:

2014-04-05. Muera (M), 65 years. Thigotha. Christian. Same as 50Phi. Visiting with housefather Ela (E).

M: Sometimes I dream about carrying (*'pü'*) a child. The child asked me to carry him.

During the day I went out and when I came home everything on me was itching. Is it the devil who wants to say something? But that is no hope. We hope in God.

HB: Do you always dream the same dream?

M: About this, always.

HB: What meaning does it have?

M: From our tradition we would have to do rituals and sacrifices. But we do not have hope in that. We hope in God.

E: Where do dreams come from?

M: I do not know. We do not like it. It comes on people, that's it. From our tradition as we have talked about '*ko o pra*' – it comes from evil spirits. Sometimes spirit doctors come and say if we were going to pay for them, they could stop it. But I do not give to them.

E: There are many who want to destroy your faith. ...

HB: We need to pray that you will dream a new dream.

28:

2014-05-14. Chilapa (Ch), from Maehatha, 65 years, longstanding Christian and evangelist. Krimuwapa (Kri) (30), evangelist, coming from Burma is married in Saswikhi (Omkoi). Dapoh (D), over 50 years, elder of Bakkha and pastor Boon Ruang (BR), Sop Lahn. Interview at the Karen center in Omkoi while we had a David Training.

HB: What do you do when you dream the old kind of dreams?

Kri I dream about raining. When I dream about the afterworld ('*plü kau*') it is raining.

Ch: Yes, it is like that. Kri: When I dream of fish my money goes away. I do not like to dream about fish. Money goes off. When I dream about my in-laws, they come to visit. Formerly I dreamed about my father.

HB: When you saw your father, were you afraid?

Kri: No, I did not fear anything.

HB: Was your father a Christian?

Kri: Yes, he was.

HB: So, this was a usual appearance?

Kri: Yes.

HB: Sometimes I hear that people dream about a deceased husband and he comes back, so people do '*ki cü*'.

Kri + Ch: Yes, yes that happens.

HB: Do people fear, they do not want it? What do you think?

Ch: Formerly I dreamed about the '*plü*' and it rained. I prayed to God about the bad dream, 'Please do not let me dream or give me better dreams.' So later I dreamed about the '*plü*', but there was no rain, but all dry. It really changed!

D: Formerly I dreamed a lot about rain, then I prayed and I did not dream about it anymore.

Appendix B 157

HB: When you dream about rain, is it a bad dream? What does it mean?

Kri: It gives us bad feelings. We are not glad when we dream about rain. We feel heavy hearted. We do not like to do things. When it rains it is not nice. Dreaming is not nice. Yet sometimes I still dream.

Ch: He dreamed about wild dogs which chased him up the tree – he cried at the wild dog. His wife heard him cry. Formerly, when you dreamed about going down a mountain that meant when you had money, you would lose money, lose your cows, buffaloes and fields. Many people would tell this when you go down a hill ... When you dream about peppers that is not nice or if you dream about fire people say you will get ill.

HB: What does it mean when you dream about an elephant?

Ch: You will have enough rice. If you dream about 3 elephants – female elephants – that meant you will have rice 3 '*pla*'. This is about female elephants.

D: I do not dream – I do not remember.

HB: That is easy.

D: If you dream about flying, you will lose hair.

HB: Have you ever dreamed?

Kri: If you want to plant peppers or tomatoes and you dream that you are going down the mountain, you will not earn any money. People will not plant it. They believe in dreams. If you dream about going up the mountain you will succeed.

Asking HB: What do you do with dreams, when you dream?

Ch: Some when they want to marry and think whether they should marry a certain girl, they say if I have good dreams, then I will marry her, if my dream is not nice I will not marry her. My brother Johapa (12J) did it that way.

HB: So he had good dreams?

Ch: Yes, he had good dreams that's why he married her. [laughter].

D: I dreamed I had wings and could fly.

Kri: Some say, Joseph in the Bible dreamed. He is an example for us. There are dreams.

HB: We can pray that God gives us dreams.

Kri: If we have good dreams, our hearts are well, if we have a bad dream, our hearts are not well.

Kri: Dreaming about fish – to which river should we go? Once we wanted to plant tomatoes well and then dreamed about '*plü*' and rain. Great rain. This kind of dream is not nice when you want to work.

HB: Dreaming about '*plü*' means what?

Ch: About people who have died – people who have already died.

HB: Is somebody going to die?

Kri: People do not die.

Ch: They have died, but they come back – they went off and become like those who have not died.

Kri: They make miracles that it is going to rain and then it is raining and destroys things. I had planted peppers and they had just been there and then I dreamed my father-in-law came to us and then he made it rain and all peppers were destroyed. I told him not to come back.

HB: What do Christians do when they dream about the *'plü'*?

Ch: Pray, that God will even give blessings through the dream.

Kri: Pray.

D: Pray.

HB: Where do dreams come from?

D: From God.

Ch: From the devil.

Kri: Yes, it can come from the devil. He can even destroy the faith.

Ch: When Joseph dreamed where did the dream come from?

HB: God gave it.

Ch: In order to understand. That he will become king.

Ch: Joseph, the husband of Mary dreamed as well. The angel told him – warned him.

HB: In the Bible I see that people who fear God do not fear in dreams but those who do not know God, fear, like Nebuchadnezzar, Pharaoh, too. They feared and did not know the meaning.

Ch: Jacob dreamed about the ladder to heaven.

HB: Explains from where dreams come.

Kri: I tell God, to have lots of dreams is not nice. It has been said: Lots of dreams – lots of illnesses. Need to go to the hospital. Pray to God to dream less.

HB: What do you think, illness comes from dreaming or you dream that you will be ill?

Ch: Dreams show what is going to happen. Hey, I have dreamed and now it has come about – that is how it happens most of the time. Some do not understand the meaning. If you dream about cucumber, it will be a boy.

D: Sometimes it really is true, they see a cucumber – a boy – and it is.

Ch: And sometimes it is a girl as seen.

D: Yes.

Ch: Those who do not worship God, dream strongly. If you dream about the mother coming to you, then the child to be born will be a girl. Sometimes the mother has not died. The mother has died and she comes in a dream, the child will be a girl.

HB: Is it because the *'k'la'* wander?

Ch: The *'k'la'* do not wander, but the mother (coming from the afterworld) wants her to be with her.

Kri: D: [Both answered]. They want the other person to be with her – it is not nice alone, in the nowhere.

Ch: If they go to God, will they come back?

HB: I explain about dreams when somebody has died – it is normal that that person appears in dreams. (*'plo so'*).

D: I need to pray that God rescues me.

HB: Rescue through prayer.

D: So that the evil does not reach me.

Ch: Pray that God does not send evil.

D: I believe that God can rescue me – I can go out and work, it is okay. If I pray about [the dream] nothing bad is going to happen.

HB: In the old tradition how did people think dreams occurred? Did they think that the *'k'la'* wandered?

Ch: In dreams? In dreams can they wander? If they wander it is different. When you get sick then the *'k'la'* wander that is when you need to do *'ki cü'*.

D: That is with those who do not worship God.

Ch: When you say the *'k'la'* wander, that is when father and mother have died. You had to do *'ki cü'* to the child.

D: In the old tradition.

Ch: Yes, when we were not worshiping God yet. If we did not do *'ki cü'* we were worried that the child will die. To dream like that is not nice at all, the child gets sick and dies.

HB: Do the parents get the child?

Ch: Yes, when mother and father will come and take the child. People fear this. But those who have died say, "Return, return we have already built a house, we have a place." They urge the child to return, it has to return – that means it has to die.

D: If we as Christians return, we will be glad. Formerly we were afraid. We did not know God. This is nice, I need not fear! Formerly, I feared, but now I do not worry much, I am glad. Because Jesus has saved us we will certainly be with him. I am glad I do not need to fear! It is great we do not need to fear, but formerly that was different. If I have a bad dream I do not need to fear because God is great, greater than anything. He has saved us. We will be with God.

HB: Have you ever dreamed about Jesus, God and the Holy Spirit?

D: Yes, once. I was revived. I saw doves. I dreamed, I saw three doves one after the other. The doves were *'rà plü'*, they could be caught. There was still a young dove. People came to worship God gladly, revival broke out. Another time I saw Jesus – went to pray – I was not free. I cried – O Lord Jesus, O Lord Jesus and then I did not see him. – I was glad.

I once went to pray and I prayed long and strongly, then I heard a big noise – when I prayed I heard a big noise, when I didn't pray I did not hear anything. I was thinking what good will come to me. What is God going to do? Whether it comes from God or not from God –you have to pray. If it is from God it will stay, if it is not from God, it will disappear.

Afterwards I did not hear anything anymore, therefore it did not come from God, but was to hinder me in prayer. I said to God, if it is true then it should stay but if not, it shall disappear.

HB: Boon Ruang, if Christians have bad dreams what do you advise?

BR: Pray – throw out the bad dream.

HB: If it comes again?

BR: Pray again. If your enemy comes to make you fear, you have to kill him all the time.

D: When we dreamed about bad things, while we did not know God well, we feared.

BR: If people say this and that, we have to look for what God's Word says. God does not destroy things, the devil destroys. If we do not listen to God's Word but listen to dreams, you have problems. When people dream of the dead they still believe. They tell it, even Christians still tell it to their children and grandchildren.

HB: Do they believe the dreams more than God's Word?

D: Yes, yes. They think the dream is bigger than God.

BR: E.g. If people want to plant tomatoes, they say when I went uphill I had a good harvest every time. If I do not dream to go uphill, I will not have any earnings – what does that mean? But if a dream comes from God, we will love to hear, it will not make us doubt.

HB: Have you ever dreamed about God?

BR: No, I have never dreamed about God.

D: If we lay our dreams in God's hand, they do not do any harm.

29:

2014-05-16. Aj. Apirak (A), Karen from KBC,[986] Chiang Mai (Interview mainly in Thai).

A: Before I started this foundation, I prayed. I dreamed and my grandfather came and he smiled at me but did not say anything. My grandfather died about 20 years ago. In my heart I wanted to serve God through this foundation [Media ministry]. The second time I dreamed, before we opened this restaurant. He said, 'Would you like to open the place here – you could do it at the old hall' [the place where they usually met when they started KBC in Thailand – about 50 meters away). I asked him whether I could open it here. He said smiling, 'Whatever

---

[986] Karen Baptist Convention

you want. If you do it, do it in a way that it will be useful.' Afterwards friends of mine came to work together for God.

HB: When did you dream?

A: Two months ago. The first dream was about one year ago. In the time between I had no dream. These dreams were a great encouragement for me to do God's work.

30:

2014-05-31. Charemo (Ch), 52 years. Pastor Boon Ruang's wife, Sop Lahn.

Ch: Our ancestors thought if somebody died you have to put a knife and hoe and rice, bananas, potatoes etc. into the grave. In the afterworld they are working as here in this world. [About old traditions when somebody died and other traditional beliefs].

HB: If you dream and you fear very much what do you do?

Ch: Our ancestors had to do some sort of ceremony. e.g. '*ki cü*'. But nowadays our children do not know how to do it. If we have bad dreams, the '*k'la*' wander. If you fear or a branch of a tree falls beside you and you are shocked, you have to go and call the '*k'la*' back.

Ch: I cannot remember much. I was 13 when we became Christians. My mother thought I would soon die. ('*ko se*' you will not live long). But God is with us. There are so many traditions. Many people fear those ceremonies. If you made a mistake when they were '*au qai*' you would die. If you were sacrificing for '*au qai*', you were not allowed to carry the meat outside the house. If you did something wrong, you had to do it again.

HB: [I tell about Pessamoh in Gebluekhi whose non-Christian husband has been appearing to her after he had died].

How can we help her?

Ch: We have to pray. The devil makes people fear.

HB: I explain a little about dreams.

Ch: Sometimes we have never thought about something, but we still can dream about it. The dreams which cause fear are caused by the devil. Sometimes we dream about things we have never seen. Some people think there is no heaven because they see people in the afterworld. Some do not believe in the kingdom of heaven. Some who did not have a nice house here see them in the afterworld and do not have a nice house there either.

Ch: Tejoamoh dreamed that my father [who had just died a few weeks before] did not have a nice house. I answered that the people who have believed in God will have a nice place to live. I do not doubt it.

Ch: Do you dream sometimes?

HB: Yes ...

Ch: If you dream that the person does not have a nice house to live in, it makes your heart sad. I think we need to trust completely in God.

HB: I explain John 14:1ff. If we believe more in dreams than in God's promises, we will see problems.

Ch: If we believe in God, we will not doubt because of dreams. If we do not really believe, we will fear a lot of things. We will worry about it.

HB: Somebody told me that when he has bad dreams, he humbles himself before God and he prays and he does not see any bad things happen.

Ch: Yes that is it. If we ask Karen about dreams they usually dream, some dream about fire which is a bad dream. If you dream about peppers, it is a bad dream. Going downhill is not good.

Ch: If you dream about fish you are glad – you will make money. I wanted to dream about my father but have not dreamed of him. I would like to see him happy. He said (before he died) he was happy and he wants his children and grandchildren to be happy. He does not want to make trouble. He did not hold on to life longer.

31:

2014-05-31. Polluphue (P), 70+ years, one of the most influential Christian in the area. Daesopa (D), 62 years, long-standing elder of Sop Lahn church and his wife Daesomo (DM), 58 years. She is the daughter of the headman who was the first believer in the area.

P: If you dream about high waters it means anger and hate. This kind of dream leads to quarrels. Non-Christians did not go out. But to the Christians it does not matter. Jesus has saved us from it.

HB: Formerly when you dreamed about this, did you fast?

P: It is the devil's working so we had to fast. If you dream that your house is destroyed, it is no good. Then you will not be well. But to Christians this does not do any harm.

HB: When you were not a Christian yet, did you sometimes dream?

P: I have never dreamed that the house will fall apart.

HB: When you were not a Christian yet did you have good dreams?

P: If I had a good dream I went hunting and I would succeed.

HB: What did you dream exactly?

P: Dreaming about a dead person, his corpse, and you go and help and then when you go hunting you will eat. Nowadays we go out and we do not eat. I do not think about dreams at all. Formerly, the devil came to tell. We believed it. Now we do not believe it anymore. If you dreamed that your gun was defective, you were going to succeed – nowadays we do not 'eat'.

HB: Where do dreams come from?

D: I do not know where they come from.

P: At night when I sleep my 'k'la' goes to Omkoi and Ban Yang Tai, while I am here. Sometimes I dreamed that I was going to fish or hunt a bird at the Maetuen river, while I am here in the house. Sometimes I dream that I am haunted and it causes fear. And when I wake up I can see nothing.

P: Do you also dream?

HB: Yes. I dream from time to time.

P: Sometimes I dream I go to Omkoi, while I am here. How this comes about, I do not understand.

D: It is the 'k'la' wandering.

P: I dreamed: People from Thichomita came down and had to cross a high river. An older woman was taken away for a short way. Three children were taken away by the high river and I went to look for them ('k'la'). The water had taken them. I went to look for them and I woke up. Formerly, we got angry. But now we pray and it is okay.

HB: Did you ever dream about the afterworld?

P: I have not dreamed of my father but I have dreamed of my mother. I have dreamed about people who have died long ago. And we went together. I do not know whether it was my 'k'la'. I just went to the afterworld.

HB: Did you fear?

P: Why fear? I did not fear.

P: When we dream about the afterworld we will eat, sometimes it is also raining. [Which is not so good].

[I tell about 28Kri]

D: Yes, if we dream about the afterworld and it is raining, things may be destroyed.

HB: When you have a bad dream, what do you do?

D: We pray.

HB: If somebody comes to you who had a bad dream and now he fears, what do you do, when he is a Christian?

P: If they worship God, we encourage him that it will be okay and we pray for him. God will save him from troubles. God does really save. I believe it.

HB: Do Christians sometimes dream about Jesus and God?

D: I do not know. Sometimes the Holy Spirit speaks to people.

HB: Did you dream this way?

D: Yes, from time to time. I went to worship in the fields/forest. When I went to sleep it was like the Holy Spirit came to me. When we worshiped God until midnight I went to sleep – not sleeping yet – I still heard the singing. The Holy Spirit came to tell me that I should wash my hands and my feet. The Holy Spirit came to me and I was so happy. I was really glad. It was like the angel coming to Mary – and she was happy. I dreamed this way once.

I went once to Ouhaetha to a revival meeting. My hand was a fist and I could not open it. I do not know the meaning. We do eat with our hands so they have to be clean. We want the Holy Spirit to be with us.

HB: Where do you think the bad dreams come from?

D: They may be the devil's temptation. We pray that God will save us. We do not stay at home. God alone can do it.

HB: When you dream that you are going down the mountain do you still go and plant tomatoes?

D: If I dream, it does not matter. If I do not earn, it does not matter. Other people do not go out. But I believe in God. So it is okay.

HB: What do Karen dream about most?

D: Dreaming often about going uphill.

HB: Did you ever dream that you will have a boy or a girl?

P: Yes. If you dream about melons – female melon which has a bit of color – male melon – you dream you will get a girl or boy respectively.

D: If you dream about water coming out of bamboo cane it will be a boy. If you dream about a well it will be a girl.

D: DM, his wife who had already 4 girls, dreamed about a gun and she had a boy.

P: She is dreaming a lot.

HB: What is she dreaming about?

DM: I am not dreaming. If you dream about the rice fields and threshing the rice and then you dream about an elephant, you will have more to eat. If you are going to plant and you dream about fishing or going up the mountains, you will get a good price for the product. If you go uphill you will not eat and if you go down you will eat – this is an experience.

[P: is amazed].

HB: So it is not certain, you may even eat when you go downhill?

DM: I went to plant tomatoes at Mahanaglo with ... and I dreamed about killing an ape and had already fried it and kept it there. Then the ape came to life and went off, the dogs were behind it, but they could not get it. The tomatoes had no price, we did not make a profit.

DM: I went to plant tomatoes. I was afraid of dreaming about buffaloes because if you dream about buffaloes the tomatoes will not be good. [From former experiences].

We wanted to plant tomatoes in the paddy fields. We prayed in the evening but at night I dreamed about stinky fish. The fish had no water, dried. We had no water, so we did not plant, otherwise we would have lost it all. The dream was a warning.

HB: If people have dreams which they fear, what do they dream?

D: If people dream that somebody or something is going to catch/hold them. Or if someone is coming to beat them or to kill them.

HB: Have you ever dreamed a dream that made you afraid?

D: Yes, sometimes.

DM: Dreams about somebody haunting you and you cannot escape – they nearly catch you. Even when waking up you are still afraid. I dreamed once something was after me and nearly got me and I really feared. It nearly got me and I was afraid.

HB: What do you do after such a dream?

DM: I did not do anything.

D: We know one thing, we pray. God saves people.

HB: Did you ever pray that you would have a good dream?

D: I pray that I will have no bad dreams at night. When I have prayed I sleep. If I dream a lot sometimes problems arise.

D: Formerly, when we had bad dreams, we did not go out.

HB: When you have good dreams, do you go out in strength?

P: In former days people dreamed and it came about. They believed but now we do not believe in dreams. We believe that God is helping us. God saves us, yes He saves us.

P: Nowadays the Holy Spirit talks to people in dreams. When you dreamed about a storm coming, you had to be careful not to quarrel. If you believe in God, it does not do any harm.

While transcribing this section, Mr. Wirot said, „If we dream about a long road we will live long – people say."

32:

2014-05-31. Pastor Boon Ruang (BR), Sop Lahn. Same as 28BR and 67BR.

BR: My father dreamed that he was crossing the river only half way and he thought he was going to die. That was about 4 years ago. I encouraged him that our life is in God's hand. And until today he is alive. I told him he does not need to believe this dream.

Some people see a plane coming to catch them. After two or three days, some people who have already been sick, sometimes dream like that and they die. Afterwards the dream is told to people and they believe it.

HB: Do people tell the dream beforehand or after something has happened?

BR: Mostly people tell afterwards when they have experienced it.

HB: Do you think dreams cause sickness or are dreams a warning that the sickness will occur?

BR: Mostly people think that the dream causes the sickness. They see it and it comes true. It is like a warning.

BR: Often people see beforehand and then it happens. After you have dreamed, it happens.

HB: Have you dreamed this way?

BR: No, I have not dreamed this way.

HB: Have you seen difficulties arise which were caused by dreams?

BR: I saw it twice. I dreamed I saw two pans – one in the upper village and one in the lower part of the village. Then the Seventh Day Adventist came to Mae Lan and we got two churches.

About Thigekhi and Maeleakhi – I saw a tree and many birds came to sit. I went to shoot birds but I had no time to shoot because a buffalo came running after me. I tried to shoot birds but the buffalo was chasing me and nearly overran me. And then it happened. [At that time four churches left ACT and joined KBC].

HB: When you dreamed this what did you think?

BR: I was not sure about the meaning. The buffalo may have been the devil. I saw the fruit of the tree which I think are the churches. Maybe there will be less? The birds came to eat the fruit. I went to shoot the birds but then the buffalo came after me. I wanted to shoot twice or three times but the buffalo came after me. I know two meanings. About God – will there be less churches? Then the birds flew away – many flew away. This made me think many churches will leave us. If buffaloes or elephants are after people, it means spirits are at work. They come to hinder. That is what Karen think.

HB: Do you think the problems in Maeleakhi have something to do with dreaming?

BR: Yes. It has. Yes, it makes me think.

HB: Can I go up to Maeleakhi and ask?

BR: Of course, you can ask.

The following happened in Sop Lahn: Somebody dreamed that they went to work and the way was blocked. And then a person got ill and this person was very unhappy. And she went to ask a spirit doctor.

HB: Which doctor?

BR: A spirit doctor in Burma, one who came over here.

HB: Was he a Christian?

BR: No, he wasn't. Formerly, he was at Suvapa's house. Then Suvapa ordered him to leave the village. He came to destroy Christians. The spirit doctor said and predicted (*'ga ta'*) the one who caused the illness had three children and lived in the west. They thought it must be Charemoh [his wife]. But then the family thought that because Charemoh is a Christian she has not done it by herself, but she may have asked somebody else to curse them. And then the man died. And then his wife went to see the spirit doctor. And he said, the spirits (*'ta mü qa'*) said nobody has caused his death, he just died by himself.

HB: The Christians still go and ask?

Appendix B

BR: Yes, some still do. Some go to ask the spirit doctor if they have not succeeded in their work. If illness is occurring through dreams, it is a big temptation.

HB: What do you do in these cases?

BR: We need to talk together and pray with people. Some have worshipped God for a long time and still go to the spirit doctor.

HB: What should we do?

We need to talk together. We have to teach them. I have taught them several times and they still go. Some believe in dreams, they believe it. If they get ill, sometimes they doubt. They think that person has done it – he has caused the illness. That is difficult. The devil lies to them. In the village (Sop Lahn) there are still many who believe it. There was one who had cancer – he went to the hospital and had an operation. Then went to the spirit doctor to ask why he had this illness. The spirit doctor said it was a certain person – people know but they did not do anything.

HB: Do people still think that Charemo did something wrong?

BR: Yes. They still think it. But I went to talk with them. You have to talk to people. If you do not go to talk, they think more and get angry.

33:

2014-06-01. Pasopa (P), 57 years, Sop Lahn. Brother-in-law of Boon Ruang.

P: If you are about to look for food and you have dreamed that you killed something or somebody – if you go and look for food, you will make money, you will succeed. If you dream that people give you food or money and then you go to look for it, you will eat. If you dream a bee has stung you that is not good. You will get sick. If you dream that a tiger or a bear or a dog bites you that is a bad dream. This causes illness. This is the devil's power to bite. If a tiger or a bear is going to bite you and you can beat them off or kill them, it does no harm. But if you cannot beat him off or kill him then you have to fear. This is the devil's power. You have to fear. If you dream about going down the mountain, that is bad or your car cannot make it up the mountain but slips back, that is not good – you will have problems. You will not succeed – you will not have the strength.

HB: If you want to plant tomatoes and you dream like that?

P: O, I will not plant – I will never earn money.

HB: If you see a dead person, is that a good dream?

P: No, you will not succeed. If I dream I killed a deer, I will not succeed in hunting.

HB: If you dream about a dead person will you succeed?

P: I went out with Dipapa – I dreamed an elephant bite me – O, we will not succeed, I told him.

HB: Where do dreams come from?

P: I do not know. What do you think?

HB: When people are not Christians what do they think?

P: O, if they have bad dreams they will fast. They will fast. As Christians we pray that God will save us. If our ancestors had bad dreams they did not go out to work.

HB: Do they think the *'k'la'* goes out?

P: Yes, it is as you say, the *'k'la'* go out. You may encounter problems. The devil can do things. Our ancestors stayed at home. If a cat or dog bites you that means the devil has his ways – it is the *'tayo'*, evil spirits. If you can overcome the cat or the dog or kill them, it does no harm.

HB: Do you remember a nice dream?

P: Whatever I dream I give it into the hands of God. I pray. I do not doubt. It is okay. God is with us. If I have a bad dream before I go and plant – that is not good. The plants will die or be destroyed. To plant in those circumstances is no good.

P: Formerly, from Penouekhi a man – Gedalaepa – he died. They had a car in Penouekhi. He dreamed before. He dreamed about 'flying'. He went by car and the car overturned and he died under it. If he had not gone, nothing would have happened to him, but he went. He dreamed and told me he flew. The car went so quickly and it overturned like flying.

HB: Do problems arise among the Karen through dreaming?

P: Dream and you go out and you may have problems. You may get sick.

HB: Did you ever dream about God, Jesus Christ or the Holy Spirit?

P: I have never dreamed about it. Did you ever dream?

HB: Yes, I dreamed once – maybe it was more of a vision – I sat on the laps of Jesus.

P: I sometimes dream about worshiping God. Singing and worshiping.

HB: Did you ever see problems arise through dreams? Or did you ever get help through a dream?

P: I cannot see any.

HB: Those who are worshiping God and those who do not – is there any difference in dreams?

P: The dreams are the same but if you do not worship God, you stay at home. But Christians do not fear, they pray. If we dream about spirits, we do not fast [we go out]. We do not respect them. We believe in God. We give them into the hands of God. If we have a bad dream, God will save us. We do not need to doubt.

HB: When your children were not yet born did you ever dream that it would be a girl or a boy?

P: Yes, I dreamed. If you dream about a female cucumber it will be a girl. If you dream about a male cucumber it will be a boy.

34:

2014-06-01. Ratanaphopa (R), 43 years. From Burma, but has lived in Sop Lahn for over 10 years. Interview in BR's house.

HB: Have you ever dreamed?

R: I dream a lot. Sometimes I remember, sometimes I do not remember. I dreamed I went to wash myself at the river and when I came back my child had a cold and was unwell. If I dream like this, it does not matter. If I dream, I pray and God will answer. This is better than before. Sometimes I dream things and I do not know the meaning.

HB: If you want to know the meaning, who will you ask?

R: I don't know. I do not ask anybody.

HB: Do you have good dreams from time to time?

R: Yes, I have. A storm from heaven came to earth. I do not know the meaning. I dreamed I was talking to the king, but I did not see him. That year I planted tomatoes and I thought, if I talked to the king, surely I will sell the tomatoes for a good price. But then they were not bought [or only for a very low price]. I do not understand the meaning. Dreams may have meaning, but I do not understand it.

HB: What do you think, how do dreams occur?

R: From time to time it is dreamed that fire is in the house – that is a bad dream. Our ancestors said you will have problems. Some say if you dream about fire, it is about God. I do not know for certain.

HB: Do you remember a dream which was very bad?

R: Yes, I do. Dreaming about '*pa te qa*' [a certain spirit]. I saw it and it ran after me. I feared it but I could not escape. I tried to overcome it but could not overcome it. After dreaming like this I felt very tired.

HB: How did the spirit look?

R: In the dream I cannot tell. It was just that I really feared it. It is more like a dog going to bite. Dreaming about wanting to escape but not being able to escape. I was really tired afterwards.

HB: In the morning when you were tired, what did you do?

R: It was still at night and I started to pray and then I slept very well! It did not do anything because God saved me. If I think about it, it was a temptation to fear. If I am thinking of having seen a ghost – just pray and it is okay. Children dream as well. But they cannot tell for sure. At night they cry, and if I ask them they cannot tell. One dreamed the sun went up but I do not know the meaning.

HB: What did your parents say – where do dreams come from?

R: I did not ask them.

HB: When your children were not yet born did you dream that they would be a boy or a girl?

R: I dreamed about cucumber and it was a boy. I dreamed that my wife went to a field and saw a lot of cucumbers – she was not pregnant at that time. Small and big cucumbers, some belonged to other people, these I did not take, but those which did not belong to anybody, I ate. I took a cucumber which was bent. After the child was born – the child was not very healthy. It was a boy and he was often sick. It was a bent cucumber. I dreamed that I was going to cook a turtle. I went to look for turtles and I saw many. I caught some and put them into my clothes and some I put into the bag. I gave some to other people to eat. Our old people said when you dream about turtles it will be a girl. They said if you dream about beans it will be a boy. Dreaming about bananas it will be a boy. I had this kind of experience.

HB: Do you like to dream?

R: No, I do not like to dream. I do not want it. There is no hope in dreams. Sometimes I really sleep very deeply, that is nice. But when I dream a lot I have not slept enough, I am tired.

HB: Did you ever dream about God, Jesus, or the Holy Spirit?

R: About Jesus I have never dreamed. I have dreamed about old stories like about the orphans. I have dreamed like a second dream – like the *'k'la'* dreaming. One is the body dreaming, the second is the *'k'la'* dreaming. I do not understand. [Double dream].

HB: Do you think the *'k'la'* wander while you dream?

R: No.

HB: Have you ever dreamed about the *'plü kau'*?

R: No. I have dreamed that I went up the sky in the wind and the clouds. But I have not seen an angel yet.

35:

2014-06-24. Talk with Nebluethupa (N), 37 years, in the car to Omkoi. He is the son-in-law of grandfather S who was accused of *'lo ta'*. Because of it, he and his family were thrown out of their village. After I had got the information of 12J, I wanted to know his view.

N: One man (Pusopa) was an enemy of my father-in-law. Because he had bad thoughts he had bad dreams. It's *'plo so'*.[987] Who knows what he really dreamed? He wanted to destroy my father-in-law. But in the meantime he has died himself.

N: Regarding cremation I think it is not right that Christians are cremated that is why my father-in-law was against it.

HB Comment: Usually Karen bury people. For those who are in the old beliefs they want to see whether the person who died was cursed to death that is why they wanted the person to be cremated. If the belly is full of meat that means the person was cursed. When Somuphue did not want that person to be cremated

---

[987] Dream about things you were doing or thinking during the day

he drew suspicion on himself – those who accused him of sorcery thought that he wants to cover up his evil deeds.

36:

2014-06-03. Luwa (L), 60+ years. Mor Kler Kee. Non-Christian.

L: Before my wife died, I dreamed that my wife entrusted the children to me and she went off. [Mr. Somu who comes from this village, explains: His wife had cancer and after he had dreamed, his wife died two or three days later].

37:

2014-06-03. Mueklapa (M), 50 years. Father of Somu. Mo Kler Kee. First Christian family in the village, not many years yet.

M: I dreamed that my son carried salt to our house, we had no salt anymore. [He had dreamed this the night before we came up. Somu gave a good meaning to it – light, God's Word].

HB: When you were not yet a Christian what did you dream?

M: I dreamed about going up a mountain or going down a mountain. Going down the mountain ['*lo'hü*' = loss!] We have to buy lots of things, and we are not well. Going up the mountain: It is easier to find food and money. We are happier in the family.

HB: Did you sometimes fast when you had a bad dream?

M: Yes. For example: I dreamed that a dog bit me, so I would not go out. Or when I dreamed about darkness, I was not going out. We do not see the way. Formerly, people said if you dream that you return to your home and see all your family that is a good dream. But if you dream that people, your '*wi k'la*', [spirit '*k'la*'] go off each one his own way it is a bad dream. I have dreamed that somebody stood up and they came.

HB: Did you dream about this?

M: Yes. I have dreamed about him [his son] to stand up and he came home. And it happened like that. If I dream about him to sit, that means he does not come back yet. When I was going to marry – but not married yet – I dreamed I went up a hill but I did not reach the top. I was rich and had a lot of buffaloes. Many envied me and then I lost one after the other. After I became a Christian my oldest daughter dreamed that people led me to the mountain. God has blessed me. A teacher gave me a plough to do the fields. Somebody said he had dreamed about buying a car and when it went uphill, it slipped backwards but many people came to help and they got it up the mountain.

38:

2014-06-03. Pecho (P) – non-Christian. Luwa (L), non-Christian. Mueklapa (M), father of Somu, same as 37M. Mueklapa's father was a spirit priest and Mueklamo (MM), mother of Somu – her father was the spirit priest and founder of Mo Kler

Khee village. She has eight siblings they are still seven. She had 13 children, seven survived. In their house.

P: If I do not get to the other side it means I will not be successful. But if I get there, I can do anything. If I swim and do not reach the other side, it is a bad dream. If I dream that I can reach the other side, I will weed the field easily. If I do not reach it, there will always be weeds to cut and I will not finish. I will not be well and therefore I will not succeed. I want to do it, but I will not be able to do it.

HB: Do you need to '*ki cü*'?

P: Yes, we have to do this, too.

HB: Do you sometimes dream about your children [who live among the Thai]?

P: Yes. If I see them, I am happy. Sometimes I dream they are not well and when I phone them they are not well.

L: I dreamed my child went up the hill, went up but did not go up to the top. I think it was a good dream.

HB: Have you had very bad dreams?

P: When you go uphill but do not succeed or when you have to walk in the dark. If I see a woman, old person or a dog which is biting people – it is no good to go out. If we go we will come back sick. If a pig or dog bites a person, we get sick, shivering ('*senjarö*'). If I dream about an elephant which is haunting us and we do not get away, but the elephant does not harm us. It causes us to fear.

L: I dreamed about a snake and I cut it up. Usually I am afraid of snakes but not in this dream. If you dream about a big snake, that means you will get old, but if it is cut up, you have to know what it means. People do not interpret it.

HB: Where do dreams come from?

P: If we dream about a snake that is cut up, you do not get very old, but if you dream about a big snake, you will get very old.

HB: Do you dream about '*k'la' ha*'?

L: Yes. If they wander into the thick forest – then I am not really healthy.

P: If you dream about '*k'la'* ha' and you do not see your children and grandchildren we have to call the soul ('*k'la'*) back. 'yo g'la' – call back the soul.

HB: Why do the '*k'la'* not come back?

P: It is because bad spirits have caught it.

HB: What do you do then?

P: Call them back. They take '*me ko*' [cooked rice nobody has eaten from yet], put it into a bamboo thing and call the '*k'la'* back with a '*no po gra:*' – a bamboostick which is cut open at the front and has some holes near the handle. They call the '*k'la'* back with it. [There are other forms of calling the '*k'la'* back – if it is a big one – that somebody is about to die, it is different]. There are so many things in our traditional ways we cannot tell everything.

HB: Have you seen the afterworld in dreams?

P: Sometimes we dream about the '*plü kau*', we go and can see it but do not go to it. Sometimes we go and cannot see the way anymore and we return. If someone who is ill dreams that he has gone to the '*plü kau*', he is going to die.

[P to Somu: Your grandfather could do things – we do not know all.]

When it is harvest time and we dream about a female elephant and a baby elephant it is a very good dream. If we dream about a male elephant it is not good, we will not have enough rice. There are two different dreams. If we see bees coming to the house, then the rice soul ('*k'la*' of the rice) is coming into the house. It is a good dream.

M: If we see an elephant with a baby elephant, it is good. If it is an elephant with tusks, it is not very good – the rice granary will not be full.

HB: Do trees have '*k'la*'?

M: Yes, they have.

HB: How many '*k'la*' do people have?

P: Many.

L: 7.

P: 7. If we had only one, we would soon die. I will be reborn – [talk about that the '*k'la*' will be born again].

M: I dreamed the child will be born [again] and then it was born.

MM: A child had a special sign on the ear and I dreamed the child will be born again and then I got pregnant and the child had the same sign. I dreamed my father came to me and asked me to go with him. I nearly died and they did a ceremony to cut me off from my father [not a Christian then]. He had come twice. And since I have become a Christian he came again and asked me to go with him but God did not give me to him. I have just recently dreamed this again and then I got very sick! [She was just recovering when we were there].

HB: If you dream about '*plü kau*', does it rain?

M: Yes, this happens. I dream a lot about the '*plü kau*'. There are two kinds of dreams about the '*plü kau*'. One is about hatred. If we dream about the '*plü kau*' a lot, bad things are going to happen. When hatred reached me I lost a buffalo – somebody stole it. I got angry and I was worrying a lot. I need to buy another. Dreams about peppers and '*plü kau*' is about the same. Quarrelling within the family will occur. You have to be careful. You have to know yourself ('*to sa*'). Fighting in the family will occur.

M: If you dream about a broad place in the river, it is a good dream – it is good to plant and you will earn well. Dreams about water coming from the tap – the child will be a boy. If you dream about a river, it will be a girl.

MM: I dreamed a lot and I lost six children.

HB: What did you dream?

MM: I dreamed the child comes back – I got pregnant. Afterwards, when the child was here, I dreamed about fire and the child died again – usually between one and three years later.

M: I do not remember all dreams.

MM: Dreams about fire mean sickness will come. Our daughter, the younger sister of Somu, dreamed about fire and this caused illness. [Their new born child has a cleft palate]. And then I, my daughter and my husband got sick. [While we were there, they were just recovering from it – not really well yet].

HB: Did you ever pray that God will give you a good dream?

MM: No.

[I tell them about dreams in the Bible – encourage them to pray for good dreams].

39:

2014-06-03. Chaemu (Ch) (Pakuepa), 34 years, Mo Kler Kee, Buddhist/Animist, in Mueklapa's (M) house. Formerly he lived in Poblakhi where many Catholics live and where there is a Catholic school.

HB: Do you sometimes have a special dream?

Ch: Yes.

HB: Do you sometimes have bad dreams? What do you do?

Then I have to pray in front of the Buddha shelf. I call '*Ywa*' – the heavenlies – and worship Buddha.

HB: Do you dream and fear sometimes?

Ch: I have dreamed that '*pa te qa*' [not a very big spirit which is not feared too much – '*ta mü qa*' are feared much more] was after me. 'Pa te qa' caught me and I was hitting my wife when I slept. I feared so much I did not go out on that day. My nephew was going to marry. At night I dreamed I was going to marry [which is not a good dream] and in the evening I was not well, I had to vomit. After dreaming this dream I got sick.

HB: Did you dare to tell your wife?

Ch: Yes, I dared to tell her. I drank a little opium and I got better.

HB: What do you do when you have a very bad dream?

Ch: You have to stay home. Christians pray but we as Buddhist do '*yo hpe*' [before leaving the house, stomp the foot in the ashes and the '*pa te qa*' spirit will not see you]. I do not do it this way, I pray in front of the Buddha shelf.

M: There are other dreams when we are going to look for food or hunting. If you dream that you have killed a person, you will find food e.g. a deer while hunting. If you dream that you have killed a pig or a deer that is not a good dream.

HB: If you dream that somebody has cursed someone else, what do you do?

Ch: If you dream that somebody has cursed you, it means that that person has blessed you!

[Somu confirms the meaning.]

HB: Do you like to dream?

Ch: Whether you like it or not I dream all the time.

HB: What do you dream, more good or bad dreams?

Ch: I have all kinds of dreams. I dreamed my *'k'la'* went to Bangkok. He slept in the house.

HB: Did you go often?

Ch: Just once.

HB: How long?

Ch: Just for one night. (You can speak Karen well).

40:

2014-06-03. Somu's father Mueklapa (M).

M tells: I dreamed about an uncle in Mokokhi who killed two pigs. Not long after, two of his children died. These two children were already married. Lakuepa and Gloesomo were the persons who died. Dreamed for another person – Two kinds of dream: If you dream of killing a pig or a deer, that is not good, but if you dream about eating fruit, that is a good dream. If you dream about melons or other fruit, you will have a child.

If you dream about fish, you will make money.

M cites a *'hta'* (poem): "Dreaming about killing a bear, grandfather remembers a corpse." [That means that somebody has to die, but he does not know who]. To dream about a bear is not a good dream. There are dreams where you go to eat (be successful) or those where you do not eat. If you dream about something big it is not good but if you dream about smaller things, like fish, it is good.

If you dream about planes, like a plane landing in Mokokhi, that means a person has to die in the village.

Somu: They dreamed about planes without having ever known or seen planes.

M: If you dream about a dried tree [a tree that has died] which is broken, that means an old person has to die. An old person is like a dried tree.

When I was still single I dreamed – when my mother was ill – the sun was blinding me and in the evening my mother died. Dreaming about the moon coming up is a bad dream.

[When their six children died, they thought they had sinned against the spirits (*'gö ma qai'*)].

41:

2014-06-03. Noh Glore (NG), 20 years, two children. Mo Kler Kee. Somu's younger sister. Husband on opium. Young Christian.

NG: In a dream, a person came to tell me this house will not be established, a girl will not get up in this house. But if it were a boy it does not matter, but a girl cannot get up.

[Noh Glore has a two month-old girl with a cleft palate and she has no milk for the child, but had fed her firstborn son for a year.]

HB: Where did this voice come from?

NG: It was not a spirit or a deceased person. It just spoke like a person and I did not fear when it spoke. I really dreamed like this – I did not see and I did not fear. I just pray that the Lord will help me and heal my daughter.

HB: It is important not to receive this dream. It is like a curse.

42:

2014-06-03. Dipamo (Mo) and Dipapa (Pa), 45 years. Non-Christians. Mo Kler Kee, 4 children, 3 girls and one boy who are not yet married. Interview took place on their porch in the evening. Somu accompanied me.

HB: Have you ever dreamed? [Explaining the reason]

Mo: Sometimes I dream about a warning. I dream about cows and money. I have dreamed about fire which caused sickness. I got ill.

Mo: Have you ever dreamed?

HB: Yes, about a dog who came to bite me, but I could keep it away.

Mo: I dream (*'plo so'*) about things which happened during the day.

Pa: Sometimes I dream about going up the mountain or going down the mountain.

Mo: Dreaming about the *'plü'* (dead people) which causes hatred (*'ta sa he'*) in the body. Dreaming (*'plo so'*) about looking for 'choemiti' [an edible root].

HB: What is the best dream you ever had?

Mo: Yes, I have. I dreamed that a single girl came to visit. Then I got money. If I dream about doing mountain rice fields and the rice looks good, then I am healthy. If I dream about a single girl, I get money. If I dream about going to wash myself – that means I will be healthy.

HB: If you were going to plant something and you have bad dreams at night, do you go and do it?

Mo: I will not go. If I have bad dreams, I will not go out.

HB: If you have a good dream, who gives the dream?

Pa: I do not know.

HB: Have you any thoughts about it?

Pa: I do not know. I want to have a good dream.

HB: Do the *'k'la'* wander sometimes?

Mo: When the *'k'la'* wander you can see many things.

Somu: When your *'k'la'* wander what do you mostly meet?

Mo: See the work. What do you do about dreams?

HB answers about what he does.

Pa: If we dream, we have to *'yo hpe'* before we go out. [*'yo hpe'* is to stamp a foot into the ashes at the cooking place].

[Somu explains what Christians do].

HB: When you dream have you ever seen the afterworld?

Mo: I have seen. Sometimes I dream about it but I did not know anybody I met. I just wandered. I sleep and the 'k'la' wander while I am dreaming.

Mo: If I could I would not like to dream at all. If I wake up after a dream it makes me think. If I dream a lot it gives me a lot to think about (worry).

HB: Have you ever dreamed about demons?

Mo: If I wake up after a bad dream, I fear and I do not go out to work. I am worrying, will the spirits do something bad?

HB: What is the dream you most fear?

Mo: I do not fear anything! It is the father and the children who do not go out. I dreamed that an elephant was running after me – in the morning I still went out to work. I go out – no problem. If you do not believe it, you can go out. If you are strong and do not fear, you can go. If I dream a big story, I sometimes do not go out.

Pa: If you dream about a deceased person who was happy and working well, it is a good dream. If you dream about a deceased person who was lazy, it is a bad dream. You will not succeed. Each person is different.

Mo: I have dreamed that the spirit caught me [meaning her 'k'la'] and I was crying out at night.

43:

2014-06-03. Buka (B) and Nouda (N) Mo Kler Kee. Inteview during late evening with candle light in the house of Buka. Nouda, from the same village, was visiting. Non-Christians.

HB: Do you have good dreams?

B: Sometimes I have good dreams.

N: I dreamed I went to Chroglo [river] and the water was flowing upwards! I saw my boy swimming in it and I kept the hands of my son. Then I woke up – that was good.

B explains: If we hold each other's hand, there will be no fighting. If you dream about going out together but each goes his own way that is not a good sign. If you dream about meeting each other and holding each other's hand, it is a good dream. You can work together. If you go together and then depart from each other, you cannot work well together.

B: I dreamed I went to a different village [in the same political entity] and when I reached the village I saw people go out in different ways. So we have no headman in our political entity of four villages. If you dream about light, or going to have a bath in clean water or going uphill that these are good dreams. If you go on the way and you see a light that is a good dream. If you dream about darkness, it is a bad dream.

B: I dreamed I went out and I came back but not into my house. This was not a good dream – I did not go out.

HB: Have you ever had a nice dream?

B: If you dream about light or if you dream you go out and come back to the house, it is a good dream.

HB: What is your best dream?

B: Going into the light or coming back home. Then I will be healthy.

HB: It is as the Bible says – go in the light – we will love our neighbors, etc

B: My son worships God and I am happy with it.

B: Pittiphue[988] is my uncle.

HB: What is your name

B: Buka. Maelotha (Sop Lahn) was the first place to worship in the area.

Somu: If you dream, where do your 'k'la' go?

B: I dreamed they did not go far. I dreamed I went to Lewa village [where his son is married] many nights. If you eat together and people use your name well, you will dream about it.

HB: Has dreaming sometimes helped you?

B: Yes, sometimes. If I dream a very happy dream, that I get a car – it will be a disappointment. I dreamed about getting a car – I was so happy. But when I woke up, I did not have one.

Somu: Have you seen dreams come true?

B: I dreamed about rice and saw a female elephant we had enough to eat. The spirit of the rice means the female elephant. If you dream about fish, you will get money. If you dream about honey or about wax, you will get a cold. It is not good.

HB: Have you ever dreamed about the afterworld?

B: I have dreamed about my parents but not about the afterworld. I have seen my father and I got homesick.

HB: When you saw him did it cause any problem?

B: Yes, we were quarreling in the family.

B: If I dream about my father, I cannot do anything good afterwards. If I dream about my father, I have to be very careful, otherwise I will have quarrels. ['to sa' to watch your heart]. After I dreamed about my father I went into the forest and lit a little fire and it became a big fire. But if you dream about the dead, sometimes they are good dreams. I dreamed about a dead person and the next time I had to bring rice from the field into the barn – I really got a lot of rice. The barn was full. If I dream about a dead person I am going to succeed. But if I see my father, we will have fights.

HB: When you have a bad dream what do you do?

---

[988] A longstanding Christian from Sop Lahn.

B: I wash my hair with *'bu chi sa'* [which is dried and then put seven beans into the water and boil it. Thai "sompoi" – fruit of the tree outside our house in CNX which works like a soap]. If you do this you will dream less! You will be happy.

HB: Have you ever dreamed about a cat?

B: To dream about a cat is no good. I have not dreamed about. I have dreamed once about a cat. Then *'tö rä'* came up. [*'tö rä'* is kind of a smaller, bad spirit]. Then my legs were hurting. I went to another village to find rice and met a spirit doctor. He asked for 30 Baht and I had to sleep a night there. He blew (*'ma hti uu'*) into the water. It got better.

B: What do you do when you dream?

HB: Pray.

HB: Has dreaming ever helped you to make a decision?

B: Yes. If we are going to do fields: If we have good dreams we go and do it – if we have a bad dream we are not going to do it. I dreamed about a big tree falling on the field and destroying a termite hill. I went to do that field and then two of my younger siblings died. Then I remembered the dream. Two of them died at the same time. When I do fields and I dream about fish or water, this is the best – the rice will be very good.

44:

2014-06-04. Tejoa (T), 35 years, Christian from a Christian family, Sop Lahn. Working with the government in the regional Malaria program.

T: If you dream about fire, you will have a "hot" heart which leads to quarrels. If you dream about water, it is a good dream – you will have a cool heart. You get along well. If you dream very nicely about a person, that is not a good omen. You will have quarrels with that person. You have to be careful. You have to find a way to solve the problem. But dreams are not always 100% true but may give you a warning.

HB: What do you think – where do dreams come from?

T: If we think a lot about something, we may dream about it (*'mimo plo so'*). If we dream about something we have never thought about, it is different. It is a real dream. If I dream about an airplane coming – I was thinking about my cows – then I saw the airplanes coming and I thought, are problems coming? It causes me to fear when the planes come to kill.

HB: Did you watch TV?

T: No. And in the end that dream did not cause any troubles.

T: In a dream it was raining so much – and the water in the rivers came very high – and I had never dreamed about this before. And I was under the water, the water went over me. It was really raining so much. And I was thinking, will this cause problems for me? That night it rained for one or two days. But if this were to cause problems for me, I knew I would escape because in the dream I could escape from the waters up to the mountain. The dream means, if I encounter difficulties today, there will be a way out. It was a great encouragement. Some people think when a child is ill we cannot go to the hospital because we have no money, nothing. But there may be a way they may still have a cow or a pig to sell.

HB: Sometimes we can see problems arise through dreams. [Explaining why I want to know about dreams].

T: For those who are not yet Christians, dreams are most important. They think what they should do. They may seek a spirit doctor. There are also some Christians who, if they dream, they think about and believe it because a dream may have deep meaning.

T tells about a man Chopä in the village of Te Go Ka. He was a Buddhist. Then he got ill and nobody could help. He became a Christian. The hospital may have been able to heal him but he did not want go. After two years he died. He could also dream about it as well as looking at bones [for clairvoyance].

45:

2014-06-04. Sachadapa (S), Spirit priest, 70 years, 7 sons and 2 daughters. Gloethipa (G), 50+ years, Thigotha. He has become a Christian very recently, only 4 months before this interview. (See also 55-56S+G). Taking the interview together with Somu.

S: If you dream about taking milk from somebody [a woman], it means that '*na hti*' a certain water spirit comes to people. If you do not have good dreams, you have to be attentive. If you go out you may get ill. If you dream about bananas, it is a bad dream, you will get sick. [In Mo Kler Kee they said you will have a boy.] If you dream about a fire outside as we do for grilling, it is not good at all. If you dream about eating with a dead person ('*plü*'), it is a bad dream. If you have cut your fields and you dream about '*plü*' the fire will burn the fields very well.

G: If you dream about the '*plü*', there are some good dreams and some bad dreams. If I dream about a friend who has died, I always get sick.

S cites a '*hta*': "If you dream about the '*k'la*' going to the afterworld your own body will not be well."

Somu: If you dream does it have meaning most of the time?

S: Yes, if you see someone's '*k'la*'.

Somu: Do you see the body?

S: No, I only see the '*k'la*'.

HB: How many '*k'la*' has a person got?

S: Seven!

HB: Do you know all seven?

S: If you dream about being so happy ['*k'la ha*' – '*k'la*' have a great feast] your body will not be well. If you dream and it predicts something good, you go out to work. If it predicts something bad, you will stay at home.

[Somu: Because he is a Spirit doctor, he knows].

HB: Do you often dream good dreams?

S/G: The bad dreams occur more often. The good dreams are less. If the *'k'la'* are in the afterworld – you are not well.

HB: If you dream about an elephant, what meaning does it have?

S: If you dream about an elephant, you have to make a ceremony (*'ta lä cho'*) that is after you have dreamed and something happened.

[*'ta lä'* = sacrifice with candles and peppers].

If you see an elephant – its *'k'la'* is a demon.

Somu: If you dream about the elephant during the harvest season...

S: That is good, if it is a female elephant. If it is a male elephant the rice is no good.

G: If you dream about a female elephant, you get lots of rice.

HB: Do you remember having a bad dream and then fasting – have you done that?

S: If you dream at night that somebody gives you meat, it is a bad dream. If you go out people will curse (*'lo ta'*) you.

HB: If you see somebody who gives the meat, does this create problems?

S/G: Yes for sure.

Somu: Is that person sinning?

S: If someone hates another person and curses him. When the person who is cursed and not well – his father goes to the spirit priest to ask for help and the spirit priest helps him, then the person who cursed the other person is not happy with the spirit priest who helped. The spirit priest fears that person.

HB: Do you like to dream?

S/G: How can we like dreams?

S: If I do not dream at night I go wherever I want, but when I dream it is different.

G: If you dream about giving pork to somebody, it is a bad dream. You have to *'yo hpe ta'*. [stamp with your toes into the ashes of the cooking place – it makes the spirit blind to your feet – therefore you can go out – this comes from a long tradition of the Karen people] and then I pray that no illness will come to me and no spirits will see me.

HB: How many children?

S: Seven sons and two daughters, the oldest name is Sachada.

G: Five children, people call me Gloethipa.

HB: When you were married but you did not have children yet, did you dream?

S: Yes.

HB: What did you dream?

S: Just a short dream. I dreamed about melons and cucumbers and then we had a child.

G: If you dream about going to get water at the bamboo water channel, it will be a boy. If you get water at the *'hti gem lö'* (well), it will be a girl. If you dream about going to get water in a well that is dry, it is a bad dream. If you then have a child, it will not survive. If you dream about going to get water in clean water where there is sand, it is a good dream, the child will be healthy.

HB: If you dream about a woman what meaning does it have?

G: If you dream about a melon, it will be a girl. If you dream about going over a bridge, it will be a boy. If you dream about going through the water, it will be a girl.

HB: If you dream, do you usually know the meaning?

S: Sometimes I know, sometimes I do not know. Sometimes there is no truth in it. If you dream about going to shoot an animal, it is not good. You will not shoot anything. I dreamed I was going to hunt a deer and then I went and I got a deer. If you dream like this and it happens then it is good. If you dream this but it does not happen, then it is a bad dream.

HB: Do you remember a very bad dream which you feared?

S/G: There are some.

G: I dreamed about buffaloes running after me and I climbed up a tree but I could not climb up. I had my legs tucked up, when I dreamed.

HB: Where do dreams come from?

S: I do not know. We just dream.

46:

2014-06-04. Former 'Phu Chuay'(P), Vice-chief of the village, non-Christian, 40 years, Thigotha. Taking the interview on his porch. Somu coming with me.

P: I have dreamed I went hunting on the mountain and I wanted to drink water and the friend said, "There is water on the other side." After having drunk, a fire was lit and I had to run up the mountain. I dreamed it during the day when I was taking a nap.

Somu: When you dream at night or in the morning, what do you think?

P: Some people do not go out after a bad dream. I do not fast.

Somu: How do you dream that you would not go out?

P: I do not stay at home. I dreamed that I went to Mae Tom. I had had some kind of a bad dream but I had forgotten. So I went to Mae Tom in the morning for a meeting [for Headmen, Phu Chuay, OPT]. I went to Thisuekhi the lower village – the headman had driven over the road in a curve and "jumped" down the forest and was rolling down the mountain. His name is Kache. He had hit his head badly and had a skull fracture. I had had a bad dream and gone out, so this happened. I dreamed by myself.

47:

2014-06-04. Former 'Phu Chuay' (P) of Thigotha, (40). Non-Christian. The same person as 46P.

HB: Do you like to dream?

P: I would not like to dream. Dreams are a temptation.

HB: What kind of a temptation?

P: It makes me think and worry. Have to think always and to worry.

HB: Where do dreams come from?

P: I do not know – I cannot think from where.

HB: Do you think *k'la* wander?

P: The *'k'la'* wander while asleep.

[Somu: There are two kinds of *'k'la ha'* – The one kind is the *'k'la ha'* at night while asleep. The other kind is when you are frightened/scared – this *'k'la ha'* is during daytime.]

P: Yes, at night – *'k'la'* wander. While my body is asleep the *'k'la'* wander. What are the *'k'la'*?

HB: If you have a good dream what happens?

P: When I have a good dream, I have good thoughts. If I have a good dream, I am not worried. I gladly go out. If I have bad dreams I am worried. Formerly, I had good dreams. As a child I was often ill. I once lost consciousness. They pinched my ear and I did not know. Then we did the ceremony of *'au qai'*. They asked me, "Have your grandparents already come?" If they had come to the patient – then they will get better. When I was unconscious I went to the *'plü kau'*. When I woke up they asked, "Have you seen your grandfather?" Yes, my *'k'la'* had met him [his *'k'la'*]. It was not far from the village. After the grandfather had eaten with them, I got better.

HB: Do you remember the *'au qai'*?

P: Yes.

HB: Do you still *'au qai'*?

P: No, we do not do it anymore for about 20 years now.

HB: Do people in this village still *'au qai'*?

P: Only one family.

HB: Have you seen spirits in dreams?

P: I have seen *'pa te qa'*. When I was a child, life was good. Our parents warned us not to eat in the forest. I once walked back home alone and I ate in the forest. Somebody or something slapped me. This is a Karen belief – and it really happened to me. I did not see anybody. In the evening my parents taught me once again, if you eat in the forest, you will be slapped in the face.

[Talking about spirits and life] *'pra mi pra htö'* it is not a spirit – not a person – you see them and then they disappear.

HB: Is it like an angel?

Somu: Yes, it is like that.

P: Formerly, we had so many beliefs.

P: Dreaming about elephants you have to make a ceremony – '*ba lä*'. If you dream about elephants, buffaloes or cows you have to do the '*ba lä ta*' ceremony.

HB: Why?

P: Because you will get ill. Elephants' '*k'la*' are bad spirits. They cause illness.

Somu: ...If we dream and we believe in it, it will happen.

P: Yes, I had it the same way. If I dream and think, then it will happen. If I do not think about it, nothing will happen. If we dream, we just have to think/worry for one day. Tomorrow, we do not have to think about it. [That's why they "fast" for one day).

48:

2014-06-05. Haesopa (HP), 40 years, and Haesomo (HM), Thigotha. Christian family, five children. Not yet grounded in their faith.

HP: When I dream about carrying ('*pü*') a child – I am not well.

HP: Many people then do a ceremony. But I did not do it. Gerdipah[989] came and brought medicine with him. If we do the ceremonies, we start to doubt.

HB: Have you ever dreamed, Haesomoh?

HM: Yes I dream, but I forget about it.

Somu: What does the dream do to you?

HP: I once dreamed about singing with a teenaged girl and we were singing to each other (anthem). And I had other bad dreams. This dream was not for myself – it was for somebody else. My oldest son got very sick. He was passing stool with blood. He had to see the doctor and he got better. Later I never again dreamed this dream. I was dreaming well. Once I dreamed about a trap and then sickness occurred.

Somu: Did you already worship God?

HP: No, later we became Christians. When I became a Christian I did not "fast" [stay home] any more.

HB: Have your dreams changed since you have become a Christian or are they still the same?

---

[989] A Christian man who sells medicine in the mountains. He also gives injections.

HP: They are still the same, but I go out and it does not matter. When we were not Christians yet, we had no hope. When we dreamed we received bad things. Since we are Christians, then we pray.

HB: Have you ever dreamed good dreams?

HP: I cannot remember. Mostly, when I dreamed, I got problems.

HB: When you did not yet have children, did you ever dream?

HP: I cannot remember.

HB: Do you like to dream or not?

HP: When you dream a lot you need to put a knife under your pillow so you will not dream so much anymore.

HB: Did it help you?

HP: Sometimes I did not dream.

HB: Where do dreams come from?

HP: I do not know.

HB: Does it come through 'k'la' wandering?

HP: I do not know.

HB: Have you ever dreamed about 'plü'?

(He cannot answer.)

49:

2014-06-05. Haegloepa (H), non-Christian, Thigotha.

H: If we dream a lot, we dream a lot.

HB: Did you dream before you went to buy a car?

H: I dream a lot, I cannot remember.

Later: H: Before I went to buy a car, I dreamed. I dreamed about a toilet and somebody asked me to take out the slurry. I could not do it. I have never dreamed this dream. But I do not know its meaning.

HB: Do you sometimes have bad dreams?

H: Yes, sometimes.

HB: If you have bad dreams what do you do?

H: I do not go out. I do not work that day, till this is gone.

50:

2014-06-05. Grandfather Thimepho (Phue), and grandmother (Phi). Christians. Thigotha.

Phi: I dreamed about carrying ('pü') a child.

Phue: What does it mean?

HB: We would like to know.

Phi: If you dream about a child it is a bad dream. (*'hpä'* is the *'k'la'* of the elephant.)

Phue tells about spirits [not dreams].

HB: If you do have bad dreams, what do Christians do?

Phi: Christians pray. Ask other Christians to come and pray if you are not well. God will heal. Ask God. Traditionally we asked the spirit doctor to come and heal.

HB: Have you ever had good dreams?

Phue: Yes, sometimes. When I dream about seeing melons ripe to eat and go out to hunt I have succeeded.

Phi: If you dream about melons, it will be a girl.

Phue: If you are newly married and you dream about water coming from 'hti mo pra' [big river], it will be a boy. If you dream about melons, it will be a girl.

HB: Did you ever dream about it?

Phue: No. If you dream about a well, it will be a girl.

Phi: When I had a girl, I had dreamed about it. If you dream you are eating part of a melon, it will be a girl.

Phue: Formerly, I dreamed and things were about to happen that way. Then my father told me I should curse the dreams so that they do not happen. If I dreamed a person would die, they died. If I dreamed that I killed a deer, I was going to kill a deer.

Somu: Do you still dream these things?

Phue: I still dream but I do not succeed. [It does not happen].[990]

Phue: In a rice field – the buffaloes were grazing – and then they bled from the mouth because of the demons. I got the field. Somebody else dreamed that the demons would not stay there because I am a Christian. Afterwards a non-Christian wanted the field, but then his buffaloes got sick again. So somebody else dreamed that the demons had come back, so he gave the field back to me. I know God loves me.

Phi: If God did not love me, I would have died a long time ago.

HB: Do you remember a good dream?

Phue: If you climb up a rock, it is a good dream. If you dream of going up a rock and you get up, it is a good dream. If you go downhill, it is a bad dream. You will not eat or earn money, but if you go uphill you will earn money.

HB: Have you ever dreamed about *'plü kau'*?

Phue: No, but I have seen my father.

HB: Do you like dreaming?

---

[990] Somu explains about praying and tells about his parents.

Phue: How could I love to dream?

Phi: I do not like dreams. If I could stop it, I would.

Phue: If you dream a lot, you are not well. Have you dreamed?

HB: Yes, sometimes but most of the time I forget about it. [I tell the dream that a dog came to bite me and I turned it off].

Phue: O, this way it is okay. It does not do anything. But if the dog had bitten you, you would have become sick.

Phi: If you dream about a cat or a dog coming to bite you, it is a bad dream.

HB: Have you ever dreamed about an elephant?

Phi: If you dream about an elephant, it is not good.

Phue: If the '*k'la*' are strong and overcome the spirits, the dreams do not matter. Now [as Christians] we can pray.

HB: Formerly you did not have this, what did you do?

Phue: '*yo hpe*' and some prayer.

HB: Do you know any poems ('*hta*') about dreams?

Phue: No, but I have dreamed about doing '*hta*' [singing poems] in my dreams.

51:

2014-06-05. Dee Hae Glae Moh (D), 37 years, Thigotha, Christian. 7 children, her husband is on opium. She is a daughter of the couple, 50Phi+Phue and the mother of the woman 21W.

D: When I have bad dreams I know the devil comes to do evil. If you dream about going downhill, you will receive suffering. If you dream about having a bowel movement, you will see sickness. ('*ta uu ta po'*) – divination/sorcery has come – I do not see any good health. I use a lot of money for many things. Thinks about whether she should give back the same way. For four years I have received money but I have to spend it all the time.

Somu: You have to give it into God's hand.

D: When people come to pray in my house I dream less.

Somu: When you were not well and dreamed a lot, what did you dream?

D: I dream mainly about going downhill and going to the toilet. I am clothing myself well – but in the body I am weak and I have no strength. The child gets sick.

HB: Does the dream come from the devil?

D: Yes, for sure. Formerly, I used the ceremony '*ba aw hti'* [a Buddhist ceremony – where you cut a bamboo and fill it with water – then you pray in front of the Buddha shelf and everybody goes to drink a little bit – this is a ceremony to overcome sickness]. There are so many ceremonies for the devil. But I do not want to do these anymore.

52:

2014-06-05. Chechapa (Ch), 60-70 years, spirit doctor, Thigotha. We went to his house and did not recognize that we should not have gone in, because he had done a ceremony and nobody was allowed to visit him for three days. Therefore the interview was very short.

Ch: I dreamed about cows and buffaloes that means there are bad spirits. It is a bad dream. I went to (*'rä lo sa'*) do a ceremony on the way [we had seen it]. I got a little better.

HB. Do you like to dream?

Ch: No, I do not like to dream.

53:

2014-06-05. Chilapa (Ch), 38 years, non-Christian, Thigotha.

HB: Have you ever dreamed?

Ch: I dream a lot but I do not remember it all. Sometimes when I have bad dreams I stay in the village.

Somu: What do you mostly dream about?

Ch: Sometimes I see the *'plü'* (afterworld), sometimes I dream about going uphill. If I dream a lot, I am not able to work a lot. If I dream about a lady who wants to marry me [He is married], it means that the *'na hti'* spirit of the water comes to eat [comes to do harm]. If you dream about peppers, it means you will quarrel (*'ta he sa'*). The same is true if you dream that you are pounding peppers or eating peppers. If you dream about peppers, you have to be careful [it is a warning] otherwise you will quarrel with your wife and children. If you have bad dreams you have to be careful – you may get angry and strike your child.

HB: Have you dreamed like this?

Ch: Yes, often.

54:

2014-06-05. Chilapa (Ch), Thigotha. The same person as 53Ch.

HB: Do you like to dream?

Ch: No, I don't like dreaming.

HB: Do you have good dreams?

Ch: Sometimes I have good dreams, sometimes bad ones.

Ch: If I have bad dreams I may be hurt, sometimes it does not matter. If I have bad dreams I may get sick, sometimes it is a child, sometimes it is me.

HB: Have you ever dreamed about the *'plü kau'*?

Ch: Yes, I do. Sometimes I dream like doing things here. There are young people there, too. I go to villages and I eat with people.

HB: What do you think – how many *'k'la'* are there with a person?

Ch: One. There may be two. Sometimes I dream about cows running after me or elephants running after me and I cannot escape. I cannot escape, but they do not get me either. It is not a good dream.

Ch: Sometimes I dream about flying in the sky.

HB: How do you fly?

Ch: Flying like a bird.

HB: If you go to the *'plü kau'*, do you talk together?

Ch: Yes, in the *'plü kau'* I talk to people. Sitting with the people who have died.

HB: If you dream like that, do you not fear?

Ch: If you dream about *'plü kau'*, for some it is a good dream, for others it is a bad dream.

HB: Some people say that when they dream about the *'plü kau'* it is raining.

Ch: Yes, it may rain. I once did the rice fields and it was not raining. Then at night I dreamed about the afterworld and then it started to rain. Sometimes when I dream about the afterworld I eat [succeed]. Some people fast [do not go out], but I do go out.

HB: Does rice possess *'k'la'*?

Ch: Yes rice has *'k'la'*.

Somu: What kind of *'k'la'*

Ch: It is the *'k'la'* of the elephant. If you dream about the elephant [during the harvest season] you will eat rice [have lots of rice]. If you dream about a male elephant, it is a bad dream and you will not eat. If you dream about a female elephant, you will eat. If you dream about a male elephant, your rice granary will not be full. If you dream about a female elephant, it will be full.

HB: If you put your rice into the house, do you need to call the *'k'la'* to come`?

Ch: No, you do not need to call them.

HB: When does the *'k'la'* of the rice come into the rice?

Ch: That is when the rice grain is formed. When the rice grain is formed and you have bad dreams it means you may not eat rice. Formerly we had to do some ceremonies – but we do not do them anymore.

Somu: If you are not a Christian, what do you do?

Ch: Formerly we sacrificed a bird or a chicken, nowadays we just use some *'kou'*, dessert. [More about *'bü k'la'* and ceremonies]. Formerly we did a lot of ceremonies, nowadays we do not so many – we cannot do it anymore. When we have planted the rice, we have to *'sae che'* [a certain ceremony].

55:
2014-06-05. Gloethipa (G), Thigotha (see also 45, 56)

HB: When you did not have children yet what did you dream?

G: Women often dream about melons and then they get pregnant. If you dream about picking and eating peppers, it is a bad dream. You will not have a child. If you dream about going to draw water and there is no water in the well [the well is dry], it is a bad dream. Because then the child to be born will be sick and die. If it lives, it will die soon after birth.

56:

2014-06-05. Gloethipa (G), Thigotha. See also 45, 55.

G: I dreamed that a 'da bo' came to sting. And when I awoke I was crying. People asked me what happened? „Oh, a 'da bo' has stung me", I said.

G: If you dream a lot, you will get sick.

HB: Where do dreams come from?

G: I do not know. Sometimes I do remember dreams, sometimes I do not remember them.

If we dream about harvesting rice, then we know that the buffaloes or cows went into the field to feed on the rice. If you dream about harvesting rice, in actual fact the buffaloes have already eaten it and the cows have eaten, too. That is what I think.

57:

2014-06-06. Aphopa (A), 55 years, Mokokhi. Christian, but does not attend church anymore. He worships in his house. Ti Cho La (Ti), 39 years, Christian who can entertain people well.

HB: Have you ever dreamed?

A: I dreamed that a woman came and kept a mirror before me. Then I did not go out ('dü ta'), otherwise a splinter would get into my eye.

HB: Have you dreamed like that?

A: I dream very often. Then I do not go out because I will be hurt.[991]

Somu: Do you dream good dreams as well?

A: Yes, sometimes I have good dreams.

Ti Cho la: What does it mean when you dream about listening to MP3 players?

A: It means you should buy one. [Jokingly].

A: If you dream that you are hunting a wild pig or a deer that means that someone is going to die and you have to go to sing 'hta'.

Ti: I dreamed that I was marrying another woman [the 'k'la' marries – actually already married]. I dreamed that this woman looked even better than the one I have married already. My 'k'la' thinks about that woman. But then I woke up

---

[991] Somu: he must have had many such experiences otherwise he would not act like this.

and I still was with my wife. But my *'k'la'* was still thinking about the other woman.

Somu: If you dream like that, what do you do?

Ti: I will go and work. Formerly, we had to fast, not go out, but since we have become Christians, we pray and go out. I pray and go. No snake has ever bitten me. God loves me. There was a rice field. Nobody could really do it. It always caused trouble. One owner then hanged himself in that field. Then, another did the field and while he was hacking the field a bamboo splinter went into his eye. When I became a Christian I went to do this field and it was good. I trusted God and went to do that field. I did not fear. God is with me.

[Tells about other experiences with God and people – how a family became Christians.]

Ti: Formerly I lived in Biotha. Then I was worshipping Buddha/Animism. My wife and children were not well – and I had to build a new house three times. Then I located in Mokokhi and became a Christian.

[Tells experiences when he was not a Christian yet.]

Somu: Do you have good dreams?

Ti: I have good and bad dreams.

Ti: I dreamed at night but did not remember. Then I went to fence in a field. One tree I had cut had not yet fallen to the ground. I had to pull it. When it fell a branch of another tree hit me behind the head to the neck. I then fell on my nose. I lost consciousness. My wife and another woman were with me. When I woke up after a while I asked, 'Where am I? I got angry at the branch which hit me.

A: I dreamed that my *'k'la'* ate meat and then, when I woke up, my stomach was so full. Isn't it funny that my *'k'la'* ate and I felt full afterwards?

HB: Where do dreams come from?

Ti: If we sleep a lot and deep. Sometimes it is not that, we just dream.

Ti: I dreamed about fish and I thought I would make a good deal. Someone from Lampang came to sell pans and I bought them for 1000 Baht. They were bad pans, we could not really use them. They got rusty.

A: I dreamed that a big woman came to ask me that I should marry her.[992] When I woke up I was thinking about that woman. I had done fields the day before and then I dreamed this. I had problems and I called the spirit doctor to do ceremonies. (I was not a Christian yet). While the spirit doctor was here a '*da bo*' [a crawler that can bite – this was a symbol for a very bad spirit] came up. But even though I did many ceremonies it did not help. When I became a Christian these problems disappeared.

A: I went to sleep in the field. I dreamed about two hills of termites. One was destroyed, the other was intact. I had two children and one got sick. I carried the sick child back to the village, it lost consciousness and it had already died when I arrived here. There must have been a power from Satan ('*ta chu*'). I dreamed

---

[992] In Karen culture in the given area, it is usually the women who ask the men to marry them.

about this then I became a Christian. Then these problems were solved. This was my dream about the termite hills.

HB: Have you ever dreamed about the afterworld?

A: To dream about the '*plü kau*' is very nice. I have seen nice things and nothing bad happened. I went to look for food and ate together. It did not do any harm to me. My '*k'la*' wandered to the afterworld with some others [from the '*plü kau*'], but in the body we did not see each other anymore.

Somu: Dreams about the '*plü kau*', are they usually good dreams?

A: It is about fifty-fifty. When we do fields we dream about it more, but now it does not matter anymore. Because we worship God. We know that God can work anything. If we were not Christians, we could not do those fields [because the child had died].

HB: As Christians do you dream differently or the same?

A: Now I have good dreams. I do not know evil dreams. Formerly, it was such a pain.

HB: Now you have good dreams, how?

A: I dream about what we do in the fields.

HB: Have you ever dreamed about God, Jesus or the Holy Spirit?

A: I have dreamed once, about God. I dreamed about grandfather Khue la pa [the first Christian in the village and a leader]. He asked me to follow him. So I followed him. We came to a fork in the road. We went one way and saw it was dark. We turned and went the other way. It was such a nice, bright way. There were two ways to the right, it was a good way – to the left, the way led into darkness. I did not want to go to the left. The other way was smooth. I think the nice way led to God. But we did not reach the end.

Formerly I went to church so gladly, even before they hit the gong. Now, I do not like to go. Maybe because I am old? I stay at home.

58:

2014-06-08. Noahmo. Ouhaeta, Omkoi. Influential Christian woman leader. Did several years of Bible training. Wife of Noahpa. Charismatic Christian. 46 years.

N: There are many kinds of dreams. There are dreams which are true. There are dreams which come from the devil. Dreams may be orders from God. Some dreams are symbols which God uses to give a message to people. Sometimes we do not know the meaning of a dream, we have to ask the Holy Spirit. E.g. The pastor of our church – his wife dreamed that a snake bit her. The poison went to her heart. She did not understand so she came to me, and told me that the snake bit her and the poison went to her heart. Then I went to prayer. Then I dreamed that the pastor was in prison. When I asked him why he is in prison, he said, "I do not know why they caught me, I have done nothing wrong." When I rose in the morning I saw the pastor. I said to him, "Last night we prayed for you and at night God revealed that you are having problems." A month later it had become obvious that he lived in adultery. The problem was now open and so it would be possible to solve the problem. We gave him a chance to repent. Now he is divorced and has married another woman and has a new child. I have dreamed myself. I saw the pastor's wife giving milk to a child but she had no milk, only milk like from an old person. I did not understand the meaning. I asked God – I do not understand. Afterwards I understood – to have no milk means there was no blessing, could not be a blessing for others. Often dreams are like a warning. Once during the women's conference I dreamed – a woman from the US who had taught at Payao Bible School – she came to me in a dream. I was happy to hug her but her clothes were dirty. Her hands were dirty. I gave her a cloth to clean her hands. Why did she come with dirty hands? She went to wash her hands. Then I saw her in new clothes as in Karen clothes. You do not need to do this, it is not necessary. I did not understand the dream so I asked God. God, what is the meaning of this? I asked, "Am I not clean?" This was just before I went to the women's conference. Then the leader of the women's work in the church association came to me. She started to tell about her family and that she was angry with her father and older brother. She came to the conference like this and she was the leader of the women in the association. The Holy Spirit told me that my dream was about this woman. If she came to the camp like this it would hinder, she had to get rid of it. I told her what I had dreamed. She had to repent of her sin that she was so angry at her older brother and father. At that time the Holy Spirit came and anointed her and she fell to the ground. I felt like laughing. When I laugh and the Holy Spirit comes I have freedom and an easy heart. After 15 min I was surprised. I saw a woman from the US – she was not the one I saw in the dream – but she came to teach at the women's conference. She wore the Karen clothes I saw in the dream.

HB: What do you do when people have bad dreams, when they fear? And if they come to you, what advice do you give?

N: Some dreams come from seeing dirty things or experiencing evil. Some watch too much TV and then they dream about that. Some keep former bad experiences in their heart. So they dream bad dreams. I dreamed that a man came to do evil. I was fighting against that man but I could not overcome him. I could not overcome. In life I married one man and I am faithful to him. Sometimes I had dreams of suffering. I dreamed that a man came to me and wanted to sleep with me and I wanted him, too. And I was angry at myself. And it created problems in my spirit. The day came when I had such problems in my spirit, deep in my heart – actually I had this problem from childhood – until about 33 years of age. It is a story of the spirit.

When I was about 3-4 years old we played "doctor" and bad sexual plays, bad thinking. I did not understand that a four year old would think like that. In actual life I did not do what I thought.

When I was not married I thought if I am married I will not have these problems anymore. But over this kind of dreams I did not have any victory. I sometimes dreamed that a deceased person ('*plü*') came to me – I could not overcome. Then I told God that I cannot understand these problems. I could not understand – I did not want it and yet it came. I thought but did not want to think about it. I had real problems.

Until the year 2000 when the Holy Spirit came to our church in Sop Umphet [Ouhaeta]. I experienced the Holy Spirit. He taught me many things in my heart. And then Ajarn Sidney brought me a CD from a teacher in Singapore, his name is Lawrence Crabb who had come to teach in Thailand. He taught leaders. Many pastors have problems with pornography. This is not a holy life. Lawrence Crabb testified that some have studied the Bible, are married and are pastors and still have these problems. He said, when I was studying I asked a lady teacher what should I do with these problems? She said, "This comes through sins of your ancestors." Then she prayed for me. Afterwards I did not have any problems anymore. I came to freedom. Then I was thinking, do my problems come from my ancestors? I started to fast. And I asked God to help me because I did not understand the problem. I did not want this kind of life. I fasted three days. After three days I dreamed, I was on a rock and there was a tree up there and on one side it was a cliff, on the other side stones as well. At that time I held onto the tree. Then I remembered the hymn "God sets us on a rock."

I dreamed about an older woman who was single [they usually wear a white dress] and the white dress was dirty and she was climbing up the rock and reached it. She tried to throw me off the rock. But I held fast to the tree with one hand – the woman tried to tear away my other hand but then the woman fell down. I went to see, but I could not see her anymore, it was so deep. Then I woke up and God had given me freedom! God had freed me from the sin of my ancestors.

Then I fasted seven days. I knew I was pure. The Holy Spirit came into my thinking. Since then I have not dreamed any bad, dirty dreams. I have overcome, I have victory in this area. God has given me freedom.

In Exodus: "the sins of your fathers – three or four generations"

[Talking about the sins of ancestors.]

N: When I looked at my family – my grandmother's sibling did not marry. Then I confessed to God. Then I started to pray for others. I went to Prachuap Khiri Khan and a lady came to me and said, "My mother married twice and I have married twice. My mother left her husband and I have left my husband."

HB explains his experiences.

N: There is a Thai lady who came to know the Lord in the US. When she returned she prayed for her sick mother who was healed. She dreamed about a Buddha statue and her spirit went off. And she did not understand and started to pray that God would show – I worship God and still there is a Buddha in my life/dream. She still feared. She still gave honor to it. Then she dreamed about swallowing the Buddha figure, which means she had overcome.

N: Last year we had problems in our family and about politics.[993] I dreamed that my husband was caught and imprisoned. It was a deep prison. I dreamed our family was driving the car. We drove to a house but there was no way anymore. The road went to that house but it did not go any further. I left the car and could see a way that goes on. A woman in that house had sued Noahpa at the district

---

[993] Her husband Noahpa is a member of the provincial parliament of Chiang Mai province.

office and they had come to catch him. The head of the district then put him into prison. My heart was angry at this woman and then I saw Noahpa – he was very small in the prison. Two ladies waited for Noahpa. And I saw a balloon and it exploded. I went to these two ladies and asked, "Why do you imprison Noahpa, he has not done anything wrong?" The two ladies went back.

Then I cried, I cried loudly. Then I saw pastor Ek. "Why do you cry?" I said, "because I am very sad. The family is not well, no happiness." I dreamed many times that our family was in danger.

When we were going to build this house I dreamed. A big fire was spreading. The fire destroyed our house. Sometimes we are warned in dreams about problems that may arise and we need to pray. These are dreams of warning to us. Our family may be in danger. Or problems may arise for Noahpa that he cannot do what he should. Or it may mean problems with money.

Noahpa was selling cabbage to Bangkok. He sold it for 108.000 Baht. Then he sold tomatoes for about 700-800.000 Baht. But the buyer did not pay one baht. As a family we could not go forward nor backwards. There was no righteousness in it. It was not our sin. But we could not see any way but we prayed. God is bigger than our problems. And I forgave the sins of those who had sinned against us. I prayed that God would bless them. I was going to pray until God answered or when he said it was enough. We prayed the whole day, prayed and prayed.

Then one day, my son came and said that he dreamed that they had imprisoned my father but in a few days he will be freed. And I also dreamed that Noahpa was in handcuffs. Then I saw the prison guard open them up with a key and he was free.

I praise God. They did not give us the money but God has helped us and helped us get through. We prayed until God said it was enough. God has helped us to build this house. This is a miracle from God.

When we did not have money, Noahpa fasted and we prayed and we have seen God's miracles often.

HB: How do you help people who dream bad dreams?

N: There was a woman in Thi Wa Sue. Her younger sister came to learn at the Bible School. And so she came to me. She was like an insane person. She was confused. She did not drink or eat. She had very bad dreams. She looked like someone had put a spell on her (*'lo'*). For two days she had not eaten. I asked her. She said, "An old man came and gave me raw pork [in the dream]. I did not eat but he forced me. I vomited it. When I awoke I thought that the old man had done sorcery to me, that I would die. Then I called the headman and village elders to talk about it."

If Karen dream like that, they think that person has done sorcery, has cast a spell on them.

She had such fear. Formerly, she was at odds with the old man and feared that he would do something bad to her. She always feared him. They had their rice fields beside each other and they quarreled. She feared and then she had this bad dream.

I told her, the way of the devil is fear. Fear creates that kind of bad dream. And then the "old man" gets power over you, because you take part in the devil's way.

Secondly, I told her, "You have to ask God to forgive your sins. Because you have accused the old man that he has done wrong to you." There are so many people who just die but the devil uses the dream to accuse people. If you pray, those dreams cannot harm you.

In Pabako there was a man, people said he was doing sorcery and they killed him, but he did not do any sorcery.

Among Karen when they dream, they believe the dream.

If you become God's people, if you have done nothing wrong, you have to be responsible to God. And I told the woman, she has to ask for forgiveness because the old man has done nothing wrong, and put everything into God's hand. If he has not done anything wrong, the sin is with you. Pray for him.

N: Problems arise through quarreling and fighting and then worrying. When I get sick people think I have dreamed about that person already. There are so many problems among the Karen because of this.

N: But there are people who do sorcery ('*lo ta*') – but if somebody gets sick they think somebody has done sorcery. This kind of thinking is not according to the truth and it is God's responsibility to judge. Noahpa's grandmother was ill with cancer of the intestines. The doctor operated on her. She thought that somebody had caused this illness. Very often when Karen are ill with cancer people think it is because sorcery is involved. If these problems occur among the Karen, they go and drink water or blow water [ceremony with the spirit doctor which should show who is guilty].

We have many people who have cancer of the liver. If this happens, many think that sorcery is involved. But this is not always the case. Karen think this is always the case.

Most problems among the Karen arise through people thinking that somebody has done something wrong to them. Many go to the spirit doctor to ask (even among Christians, many go to read palms). Their faith is not firm. They have not grown in faith. They worry.

Those who know God will die in God's hand and they will live in God's hand. They do not think about the other things. But among the Karen we find the other things so often. You can get tired!

HB: If I see people go just one way I am happy. But many do not. If people are not well, I ask them whether they have gone and seen a spirit doctor.

N: In the end they seek help with "drinking water or blowing water" [ceremonies]. Afterwards they come back and repent. ... Some do everything until the child dies ...

I remember Charepa – they asked him to drink water [which was cursed if he had done any wrong]. I remembered that Aj. Somsak[994] said it will not harm you.

---

[994] Head of Payao Bible School, when she attended.

We had a family in the village. The wife had done something wrong and they went to drink that water. The family was later destroyed.

HB: Some people believe more in dreams than in God's Word?

N: If we have bad dreams we must remember that God is bigger than anything. God can change the evil into good. If I have bad dreams I rise and I pray: Jesus, I do not receive this dream. And God is greater than that dream.

HB: I do it the same way.

N: But some people believe in the dream more than in God.

N: After we had moved house I had bad dreams the whole month.

What was this? I could not understand. Then one young person came home and said he would sleep in that place. And he had bad dreams. I thought, this is unusual. I thought it might be a bad spirit which was sent by the devil.

I went to teach at the Bible school and came back at midday. I took oil and declared God's reign and drew crosses on the wall and I prayed, "In the name of Jesus Christ, devil disappear!" I drew crosses in each room. I asked that the blood of Jesus would come to reign. If there were any gods or any fornication, I asked God for forgiveness. Then when I prayed, there was a noise. I got a chicken skin and it was exactly midday. Then I knew that the devil still had had a stronghold.

Then I dreamed at night. I saw the devil leaving through the curtain. Afterwards I was freed from the bad dreams.

Sometimes when I do not pray much and am not watchful, the dreams come back. I remember Joshua – ... wherever you put your foot, God will give you.

When we moved into the new house ... we had to pray ...

N: When we put the posts of the house I dreamed that an old person came to sleep in the hammock and he slept well. Then I called the children to come and worship in the house. We asked God to protect the house/land so that nothing bad would happen. That God would clean everything. If there is anything evil on this land, may God throw it out. ....

N: Once a pastor came to see Noahpa and said that he dreamed that a snake had bitten him. What does that mean? Noahpa: It could be that your wife has been unfaithful. He said, "No not us." Later he phoned again and said they were quarreling and they are now divorced.

Dreams do not always have the same meaning.

N: If I dream about fish I get money. If Noahpa dreams about fish, he loses money. Sometimes if I dream about fish, people believe. Sometimes people come with problems to me and I can pray and they are healed.

When we are about to plant tomatoes and I dream about fish, then the tomatoes will have a good price.

N: If I dream about dogs, I will have problems. Once Noahpa did a field in Le Pado. He had a man from Burma as a servant. He was angry and scolded him. One day, Noahpa should take rice and a knife to him. The Burman man said, "I will kill you. You have scolded me so much." ... We thought if this man is with us, he will cause problems. He was a former Karen soldier.

Then he received two men from Kosuleh[995] who hated the Burmese. They came and later they killed him and buried him there.

I dreamed about wolves and they bit me. They had such big teeth. I really feared and while I feared I saw the wolves become children. At first I did not understand but later I understood.

God saw that I had big problems but it was not about me, but about the three men.

The Bible tells us that the enemy comes one way but God gives us seven ways to overcome, it says in Deuteronomy.

N: I once dreamed about a yellow serpent, a yellow one. When I walked it followed me. It knew my heels. When I went into another house it followed me, too. It was waiting on the ceiling hanging down. But it did not bite me at all. In the dream I thought, I do not like this snake. I thought, I am going to cut her head off. I did not know the meaning of this dream. Then I looked the meaning up in the book "Dream On". It explains about the snake that it has two meanings. One is for the devil. But the other is about healing – Jesus – the serpent in the OT – whoever looked up was healed. It is a symbol for Jesus.

About the yellow snake which followed me – I felt it wanted to come into my bedroom and the devil with it – therefore I better cut her throat. In my life, I know God is really with me.

59:

2014-06-08. Noahpa (N), Ouhaeta, Omkoi. Evangelist, Bible teacher, business man, member of provincial parliament. Most influential leader in the Omkoi area. Son of 31P.

HB: Have you ever dreamed?

N: God has given me dreams all the time about matters. When problems arise God gives me dreams. When I dream that a fire comes up, I will see problems. When I dream about lots of water, pure water, then it is a dream about the heart/spirit. If I dream about dirty water, I will see hindrances and problems. If I work and dream about fish, I will get money. If I dream about a deer, I will not earn anything. During the women's conference in Sop Lahn, a lady dreamed that there was no fence around. The field was without a fence. Cows and buffaloes could enter. She dreamed there was no fence around. Then we prayed about it and that God would bless.

60:

2014-04-05. Talk with Ela (E), (Genjomuepa), hostelfather in Thibokhi, 26 years. Talk in the car driving from Thigotha to Thibokhi.

E: If I have a bad dream, I do not tell anybody but God alone.

HB: Why?

---

[995] Karen state in Burma.

E: If I tell people, they will advise me to do things which are not according to God's Word. If we tell our bad dreams to people, we give too much attention to the devil's work! In our old beliefs people think the 'k'la' go out when they dream and they may be caught by spirits, and not come back. So they have to sacrifice to the spirits so they let them go and then they have to make a "calling back 'k'la' ceremony" by tying the hand wrist.

61:

2014-06-06. Sera Tho Joe (ST), Christian from Burma – many years in Thailand. Phue KueLaPa (P), first Christian in Mokokhi, 70 years. Mokokhi.

ST: If you dreamed you had to do accordingly (in the old ways). Since we have become Christians, we offer the dream to God. If it is a good dream, God will give it to us. If it is a bad dream, God will protect us. I have not seen difficulties from dreams because God redeems us from it. Everybody dreams.

Somu: In the old tradition we had to fast ...

ST: In former days, when you dreamed and you were stubborn then bad things were going to happen to you.

P: When we were still with the devil we only had to carry heavy burdens.

Somu: Did you ever see God in a dream?

ST: This has not happened to me. Often when I dream I see evil spirits from the afterworld/Hades. If you dream about Hades, you will see difficulties. If you dream about hell, you will see suffering. I once dreamed during the day and I saw hell with lots of suffering. When I dreamed like that I hardly could breathe anymore. I have never dreamed about heaven. I once dreamed about a house which was very nice but it had no walls yet. It was not finished yet. Meaning: Anything we do in this world is not perfect. If we want it perfect, that will be with God.

Somu: Were you happy when you dreamed that?

ST: I was happy.

Somu asks Phue: Before you were a Christian and now since you have become a Christian, have your dreams changed?

P: It is different. When we were still in the devil's hand there were only heavy burdens and we had to fast [stay home]. When we had bad dreams we had to fast. Now since we have become Christians we leave it to God and he redeems us. There was a guy – his parents were pastors of a church – but he did not follow and went his own way, drinking alcohol. Then he dreamed that he saw two men, one clothed in white the other in black. The dark guy drank alcohol and while he drank the guy in white was sad. But the dark guy who was drinking felt well. But when he put the bottle of alcohol aside the guy in white was glad and the guy in black felt sad. Then the guy in black stopped drinking alcohol. He changed his life.

Somu: So you think that dreaming can change someone's life?

P: Yes, some.

62

2014-06-06. Pue KueLaPa (Pue) (Same as 61P). His son-in-law PenYoPa (PenY), Mokokhi. PenYoPa is the pastor of the Baptist church in Mokokhi. Interview in his house.

Pue: There was a [non-Christian] guy in Thigoglo who was warned in a dream not to go out. But he still went out to catch mice. When he went back home in the evening he became very ill. After two or three days he died. God does not give evil dreams, but if you have a bad dream then you have to pray to God.

Pue: I was called to MoGePa's house to worship [Hmong man in the Hmong village]. He still had an idol in his house and wanted to get rid of it. I threw it out and when I went home to sleep I dreamed:

I lost my way. I came to a village which was very different – a village people would not live in, which was dirty (*'plü kau'*). Then I dreamed that I [his *'k'la'*] went to see but did not know anybody in this place. They called me 'older brother' but I did not know anybody. There were young people and old people – I had lost my way – someone asked me, "Where are you going?" And I said, "I am looking for my way." The person said there is a way for you when you go. But he did not show me the way, he only said that there is a way. I went and went until I came to the last house. I saw a single person not married yet. He said, "if you go there is a way." Then I passed the house and I saw a wonderful way. O, I see the way – the one who seeks will find.

MoGePa dreamed as well. He saw a fountain on top of the hill and water came down to his house. That was God's blessing for him.

Pue: I felt this must have been a very strong spirit I threw out, so I said to MoGePa "What kind of spirit did you feed?" He said that the Hmong sacrifice three or four cows and buffaloes in a place in their village.

Pue: You must have strong spirits that I dreamed like that.

MoGePa became a strong Christian. Formerly I visited him but now I have not got the strength anymore.

HB: When you dream do the *'k'la'* wander? In the old days.

PenY: [gives no answer but says] If we had bad dreams, in the old days, we did *'yo hpe'* or we stayed at home [fast] and we had to do that often and we could not work. When we have bad dreams now, we pray to God that God will guide us. Sera Tho Joe (ST) went to Thigotha when nobody was a Christian yet. People said if you dream about a "yak" it will come and eat you. He went back to his village and dreamed:

I went to a wedding and they were cutting meat. After the meat was cooked they came to invite for the meal. I said, "I will not eat yet and I ask you all not to eat yet. I dreamed that I had a stone in my hand and I will produce some medicine from it and then we will go and eat." I did not eat and then I awoke.

Formerly, when you dreamed about eating meat it was a bad dream. [It means sorcery so that people die].

But I had a stone – that means I went with the Bible – it is the most valued thing.[996]

---

[996] He does not explain but it means that it is God-s Word that can heal. The Bible gives them a firm stand.

63:

2014-06-06. JaeMoPa (Jae), Mokhokhi and his wife (W), non-Christian – formerly in lower village of Mokokhi which has hardly any Christians. (The wife's relatives are mainly Christians).

Jae: My wife was not well for five days. I and my wife went to the field to sleep, and I dreamed about '*plü*' which was not nice. I dreamed about my older sister [who had already died and had lived in the same house]. My wife dreamed about her mother which was a bad dream, too. After that we came back to the village and my wife got sick. Sometimes when I have bad dreams like that sickness will occur.

HB: If you dream about the '*plü*'?

Jae: Yes, when I dream about the '*plü*' and dreaming about my sister who had died.

W: When I dream about going up the mountain it is a good dream. I have dreamed about washing myself, that is a good dream.

Jae: If you dream about going up a tree, it is a good dream. If we have bad dreams, we do '*yo hpe*' and pray.[997]

Jae: We pray too, because when we go without we may feel that we have made a mistake, so we pray that we may be excused. Speaks about '*ga ta*' [clairvoyance done on bones or on a woman's skirt].

Jae: I once dreamed that I went up a mountain. I went up to a Buddhist temple and I saw idols and a Buddha statue which was not on the top. Then I awoke. I thought it was a good dream. And then I went to the wedding of my son. After I came back from the wedding [which was far away], it was not long after that a storm came and my house was destroyed.

[I could see the destroyed house – we were taking the interview on a small porch of a provisional hut he had built].

Somu: When you dream do you believe the '*k'la*' wander?

Jae: Yes, the '*k'la*' wander – it is not the body.

Somu: Do you believe you have '*k'la*'?

Jae: There are six or seven '*k'la*'. The Karen have seven '*k'la*'.

HB/Somu: The main '*k'la*', does it wander, too?

Jae: There is a disabled ['*k'la wi:wa:*'] '*k'la*'. This one will always be with you. It will not go away. It will watch you. The others go out.

Jae: If we dream about fleeing from something and we cannot get away and then we wake up – the '*k'la wi:wa:*' will protect us.

Somu: Do you like to dream?

Jae: Sometimes I like it, sometimes not.

---

[997] I asked Somu, "To whom do they pray?" He said that he has done the same when he was a child – he prayed but he did not know to whom he prayed. It was just praying to relieve the inner pressure.

I want to dream but I want to have good dreams. I do not want to dream bad dreams. But good dreams, I really want to dream them.

Somu: When you dream a lot do you think that sickness will occur?

Jae: If you sleep a lot, you will dream a lot. If you cannot sleep, you do not dream. If you are healthy, then you do not dream a lot.

If you are not well, you sleep and you dream a lot. The *'k'la'* wander a lot. But if you are healthy, you do not dream, the *'k'la'* do not wander.

HB: Does it mean the *'k'la'* are there?

Jae: When you are not well you will sleep – the body will be here, but the soul (*'noh sa'*) will wander.

[Explains about the *'ta plo so'*] It is a dream which comes about when you have worked in the field and then you dream about that work – Karen do not give much meaning to it.

Jae: If you are healthy, you will not dream very much.

HB: If you dream about Hades (*'plü kau'*) do you fear?

Jae: There is also fear. If I have bad dreams I fear. If I see a cow coming against me, I will fear. If I see a snake, I fear (even if I see it in the body, I fear it too).

64:

2014-03-19. Choerepa (Ch), lay evangelist. Tarolekhi. When he was young he lived in Tak province, was married and had 3 children, smoking opium. Was threatened to be killed. Came to Tarolekhi where he married a Christian. Became a Christian and later stopped smoking opium. Is now going to bring the Good News to the area he lived in the past.

Ch: If you believe dreams, they may occur in reality. I dreamed I was riding an elephant which was running. When I woke up I went up a tree and fell down. I could not walk for two months. Others who dream about riding an elephant say they got a fever afterwards.

Ch: Since we worship God as Christians we do not dream the same way. Before, when we dreamed about riding an elephant, we got sick. Now it is not that way, we trust in God and evil does not happen. I pray that God will guide me today. Whether I have good dreams or I have bad dreams it does not matter, I leave it in God's hands. Afterwards I did not dream anymore. Formerly, we looked at the devil, and what we dreamed and believed occurred. Later I did not believe in it anymore. If I dream bad things now, no bad thing happens to me anymore. I understand it this way. Formerly, we believed the devil is going to do things, and so it happened. When the devil caused people to dream the evil really happened. In God's kingdom it is different. Whatever we dream it does not happen. For those who really believe in God, the evil things do not come about.

HB: Do you think that dreams also can come from God?

Ch: I have never dreamed about God. If the dream comes from God, it is something else. For example when my child, my wife or myself are not well and I dream about Charepa, you, Supopa (God's children) then they get better. The sickness heals. I see that God works in this way. Sometimes when I dream about ancestor worship or spirit doctors, then I may not feel well. When I go and pray nothing bad is going to happen. But if I dream about Supopa [evangelist] and I pray, the sickness will be healed. I believe that God works this way.

HB: If you are not well and then you see Supopa in a dream, it will heal, is it that way?

Ch: If I dream about people who belong to God and do God's work, sickness is going to be healed. But we need to pray all the time. If we pray, it will heal quickly.

HB: When you were not a Christian yet what kind of dream did you have?

Ch: When I was not a Christian yet I got evil things through dreams as well.

HB: Where do dreams come from?

Ch: I do not fully understand. I think the devil does these things. As I have said, the devil causes people to dream. Some people dream and they really get into troubles. They believe in these dreams. Sometimes they do not go out. They stay in the house. So if you fasted [because of a dream] once, then later you had to fast each time when you dreamed that way. But if you still went, then you would be hurt. They think that way and fear it.

HB: Do you think that the *'k'la'* wander when you dream?

Ch: Yes, it is that way. Karen fear and are startled when the *'k'la'* wander. They fear and get sick. Then they go and do a ceremony to call them back and they get better. I think Karen have *'k'la'*. If you dream and you are startled, then you will become ill.

Ch: Do you have this kind in your country?

Ch: Dreams can cause lots of thinking and a heavy heart. There are so many kinds of dreams. Sometimes I dream and I forget it.

HB: How many *'k'la'* are there?

Ch: There are over thirty. There are 33 *'k'la'*.

HB: Is there a head?

Ch: There is one disabled – he cannot walk. There is another one who is very intelligent (*'le ge de'*). He has knowledge. The one who cannot walk is a good one. Because he stays with you on the fontanel. When this one goes away you will die.

HB: When Karen die where do they believe the *'k'la'* go to where?

Ch: When the Karen die, the *'k'la'* goes to the *'plü kau'*. Goes back to the Hades.

HB: Not all?

Ch: Just the one.

HB: What happens when there is a noise after a person has died? Does it come back?

Ch: '*Pra tö qa*' [the '*k'la*' who went to the '*plü kau*' has come back as a spirit] there are those. When the Christians die the '*k'la*' goes back to Father God. Non-Christians believe that people who died a forceful death do not go back to the '*plü kau*'. I have seen many people.

Ch: After my aunt died, she came back. She really came back. Sometimes we went to sleep to a place and she appeared. Afterwards, when I slept at night, I feared that she would appear. Then, I went to sleep and I took my rifle with me. I shot, made such big noise, and she never came back.

Ch: About dreams, it is hard to say. Until today people believe in dreams. They dream and believe it. I learnt from evangelists, fear God, do not give significance to dreams. They said, "Fear God and do not trust in dreams." As evangelist Ela said, do not tell your dreams to people, but fear God. In days gone past, we did not fear God. We feared dreams. But now, we fear God. When we fear God, dreams cannot do any harm to us. But if you do not fear God, they do.

HB: I have seen people to believe more in dreams than in God's Word.

Ch: Yes, they believe more in dreams.

HB: Sometimes, after I had a bad dream, I told God that I will not accept this dream. "In the name of Jesus, go away!" Then I did not see any problems coming from dreams.

Ch: This is my experience, too. I have told God, I do not accept dreams. I have accepted Jesus Christ. If God leads me I do not need dreams. There are many verses in the Bible that we should accept God and fear God. Do not fear dreams, because if you fear dreams you will receive the bad things you dream.

65:

2015-04-29. Dinapa (HT), 45 years. Headman Thigoglo, Omkoi. Active Christian from a Christian family.

HB: Do dreams have meaning?

HT: Dreams have meaning. If you go downhill, it is not good. You will have problems.

HB: Have you seen this happen?

HT: Once, I dreamed about a dead person ('*plü*'). The person had died but the '*k'la*' can still be seen. My '*k'la*' wandered and it ('*k'la*') went downhill with the other '*k'la*', even running down. This is not good.

HB: You dreamed this way. And what happened afterwards?

HT: It happened to my possession, cows died. Sometimes nothing happens to the possession but something may happen to you so that you will have problems. I remember this. If you dream about the '*plü*' many things can happen. Some dream about it and if they go out they will be hurt. Just recently, there was one man in the village. His child had a bad dream and it said to the father, "Do not go out." He went out and he was caught by the police.

HB: In your village?

HT: Yes, in my village. He said he has never smoked opium. And I know he has never smoked opium. But the police checked his urine and they said he has smoked opium. He said I have never smoked and I do not understand why they said, they saw he has smoked. The police did not believe him because they said if he had not smoked they would not have seen it in his urine. Before this problem arose the child had already dreamed about.

HB: Where do dreams come from?

HT: O, I do not know. Today, if I go out and if I come home and sleep, my '*k'la*' is wandering.

HB: Does the '*kl'a*' see things?

HT: Yes, the '*kl'a*' sees things – it goes out to the mountains and the forest and sees all as if we go out every day. The old people have told us this. If we have a bad dream, we may get problems.

HB: What do you do when you have a bad dream?

HT: We can do nothing. Sometimes we pray, asking God to save us from the bad things. Do you sometimes dream?

HB: Yes, I sometimes dream. I think all people dream. Some dreams I remember.

HT: If someone has died and we are still alive we dream about them and we walk together. This we call dreams of the afterworld ('*mimo plü*').

HB: Some see dreams of the afterworld and it rains.

HT: Sometimes it may rain.

HB: Have you ever dreamed well?

HT: Yes, I have. Sometimes we think we are going to plant tomatoes and I dream going uphill and then sometimes you succeed. Sometimes we plant some things and we dream about going downhill, we will not earn anything.

HB: If you plan to plant rice the next day but at night you dream badly, are you going to do it?

HT: In this case some people will not go out to plant. Actually, if you plan to plant rice and you have a bad dream, you will not eat, so you better wait one or two days until you go to plant.

HB: Do Christians and non-Christian do the same or is there any difference?

HT: As Christians we pray. If they are non-Christians, most of them would not do it. But some still do many things. They may do a ceremony in order to be saved from the bad omen. Christians sometimes kill a pig and eat together and thank the Lord. Non-Christians do their own rituals. They kill a pig and they '*ki cü*'. But as Christians we ask God that he will go with us every day and save us from the bad things. Non-Christians who do '*ki'cü*', they also will ask for blessings.

HB: Those who are not Christians, if they go and ask the spirit doctor, does the spirit doctor dream about what he is going to advise them?

HT: I am not sure about it. But there is one in the village of Uhaekhi he is going to pray to some lord and if that one comes on him his voice is changing. He knows so much. From our village people have gone to him to ask. If you go to him from any village he will know where you come from. And he knows where your house stands and what you do. Sometimes he is really right, but sometimes he is not right.

HT: Sometimes people accuse another person that he has seen in a dream one person giving meat to another and then this creates great problems. Sometimes older people tell us this and it happens like that. On this earth many things happen.

HB: Do dreams come from God?

HT: I do not know. If I dream I just dream.

66:

2014-10-14. Somu, 22 years. From Mo Kler Kee. His grandparents from mother's as well as from father's side were spirit priests. Student at Rahjabaht university. Studying teacher. Has become a Christian in the hostel during high school years. Lives in our community in Chiang Mai and has helped with interviews.

If people dream about a wedding it is not good – the person may die soon, people say.

A child's spirit is more feared then the spirit of a mature person. Therefore, if you dream about carrying ('*pü*') a child, it is a bad dream!!

My father dreamed that his newly built house needed to be lowered and that he needed to improve the foundation. Then he saw a big storm coming. My father interpreted the dream that his life would be shorter. But I told him that was not the right interpretation, it meant that he needed to be humble. He needed to strengthen his foundation in Christ. Then a storm came – the headman got very unhappy about me – and the father had to be humble so that the storm did not damage our house/family.

67:

2015-06-11. Pastor Boon Ruang (BR) and his wife Charemo (Ch) from Sop Lahn.

HB: Would you like to dream?

BR: I do not want to dream. I do not understand it. Dreaming is not enjoyable. If I do not dream I do not think anything but when I dream it makes me think/worry. Sometimes dreams are believed.

HB: Some people say that dreaming causes temptation? What kind of temptation do they mean?

BR: If you have bad dreams, e.g. about pepper, people believe and quarreling occurs in the family. When you dream about fire – you will be stressed. What is not good, will happen to you. When you are about to plant tomatoes or peppers and you go uphill you will succeed – if you go downhill it will be destroyed. It is not good. Some people do not dream about uphill or downhill but about lots of fish. Then you will make a lot of money. My older brother [who is a pastor with KBC] was planting and he was dreaming going uphill but in the end he did not earn anything. Afterwards he thought this is not always true! I do not like to dream.

HB: How should we teach Christians about dreaming?

BR: All is in God's hand! Do not believe in dreams! But if dreams come from God, God will help to understand it.

HB: How do you know it comes from God?

BR: God will show that it comes from him. Dreams do not often come from God, maybe once in a while, I do not know.

HB: Have you ever had a dream from God?

BR: I do not think about dreams very much. Whether I have a good dream or a bad one. I do not think about it. My life is in God's hand. Some dream a lot but they do not understand the meaning. I believe that the bad things do not come through dreams.

HB: I think sometimes dreams are like a mirror of our soul.

BR: Old Karen tradition is, if you have a bad dream, you do not go out. You fast [not going out]. People say, "I had a bad dream last night, therefore I do not go to work."

HB: If you have to go what do you do?

BR: They just fear, if they do not believe in God. The Christians have to be careful. If you really believe in God whether you have a good dream or a bad one, you are in God's hand.

BR: I do not believe in dreams. God is great. I do not wonder whether dreams come from God or not. It does not matter. I am in God's hand. Many people have come and asked me about the meaning of dreams. I do not know. I tell them to leave it in God's hand. Those who have died, some still dream of them that they do fields, some build nice houses, others not so nice. So they think if you die you will still have to work. They believe in this: You still have to do fields and build houses and they think it is that way. They believe, after death they still have to do things. They do not believe that they are with God in His kingdom. They still have to do things. Therefore, when a person dies, they give him knives, rice seeds and potatoes and other things to plant. They believe this.

HB: Do Christians believe this?

BR: There are those who believe this. It is a deep faith. They dream of it and they believe in those dreams. They believe in dreams. They think they have to do this. They think they do not go to heaven yet.

HB: Does this belief come through dreaming?

BR: Yes, it comes through dreaming!

HB: The dreams need to change.

BR: It is not right to give such high significance to dreams. I teach them that they need to have faith in God and obey. Often they go to ask people who do not know God and believe them.

68:

2014-06-07. In the village of Nadaglo. Talk with Sokue (S), lay pastor of the church. 32 years, married, two children.

S had an impressive dream. He was sure, the dream came from God. In the dream he saw a large house which was built on a mountain. A stream of people were moving to the house. His interpretation is, that this is a picture for revival. Many will come to worship God. The dream has been an encouragement to him and it has caused him to expect more of God working among the Karen people. It has also encouraged him to visit other villages.

Since S has married into this village and has become the pastor (part-time), the church has grown. Before, it had stayed the same for many years, half of the village Christian, the other half Animist-Buddhist. Now it is only about a quarter of the village who have not become Christians yet. He also has started to visit the neighboring village where more families have believed since then.

69:

2014-06-07. In the village of Nadaglo. Talk with Pathi (P), first Christian in the village. 59 years. Has been a Christian for over 30 years.

Pathi has dreamed that he was nailed to a cross. He suffered, and he was perplexed about the dream. He talked to Sokuepa. Sokuepa then had a similar dream about him.

Sokuepa interpreted the dream, saying that the dream shows his suffering, it is a suffering for Christ which he should accept. God will use him in this. Actually, through Pathi's prayer, God has healed several people.

My own observation: Pathi is still not the happiest man, but he has been encouraged a lot by his dream and its interpretation. It has given him hope and the suffering has got a meaning – it is not just the devil's work as he thought.

70:

2011-12-10. Notes taken from a talk on dreams with Chilapa (Ch) from Maehatha in Mae San district Si Satchanalai on an evangelistic trip. Same person as 28Ch.

Ch: "For Karen who are not Christians dreams are very important. You can see the future. You can see things you cannot see with your body. If you have a bad dream it bothers people greatly. They may go to somebody who can explain the dream and who may give some advice what to do about it."

Examples of interpretation:

Ch: "Dreams about pepper or fire means suffering is to come. Going downhill will result in losing money. The contrary is true too: Going uphill means to be more blessed with buffaloes and money. Dreaming about dead people ('*plü*') or drinking alcohol means it is going to rain. If you have a bad dream you may fear to lose your life or somebody who is near to you may die."

HB: What do people do in such a case?

Ch: "Ask a spirit doctor to do a ceremony, calling back the 'k'la' [soul] and tying your wrist with strings. You may live some more years but the fear to die stays on."

HB: How important are dreams for Christians?

Ch: "Christians still fear bad dreams! I dreamed a lot about deceased people appearing to me. I prayed and I am not bothered anymore by it.

Pray with people – God is in control – bad things may not happen!"

HB: Dreams play a certain role in the Bible ...

Ch: "If great Kings like Pharaoh or Nebuchadnezzar feared dreams – what about normal people?"

Appendix C:
Area Map

Map of the area in which the Research was conducted

Δ   Villages of interviewees

Appendix D:
Glossary of Sgaw Karen Termini used

au qai	အီၣ်ယၢၤ	ancestor cult, ceremony for healing of the sick
ba aw hti	ဘါအီထံ	a Buddhist ceremony – where you cut a bamboo and fill it with water – then you pray in front of the Buddha shelf and everybody will drink a little bit – this is a ceremony to overcome sickness.
da bo	ဒးဘိ	a creeping animal with many feet whose sting is very painful. Centipede. A symbol for a very bad spirit.
doo s'wau	ဒူသဝီ	'doo' means forest. 's'wau' means village. Pleasant place.
doo lau ra	ဒူလရၢ်	'lau ra' means roll down or to drop. Place of falling. Hell.
dü ta;	ဒုၣ်တၢ်	to fast
ta dü ta htü	တၢ်ဒုၣ်တၢ်ထူ	taboo. In connection with dreams it means you will not leave the house
ga ta	ကၢ်တၢ်	to predict, clairvoyance done with reading bones or reading a skirt
gera	ကရၣ်	spirit doctor
gö ma qä		certain spirits
hkoo sei hkau klai		guard at the entrance of the land of the dead
hpä	ဖၢ်	is the 'k'la' of the elephant
hpä – gö rä – na hti	ဖၢ်ကရၢ်နါထံ	three different spirits which are similar. They are not demons but they are like the police. They may be in the forest and if you have done something wrong they may catch you. (Somu)
hsai k'si	သၢၣ်ကသံၣ်	ritual in order to be relieved from ancestor cult

hta	ထါ	traditional poems from 'old times'. Karen poems which will be chanted at traditional funerals or weddings or at some other occasion
hti gem lö		well
hti mo pra	ထံမိၢပှၢ်	big river
kau	ကီၢ်	area, land, a territorial unity
kau k'ca	ကီၢ်ကစၢ်	'Lords of the land', strong Guardian Spirit
ki'cü	ကီၢ်စူ	put strings around the wrist in order to bind the 'k'la'
k'la	ကလၤ	soul, life force
k'la hko hti	ကလၤခိၣ်ထံ	the main soul/life force of a person
k'la wi:wa:	ကလၤဝီးဝး	a disabled 'k'la' which does not wander. It is always with the person. It does not go away. When it goes away, the person dies
lä ta		to make a certain sacrifice
lo ta		to cast a death spell, to bewitch, sorcery, to curse s.o. to death
ma hti uu	မၤထံအူ	to blow into the water as a ritual
me ko	မ့ၢ်အဉ်	cooked rice nobody has eaten from yet
me to		rice cooked in leaves which are bound together
mi mo ta	မံမိၢ်တၢ်	to dream
moh le pa la	မိၢ်လၢပၢ်လၤ	according to the Karen tradition
mü kau li	မှၣ်ကီၢ်လံၢ်	devil, (female form)
mü qa		soul of the ancestor
na hti	နံထံ	a spirit of the water
no po gra	နိၣ်ပိၢ်ကြး	bamboo stick which is cut open at the front and has some holes near the handle

Appendix D

pa te qa		not a very strong spirit which is not very much feared, 'ta mü qa' are much more feared
po tö qa		a certain spirit
pra tö qa		the 'k'la' who went to the 'plü kau' and has come back as a spirit
plo so		to dream about daily work and cores or things you have been thinking about a lot.
plü	ပျူ၊	the Dead
plü kau	ပျူ၊ကိ်	realm of the dead, afterworld, Hades
pra mi pra htö	ပြၢမိပျၢထော၁	It is not a spirit. It is not a person – you see them and then they disappear.
pü	ပု်	to carry a child on the back
rä lo sa		a certain ceremony which is done on the way
soe goe re, soe ta na, ta ju ta plae	စၢဂေ၂်ရဲ့, စၢတၢ်နံ့, ဂျၢယှံဉ်တ၁်ပျ	appease the bad spirits
ta he sa	တ၁်ဟုသး	quarrel, hatred
ta lä cho		a ceremony which has to be done after you have dreamed and something has happened
ta lä/ba lä ta		ceremony with candles and peppers
ta mü qa	တ၁်မု်ဃါ	collective term for all kinds of spirits
ta plo so		a dream about things you were doing or thinking during the day. This kind of dream is thought to be trivial
ta yo		an evil spirit who eats people
sa	သး	heart, soul, spirit
tö rä		kind of a smaller, bad spirit
to sa		to watch your heart

uu ta	အူတၢ်	to blow – magic blowing into water
yo hpe hoko	ယဲး၀့ၤးဟိၣ်ခိၣ်	to stamp the earth (similar to 'yo hpe yo blo' or 'yo hpe' but done outside in the dust)
yo hpe yo blo	ယဲး၀့ၤးယဲးဘၠီ	to stamp into the ashes so dust will come up in order to make the spirit not see your feet
yo hpe	ယဲး၀့ၤး	before leaving the house to stomp the foot in the ashes and then the 'pa te qa' spirit will not see you
yo k'la	ယၢ်ကလၢ	call back the 'k'la' (soul)
Ywa	ယွၤ	High God in Karen mythology, term used in the Bible for God

Bibliography

Albani, Matthias. "Traum/Traumdeutung. Alter Orient und Altes Testament." In *RGG⁴* Vierte, völlig neu überarbeitete Auflage, Band 8 (563-574). Tübingen, Germany: Mohr Siebeck, 2005.

Allen, Leslie C. *The Books of Joel, Obadiah, Jonah and Micah.* Grand Rapids, MI: Williams B. Eerdmans Publishing, 1976.

American Anthropological Association. "Statement of Ethics" http://ethics.aaanet.org/ethics-statement-1-do-no-harm/ (22.05.2014).

Andersen, Francis I. *Job. An Introduction and Commentary.* Leicester, United Kingdom: Inter-Varsity Press, 1976.

Angrosino, Michael V. "Altered States of Consciousness." *Encyclopedia of Religious Rites, Rituals, and Festivals.* Ed. Frank A. Salamone, 31-33. New York, NY: Routledge, 2004.

Arzi, Abraham. "Dreams. In the Talmud." In *Encyclopaedia Judaica* Vol. 6. 210. Jerusalem, Israel: Keter Publishing House, 1971.

Ayoub, Mahmoud. "Foreword." In Muhammad Ibn Seerin's Dictionary of Dreams: According to Islamic Inner Traditions. Philadelphia, PA: Pearl Pub. House, 1992.

Bakon, Shimon. "Genesis 31: Jacob's peculiar dream." *Jewish Bible Quarterly 40,* no. 4 (October 1, 2012): 259-260. ATLASerials, Religion Collection, EBSCOhost (25.02.2015).

Baldwin, Joyce G. *Daniel. An Introduction and Commentary.* Leicester, United Kingdom: Inter-Varsity Press, 1978.

Bär, Hans. *Heilsgeschichtlicher Bibelunterricht. McIlwains Programm 'Building on Firm Foundations' im Einsatz unter den Karen im Bezirk Omkoi* (Nordthailand). Bonn, Germany: Verlag für Kultur und Wissenschaft, 1998.

Barth, Karl. *Die kirchliche Dogmatik: Registerband.* Zürich, Switzerland: EVZ-Verlag, 1970.

Bauer, Walter. *Wörterbuch zum Neuen Testament.* Berlin, Germany: Walter de Gruyter, 1971.

Berger, Rose Marie. "Stammering through Dreams." *Sojourners Magazine,* 07, 2009. 44.

Bräumer, Hansjörg. "Exkurs III: Träume und ihre Deutung im Alten und Neuen Testament." In *Das erste Buch Mose, 3. Teil.* 112-130. Wuppertal, Germany: R. Brockhaus Verlag, 1990.

Buadaeng, Kwanchewan. *Negotiating Religious Practices in a Changing Sgaw Karen Community in North Thailand.* A thesis submitted in fulfilment of the requirements for the degree of Doctor of Philosophy. University of Sydney, 2001.

Bubeck, Mark I. *The Adversary. The Christian Versus Demon Activity*. Chicago, IL: Moody Press, 1975.

Bulkeley, Kelly. *Dreaming in The World's Religions. A Comparative History*. New York, NY: New York University Press, 2008.

Burnett, David. *World of the Spirits. A Christian Perspective on Traditional and Folk Religions*. London, United Kingdom: Monarch Books, 2000.

Busch, Eberhard. *Glaubensheiterkeit: Karl Barth, Erfahrungen u. Begegnungen*. Neukirchen-Vluyn, Germany: Neukirchener Verlag, 1986.

Calvin, John. *Commentary on Genesis – Volume 1*. Grand Rapids, MI: Christian Classics Ethereal Library.

Calvin, John. *Commentary on Genesis – Volume 2*. Grand Rapids, MI: Christian Classics Ethereal Library.

Calvin, John. *John Calvin's Commentaries On Joel, Amos, Obadiah* (Extended Annotated Edition). Altenmünster, Germany: Jazzybee Verlag Jürgen Beck, 2012.

Craigie, Peter C. *The Book of Deuteronomy*. Grand Rapids, MI: Williams B. Eerdmans Publishing, 1976.

Cross, E.B. "On the Karens." In *Journal of the American Oriental Society* 4 (1854): 289-316.

Dautzenberg, Gerhard. "Zum religionsgeschichtlichen Hintergrund der 'diakrisis pneumaton' 1Ko 12,10." In *Biblische Zeitschrift* 15 (Paderborn, 1971): 93-104.

Dawson, Catherine. *Introduction to Research Methods. A practical guide for anyone undertaking a research project*. Oxford, United Kingdom: How To Books Ltd, 2009.

Day, Michael James. *The Function of Post-Pentecost Dream/Vision Reports in Acts*. Ph.D. diss., Southern Theological Seminary, 1994.

Dodds, E. R. *The Greeks and the Irrational*. Boston, MA: Beacon, 1957.

Doyle, Tom. Webster, Greg. *Träume und Visionen. Wie Muslime heute Jesus erfahren. 23 Geschichten*. Giessen, Germany: Brunnen Verlag, 2013.

El-Aswad, El-Sayed. *Muslim Worldview and Everyday Lives*. Plymouth, United Kingdom: AltaMira Press, 2012.

Ehrlich, E. L. "Der Traum im Alten Testament." *BZWA*, 73, Berlin, Germany, 1953.

Ehrlich, E. L. "Traum." In *RGG*, 6. Band, 3. Auflage (1001-1005). Tübingen, Germany: J.C.B.Mohr, 1962.

Foster, Richard. *Celebration of Discipline. The Path to Spiritual Growth*. London, United Kingdom: Hodder & Stoughton, 1980.

France, R.T. *Matthew. Tyndale New Testament Commentaries.* Leicester, United Kingdom: Inter-Varsity Press, 1985.

Freud, Sigmund. *The Interpretation of Dreams.* Translated by A. A. Brill. Ware, Hertfordshire, United Kingdom: Wordsworth Editions, 1997.

Frey, Hellmuth. *Das Buch des Kampfes. Kapitel 25-35 Des ersten Buches Mose.* Stuttgart, Germany: Calwer Verlagsbuchhandlung, 1938.

Garison, Jason A. "Nebuchadnezzar's Dream: An Inversion of Gilgamesh Imagery." *Bibliotheca Sacra* 169 (April – June 2012), 172-187.

Gaster, Theodor H. "Dreams. In the Bible." In *Encyclopaedia Judaica,* Vol. 6. 209-210. Jerusalem, Israel: Keter Publishing House, 1971.

Gesenius, Wilhelm. *Hebräisches und aramäisches Handwörterbuch über das Alte Testament.* Berlin, Germany, Springer Verlag 1962.

Gnuse, Robert Karl. "Book Review on Husser, Jean-Marie. Dreams and Dream Narratives in the Biblical World." Sheffield: Sheffield Academic Press, 1999. *The Catholic Biblical Quarterly,* 61 (2000), 522.

Gollnick, James. "Implicit Religions in Dreams." *Implicit Religions* 8.3 (2005): 281-298.

Gravers, Mikael. "Waiting for a Righteous Ruler: The Karen Royal Imaginary in Thailand and Burma." *Journal of Southeast Asian Studies,* 42, 2 (June 2012): 340-363.

Gregerson, Marilyn. E-mail: fishnet-bounces+jldeal=comcast.net@lists.bethel. edu. March 28, 2014.

Grudem, W. "A Response to Gerhard Dautzenberg on 1 Cor 12:10." *Biblische Zeitschrift* 2 (Paderborn, 1978): 253-270.

Grün, Anselm. *Träume auf dem geistlichen Weg.* Münsterschwarzach, Germany: Vier-Türme-Verlag, 1989/2001.

Grünebaum, G.E. von. "Introduction: The Cultural Function of The Dream As Illustrated by Classical Islam." In *The Dream and Human Societies,* ed. G.E. von Grünebaum and Roger Callois, 3-21. Berkely, CA: University of California Press, 1966.

Hale, Keith. Personal e-mail to the author. 18th May, 2014.

Hall, J. "Religious Images in Dreams." *Journal of Pastoral Care,* 18.4 (1979): 327-335.

Hanson, John S. "Dreams and Vision in the Graeco-Roman World and Early Christianity." *ANRW* 23.2: 1395-1427. Edited by H. Temporini and W. Haase. New York, NY: De Gruyter, 1980.

Hark, Helmut. *Der Traum als vergessene Sprache. Symbolpsychologische Deutung biblischer und heutiger Träume.* Opus magnum, 2004.

Harrison, Jane. *Prolegomena to the Study of Greek Religion.* New York, NY: Meridian Books, 1960.

Hayami, Yoko. *Between Hills and Plains. Power and Practice in Socio-Religious Dynamics among Karen.* Kyoto Area Studies on Asia, Volume 7. Kyoto, Japan: Kyoto University Press, 2004.

Heininger, Bernhard. "Traum/Traumdeutung. Neues Testament." In *RGG[4]* Vierte, völlig neu überarbeitete Auflage, Band 8 (563-574). Tübingen, Germany: Mohr Siebeck, 2005.

Hendel, Ronald S. "The ladder of Jacob: Ancient Interpretations of The Biblical Story of Jacob And His Children." *Interpretation* 62 no 2 (April 2008): 182-184.

Hendel, Russell Jay. "Joseph: A Biblical Approach to Dream Interpretation." *Jewish Bible Quarterly* 39, no. 4 (October 1, 2011): 231-238. ATLASerials, Religion Collection, EBSCOhost (25.02.2015).

Henry, Matthew. *Matthew Henry's Commentary on the Whole Bible. Volume 2, Joshua to Esther.* New Modern Edition. USA: Hendrickson Publishers, 1991.

Hinton, Peter. "The Pwo Karen of Northern Thailand: a Preliminary Report." Chiang Mai, Thailand, 1969. Unpublished paper.

Hobson, J. Allan. *Dreaming. A Very Short Introduction.* Oxford, United Kingdom: Oxford University Press, 2002.

Hollan, Douglas. "The Personal Use of Dream Beliefs in The Toraja Highlands." *Ethos*, Vol. 17, No. 2 (June 1989): 166-186.

Hollan, Douglas. "The Cultural and Intersubjective Context of Dream Remembrance and Reporting." In *Dream Travelers. Sleep Experiences and Culture in the Western Pacific,* ed. Roger Ivar Lohmann, 169-187. New York, NY: Palgrave Macmillan, 2003.

Hollan, Douglas. "To the Afterworld and Back: Mourning and Dreams of the Dead among the Toraja." *Ethos,* Vol. 23, No. 4 (Dec. 1995): 424-436.

Holland, Martin. *Judasbrief.* Neuhausen-Stuttgart, Germany: Hänssler-Verlag, 1996.

Hovemyr, Anders. *In Search of the Karen King.* Uppsala, Sweden: Studia Missionaria Uppsaliensia, 1989.

Howe, Leroy. "Dream Interpretation in Spiritual Guidance." *Journal of Pastoral Care* 40.3 (1986): 262-272.

Hubbard, David Allan. *Joel and Amos. An Introduction and Commentary.* Leicester, United Kingdom: Inter-Varsity Press, 1989.

Hudspith, Edwin J. "Tribal Highways and BYways: A Church Growth Study in North Thailand." M.A. Miss. Thesis, Fuller Theological Seminary Pasadena, 1969.

Hume, Lynne. "Accessing the Eternal: Dreaming 'The Dreaming' and Ceremonial Performance." *Zygon* 39 no 1 (2004): 237-258.

Husser, Jean-Marie. *Dreams and Dream Narratives in the Biblical World.* Sheffield, United Kingdom: Sheffield Academic Press, 1999.

Jariyaphruttipong, Worapong. "Transformation in Omkoi, Thailand." www. Sentinelgroup.org/fire-quest/asia/Thailand/introduction/. Accessed 29th July 2015.

Jentsch, Werner. *Der Seelsorger: Beraten, bezeugen, befreien. Grundzüge biblischer Seelsorge.* Moers, Germany: Brendow, 1984.

Joll, Christopher Mark. *What Muslims in Cabangtiga Mean by Merit: Merit Making Rhetoric, Islamic Discourse and the Thai Milieu.* A Dissertation for the Doctor of Philosophy. Bangi, MY: University Kebangsaan, 2009.

Jung, Carl Gustav. *Dreams.* From The Collected Works of C.G. Jung, Vol. 4,8,12,16. Bollingen Series XX. Translated by R.F.C. Hull. Princeton, NJ: Princeton University Press, 1974.

Käser, Lothar. *Animismus.* Bad Liebenzell, Germany: Verlag der Liebenzeller Mission, 2004.

Käser, Lothar. *Fremde Kulturen. Eine Einführung in die Ethnologie.* Erlangen, Germany: Verlag der Evang.-Luth. Mission, 1997.

Kelsey, Morton T. *God, Dreams, and Revelation. A Christian Interpretation of Dreams.* Revised and Expanded Edition. Augsburg, MN: Augsburg Books, 1991.

Kemlin, M. M. J. "Les Songes et Leurs Interprétation Chez les Reungao." *Bulletin de l'Ecole Francaise d'Extrême Orient* 10:507-538.

Keyes, Charles F. *Ethnic Adaptation and Identity. The Karen on the Thai Frontier with Burma.* Philadelphia, PA: Institute for the Study of Human Issues, Inc., 1979.

Keyes, Charles F. "The Politics of 'Karen-ness' in Thailand." In *Living at the Edge of Thai Society*, ed. Claudio O. Delang, 210-218. New York, NY: RoutledgeCurzon, 2003.

Kidner, Derek. *Genesis. An Introduction and Commentary.* Westmont, IL: InterVarsity Press, 1967.

Kinberg, Leah. "Dreams and Sleep." *Encyclopaedia of The Qur'an. Volume One A-D*, ed. Jane Dammen McAuliffe, 546-553. Leiden, NL: Brill, 2001.

Kroeker, Jakob. *Patriarchen. Die Grundlagen des Glaubens.* Giessen, Germany: Brunnen Verlag, 1959.

Lackner, Michael. "Wandering Spirits: Chen Shiyuan's Encyclopedia of Dreams." *Journal of Chinese Religions* no. 36 (2008): 196-198. ATLASerials, Religion Collection, EBSCOhost (accessed February 14, 2014).

Larchrojna, Somphob. *Karen Medicine.* A Thesis Submitted in Fulfillment of the Requirements for the Master of Arts Degree. Sidney, AU: Sidney University, 1975.

Lebar, Frank M., Gerald C. Kickey, John K. Musgrave. *Ethnic Groups of Mainland Southeast Asia.* New Haven, CT: Human Relations Area Files Press, 1964.

LeCompte Margaret D. & Schensul Jean J. *Analyzing and Interpreting Ethnographic Data.* Walnut Creek, CA: AltaMira Press, 1999.

Lewis James R. and Oliver, Evelyn Dorothy. *The Dream Encyclopedia.* Detroit, MI: Visible Ink Press, 2009.

Lewis, Paul and Elaine. *Peoples of the Golden Triangle.* London, United Kingdom: Thames and Hudson Ltd., 1984.

Lewis, Paul und Elaine. *Völker im Goldenen Dreieck.* Stuttgart, Germany: Edition Hansjörg Mayer, 1984.

Lohmann, Roger Ivar. "How Evaluating Dreams Makes History: Asabano Examples." In *History and Anthropology*, Vol. 21, No. 3, (September 2010): 227-249.

Lohmann, Roger Ivar. "Supernatural Encounters of the Asabano in Two Traditions and Three States of Consciousness." In *Dream Travelers. Sleep Experiences and Culture in the Western Pacific*, ed. Roger Ivar Lohmann, 189-210. New York, NY: Palgrave Macmillan, 2003.

Lohmann, Roger Ivar. "The Role of Dreams in Religious Enculturation among the Asabano of Papua New Guinea." In *Ethos*, 28 (1) (2000): 75-102.

Luce, Gordon H. "Introduction to the Comparative Study of Karen Languages." In *Journal of the Burma Research Society* 42, 1 (1959): 1-18.

Maier, Gerhard. *Matthäus-Evangelium.* Stuttgart, Germany: Hänssler-Verlag, 1979.

Mandryk, Jason. *Operation World.* Completely Revised 7th Edition. Colorado Springs, CO: Biblica Publishing, 2010.

Maniratanavongsiri, Chumpol. *Religion and Social Change: Ethnic Continuity and Change among the Karen in Thailand with Reference to the Canadian Indian Experience.* A Thesis for the Degree of Master of Arts. Peterborough, Ontario, Canada: Trent University, 1993.

Marshall, Harry Ignatius. *The Karen People of Burma. A Study in Anthropology and Ethnology.* Bangkok, Thailand: White Lotus Press, 1997 (1922).

Mason, Francis. "Religion, Mythology, and Astronomy among the Karens." In *Journal of the Asiatic Society of Bengal,* Vol. XXXIV, No. III, Part II (October 1865): 173-250.

Mason, Francis. *The Karen Apostle.* Revised by H. J. Ripley. Boston, MA: Gould, Kendall, and Lincoln, 1847. Copyright: BiblioLife, LLC.

Mathews, Kenneth A. *The New American Commentary. An Exegetical and Theological Exposition of Holy Scripture. Genesis 11:27-50:26.* Nashville, TE: Broadman and Holman Publishers, 2005.

Miller, James E. "Dreams And Prophetic Visions." *Biblica* 71 (1990): 401-404.

Miller, John, B.F. *Convinced That God Had Called Us: Dreams, Visions and the Perception of God's Will in Luke-Acts.* Leiden, NL: Brill, 2007.

Milligan, Ira. *Träume deuten, Träume verstehen. Ein biblisches Handbuch, um Gottes Stimme zu hören.* Berlin, Germany: Aufbruch Verlag der Gemeinde auf dem Weg e.V., 2007.

Milligan, Ira L. *Understanding the Dreams You Dream. Biblical Keys for Hearing God's Voice in the Night.* Shippensburg, PA: Destiny Image Publishers, 1997.

Mischung, Roland. *Religion and Wirklichkeitsvorstellungen in einem Karen-Dorf Nordwest-Thailands.* Wiesbaden, Germany: Franz Steiner Verlag, 1984.

Mischung, Roland. "When It Is Better to Sing Than to Speak: the Use of Traditional Verses (*Hta*) in Tense Social Situations." In *Living at the Edge of Thai Society*, (130-150), ed. Claudio O. Delang. New York, NY: RoutledgeCurzon, 2003.

Morris, Henry M. *The Genesis Record. A Scientific and Devotional Commentary on the Book of Beginnings.* Grand Rapids, MI: Baker Book House, 1976.

Nakashima Degarrod, Lydia. "Dreams and Visions." In *Shamanism. An Encyclopedia of World Beliefs, Practices, and Culture.* Edited by Mariko Namba Walter and Eva Jane Neumann Fridman. 89-94. Santa Barbara, CA: ABC-CLIO, 2004.

New International Version, *NIV Study Bible*, Fully Revised. Grand Rapids, MI: Zondervan, 2002.

Newton, Nigel. "The Use of Semi-structured Interviews in Qualitative Research: Strengths and Weaknesses" (2010). https://www.academia.edu/1561689 (21.05.2014).

Novak, Simon. "Jacob's Two Dreams." In *Jewish Bible Quarterly*, 24, no 3 (1996): 189-190.

Nygren, Anders. *Agape and Eros, Part I and Part II.* Philadelphia, PA: The Westminster Press, 1953.

Olyott, Stuart. *"Unbestechlich!" Daniel – Treue um jeden Preis.* Friedberg, Germany: 3L Verlag, 2001.

Omori, Kinuko. Greksa, Lawrence P. "Morbidity and Mortality Patterns, Health Beliefs, and Health Risk Factors of Karen Highlanders of Northwest Thailand." *Southeast Asian Journal,* Vol. 30, No. 4 (Dec 1999): 789ff.

Peleg, Yitzhak. "Going Up and Going Down: A key to Interpreting Jacob's Dream (Gen 28,10-22)." *Zeitschrift Für Die Alttestamentliche Wissenschaft* 116, no. 1

(January 1, 2004): 1-11. ATLASerials, Religion Collection, EBSCOhost (25.02.2015).

Pentony, B. "Dreams and Dream Beliefs in North Western Australia." In *Oceania*, Vol. 32, No. 2 (Dec., 1961): 144-149.

Pfeifer, Samuel. *Schlafen und Träumen. Schlafstörungen - Diagnose und Therapie*. Riehen, Switzerland: Psychiatrische Klinik Sonnhalde, 2009.

Pfeil, Gaby. "Unseren Träumen auf der Spur ...". Notes given out at a Seminar on Dreams in Amden, CH, 25th-29th September 2014.

Pinker, Aron. "A Dream of a Dream in Daniel 2." In *Jewish Bible Quarterly* 33 no 4 (2005): 231-240.

Pratt, Christina. *An Encyclopedia of Shamanism*. New York, NY: The Rosen Publishing Group, Inc., 2007.

Pruett, Gordon E. "Through A Glass Darkly: Knowledge of the Self in Dreams in Ibn Khaldun's Muqaddima." In *The Muslim World*, 29-44. Massachusetts, MA: Northeastern University Boston.

Priest, Robert J. Anthropology of Dreams. E-mail: <fishnet@lists.bethel.edu>, 16th October 2013.

Renard, Helene. *Traumgeschichten der Bibel. Ausgewählt und eingeleitet von Helene Renard*. Deutsche Bibelgesellschaft.

Renard, Ronald D. *Kariang: History of Karen-T'ai Relations from the Beginning to 1923*. A Dissertation for the Doctor of Philosophy in History. Hawaii, HI: University of Hawaii, 1980.

Renard, Ronald D. "Studying Peoples Often Called Karen." In *Living at the Edge of Thai Society*, ed. Claudio O. Delang, 1-15. New York, NY: RoutledgeCurzon, 2003.

Rinpoche, Namkhai Norbu. *Mi-Lam. The Dream Practice*. Arcidosso GR, Italy: Associazione Culturale Comunita Dzog-chen Merigar, 1989.

Rogers, Benedict. *A Land Without Evil. Stopping the Genocide of Burma's Karen People*. Oxford, United Kingdom: Monarch books, 2004.

Ruble, Richard L. The Doctrine of Dreams, *Bibliotheca Sacra*, (October 1968): 360-364.

Rüegg, Robert. Rieser Ewald. *Träume und Bilder und ihre Deutung in biblischer Sicht*. Zürich, Switzerland: Vereinigte Bibelgruppen, 1973.

Ruthe, Reinhold. Ruthe-Preiss, Lydia. *Traumbotschaften. Deutungshilfe für die Seelsorge*. Wuppertal, Germany: R. Brockhaus Verlag, 1994.

Ruthe, Reinhold. *Träume - Spiegel der Seele. Krankheiten - Signale der Seele*. Moers, Germany: Brendow Verlag, 2007.

Ryle, James. *Ein Traum wird wahr. Spricht Gott auch heute durch Träume und Visionen?* Fürth, Germany: Verlag R. Hassmann, 1999.

Sanford, John A. *Dreams and Healing. A Succint and Lively Interpretation of Dreams.* New York, NY: Paulist Press, 1978.

Sanford, John A. *Dreams: God's Forgotten Language.* New York, NY: HarperCollins Publishers, 1989.

Saw Hay Moo. *Doing Theology in the Karen Church: The Gospel As Incarnation (John 1:1-14) within the Karen YWA (God) Tradition.* A Dissertation for the Doctor of Missiology. Pasadena: Fuller Theological Seminary, 2002.

Schweizer, Eduard. *Das Evangelium nach Matthäus.* Göttingen, Germany: Vandenhoeck & Ruprecht, 1981.

Seow, Choon Leong. *Daniel.* Louisville, LA: Westminster John Knox, 2003.

Song Saeng, Tongkham. "*Demonology Among the Karens.*" Bachelor of Theology Thesis. Chiang Mai, Thailand: The Thailand Theological Seminary, 1964.

Spiro, Melford E. *Burmese Supernaturalism.* Philadelphia, PA: Institute for the Study of Human Issues, 1978.

Spradley, James P. *The Ethnographic Interview.* Belmont, CA: Wadsworth Group, 1979.

Stanner, W E H. "Some Aspects of Aboriginal Religion." *Colloquium* 9, no. 1 (October 1, 1976): 19-35.

Steinmetz, David C. "Luther and The Ascent of Jacob's Ladder." *Church History* 55, no. 2 (June 1, 1986): 179-192. AtlaSerials, Religion Collection, Ebscobhost (25.02.2015).

Stern,Theodore. "Ariya and the Golden Book: A Millenarian Buddhist Sect Among the Karen." *The Journal of Asian Studies* 27, 2 (1968): 297-328.

Stewart, Charles. "Dreams." In *The Routledge Encyclopedia of Social and Cultural Anthropology.* Ed. Alan Barnard and Jonathan Spencer, 2nd ed., 202-204. New York, NY: Routledge, 2010.

Steyne, Philip M. *Gods of Power.* Houston, TX: Touch Publications, 1990.

Steyne, Philip M. *Machtvolle Götter.* Bad Liebenzell, Germany: Verlag Liebenzeller Mission, 1993.

Strack, Hermann L. und Billerbeck, Paul. *Das Evangelium des Matthäus erläutert aus Talmud und Midrasch.* München, Germany: C.H. Beck'sche Verlagsbuchhandlung Oskar Beck, 1922.

Strickling, Bonnelle Lewis. *Dreaming about the Divine.* Albany, NY: State University of New York Press, 2007.

Thawnghmung, Ardeth Maung. *The "Other" Karen in Myanmar.* Lanham, ML: Rowman & Littlefield Publishers, 2012.

Thümmel, U. "Traum." In *Das grosse Bibellexikon,* Hg. Helmuth Burkhardt, Fritz Grünzweig, Fritz Laubach, Gerhard Maier. Wuppertal, Germany: R. Brockhaus Verlag, 1987.

Tonkinson, Robert. "Anthropology and Aboriginal Tradition: The Hindmarsh Island Bridge Affair And the Politics of Interpretation." In *Oceania* 68 (1997): 1-26.

Tuzin, Donald. "The Breath of a Ghost: Dreams and the Fear of the Dead." *Ethos* 3 (1975): 555-578.

Van Rheenen, Gailyn. *Communicating Christ in Animistic Contexts.* Grand Rapids, MI: Baker Book House, 1991.

Von Rad, Gerhard. *Das Alte Testament Deutsch. Das erste Buch Mose. Genesis.* Berlin, Germany: Evangelische Verlagsanstalt, 1972.

Wade, Johnathan, and Mrs. Bennett, S.K. *A Dictionary of the S'gau Karen Language,* Vol. 1+2. Rangoon, Myanmar: Karen Baptist Press, 1896.

Wade, J. *Thesaurus of Karen Knowledge,* Vol.1. Rangoon: U Maung U, 1963. First Published in Karen: Wade, John and Kau-Too (compilers). Thesaurus of Karen Knowledge. Tavoy, Myanmar: Karen Mission Press, Vol. I, 1847.

Walliman, Nicholas. *Social Research Methods.* London, United Kingdom: Sage Publications, 2006.

Wellenkamp, Jane C. "Fallen Leaves: Death and Grieving in Toraja." In *Coping with the Final Tragedy: Cultural Variation in Dying and Grieving,* eds. D.R. Counts and D.A. Counts, 113-136. Amityville, N.Y. Baywood Publishing, 1991.

Westermann, Claus. *Biblischer Kommentar Altes Testament. Genesis. 2. Teilband.* Neukirchen-Vluyn, Germany: Neukirchener Verlag, 1981.

Westermann, Claus. *Biblischer Kommentar Altes Testament. Genesis, 3. Teilband.* Neukirchen-Vluyn, Germany: Neukirchener Verlag, 1982.

Wikenhauser, Alfred. "Die Traumgeschichte des Neuen Testaments in religionsgeschichtlicher Sicht." In *Pisciculi: Studien zur Religion und Kultur des Altertums: Franz Joseph Dölger zum sechzigsten Geburtstag dargeboten von Freunden, Verehrern und Schülern*. Edited by T. Klauser und A. Rücker. Antike und Christentum Ergänzungsband I. 320-333. Münster, Germany: Aschendorf, 1939.

Wilson, Stephen. "Introduction." In *The Interpretation of Dreams*, Sigmund Freud. Ware, United Kingdom: Wordsworth Editions, 1997.

Winkler, Jakob. "Glossary of Tibetan Terms and Names for the Dzogchen Community." (Sixth version August, 2004). http://www.scribd.com/doc/169835462/Glossary-of-Tibetan-Terms-and-Names-for-the-Dzogchen-Community-Winkler. (18.02.2014).

Wolff, Hans Walter. *Joel and Amos: A Commentary on the Books of the Prophets Joel and Amos.* Philadelphia, PA: Fortress Press, 1977.

Yamamoto, Kumiko. "Religion and Religious Change in A Hill Karen Community of Northwestern Chiang Mai Province." *JSS* Volume 79, (1991): 124-137.

Yong, Amos. "Dreaming About the Divine." *Pneuma* 32, no. 3 (January 1, 2010): 470-471. ATLASerials, Religion Collection, EBSCOhost (14.02.2014).

Young, Gordon. *The Hill Tribes of Northern Thailand.* Bangkok, Thailand: The Siam Society, 1962.

Young, Robert. *Analytical Concordance to the Holy Bible.* Eighth Edition. London, United Kingdom: Lutterworth Press, 1977.

Yoshimatsu, Kumiko. *"The Karen World: The Cosmological and Ritual Belief System of the Sgaw Karen in North Western Chiang Mai Province."* Final Research Report Presented to the National Research Council of Thailand, Bangkok, Thailand. 1989.

Young Serinity. *Dreaming in the Lotus: Buddhist Dream Narrative, Imagery, and Practice.* Somerville, MA: Wisdom Publication, 1999.

www.ingramcontent.com/pod-product-compliance
Lightning Source LLC
Chambersburg PA
CBHW050143170426
43197CB00011B/1945